OLD MAN LOGAN

THE LAST RONIN

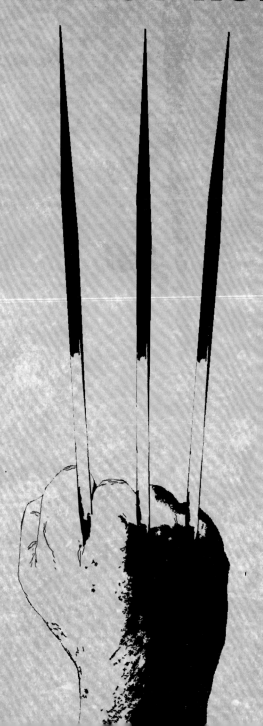

OLD MAN LOGAN

THE LAST RONIN

WRITER **JEFF LEMIRE**

ARTIST **ANDREA SORRENTINO**

COLORIST **MARCELO MAIOLO**
LETTERER **VC'S CORY PETIT**
COVER ARTISTS **ANDREA SORRENTINO & MARCELO MAIOLO**

ASSISTANT EDITOR **CHRISTINA HARRINGTON**
EDITOR **MARK PANICCIA**

COLLECTION EDITOR **MARK D. BEAZLEY**
ASSOCIATE MANAGING EDITOR **KATERI WOODY**
ASSOCIATE EDITOR **SARAH BRUNSTAD**
SENIOR EDITOR, SPECIAL PROJECTS **JENNIFER GRÜNWALD**
VP PRODUCTION & SPECIAL PROJECTS **JEFF YOUNGQUIST**
SVP PRINT, SALES & MARKETING **DAVID GABRIEL**
BOOK DESIGNER **ADAM DEL RE**

EDITOR IN CHIEF **AXEL ALONSO**
CHIEF CREATIVE OFFICER **JOE QUESADA**
PUBLISHER **DAN BUCKLEY**
EXECUTIVE PRODUCER **ALAN FINE**

WOLVERINE: OLD MAN LOGAN VOL. 3 - THE LAST RONIN. Contains material originally published in magazine form as OLD MAN LOGAN #9-13. First printing 2017. ISBN# 978-1-302-90314-5. Published by MARVEL WORLDWIDE, INC., a subsidiary of MARVEL ENTERTAINMENT, LLC. OFFICE OF PUBLICATION: 135 West 50th Street, New York, NY 10020. **Printed in Canada.** ALAN FINE, President, Marvel Entertainment; DAN BUCKLEY, President, TV, Publishing & Brand Management; JOE QUESADA, Chief Creative Officer; TOM BREVOORT, SVP of Publishing; DAVID BOGART, SVP of Business Affairs & Operations, Publishing & Partnership; C.B. CEBULSKI, VP of Brand Management & Development, Asia; DAVID GABRIEL, SVP of Sales & Marketing, Publishing; JEFF YOUNGQUIST, VP of Production & Special Projects; DAN CARR, Executive Director of Publishing Technology; ALEX MORALES, Director of Publishing Operations; SUSAN CRESPI, Production Manager; STAN LEE, Chairman Emeritus. For information regarding advertising in Marvel Comics or on Marvel.com, please contact Vit DeBellis, Integrated Sales Manager, at vdebellis@marvel.com. For Marvel subscription inquiries, please call 888-511-5480. . **Manufactured between 11/25/2016 and 1/2/2017 by SOLISCO PRINTERS, SCOTT, QC, CANADA. .**

10 9 8 7 6 5 4 3 2 1

After surviving a future where everything good in the world was destroyed, Old Man Logan awoke in the present, determined to prevent the death of his wife and children. Even after accepting that the past he remembers is not real, he is still haunted by his lost family.

Logan recently traveled to Killhorn Falls, a mining town in northern Canada. While he was there, Lady Deathstrike and her band of Reavers attacked. Their target was Logan, but in the end only innocent people were killed.

Meanwhile, in his past, Logan has seemingly found safety with a group of refugees who have settled in the old Weapon X bunker. He has also found love with a young woman named Maureen.

OLD MAN LOGAN
THE LAST RONIN

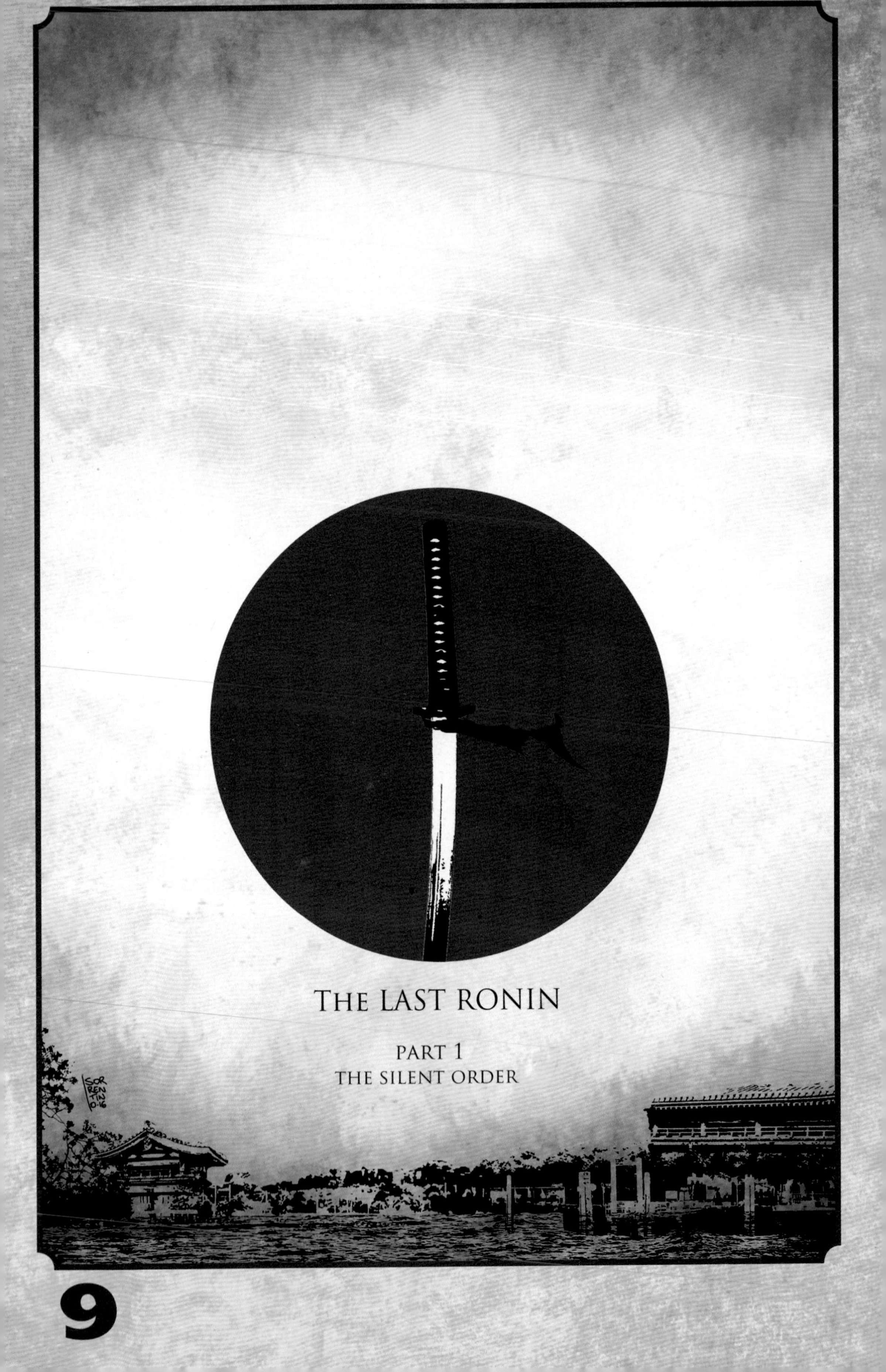
THE LAST RONIN
PART 1
THE SILENT ORDER

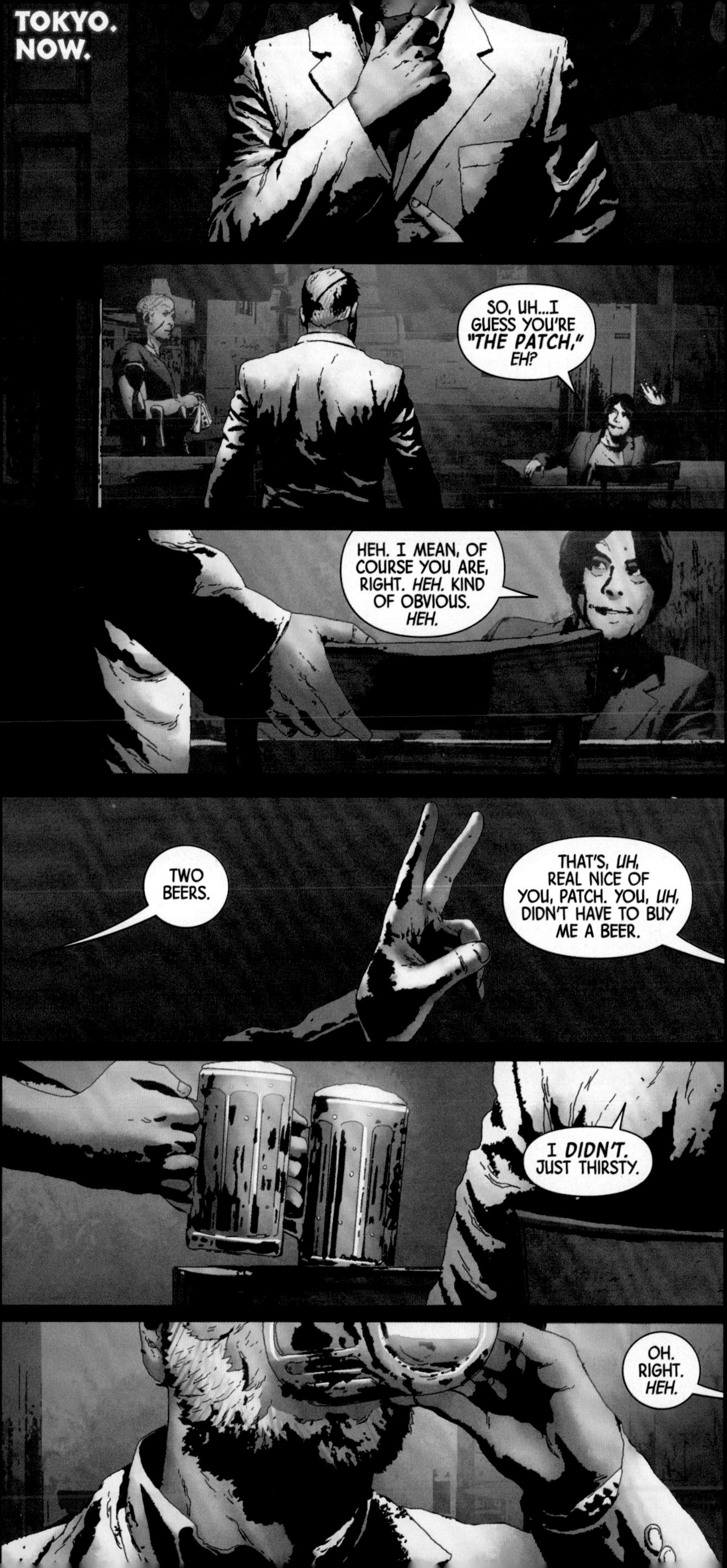
TOKYO. NOW.
SO, UH...I GUESS YOU'RE "THE PATCH," EH?
HEH. I MEAN, OF COURSE YOU ARE, RIGHT. HEH. KIND OF OBVIOUS. HEH.
TWO BEERS.
THAT'S, UH, REAL NICE OF YOU, PATCH. YOU, UH, DIDN'T HAVE TO BUY ME A BEER.
I DIDN'T. JUST THIRSTY.
OH. RIGHT. HEH.

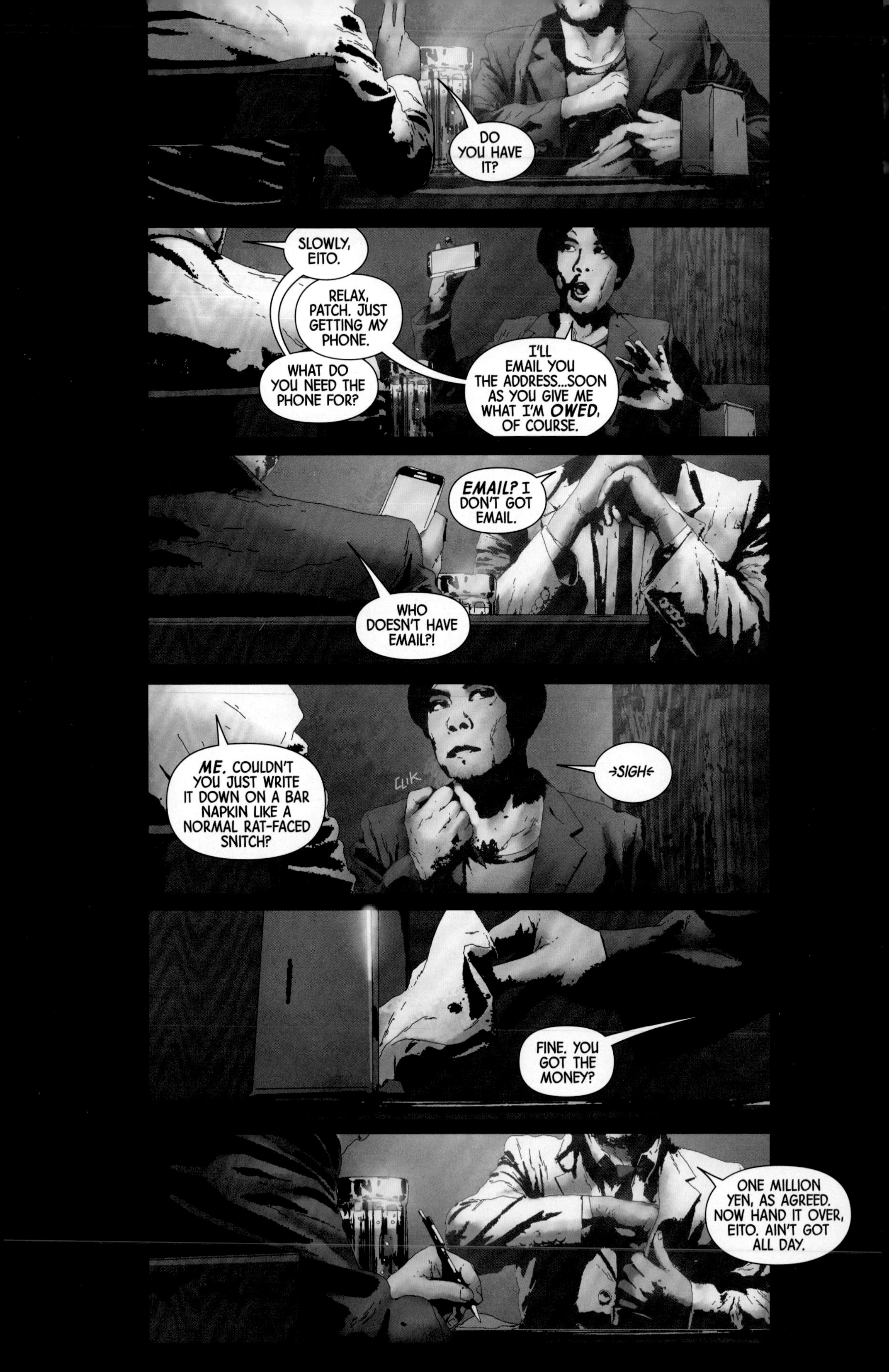
DO YOU HAVE IT?
SLOWLY, EITO.
RELAX, PATCH. JUST GETTING MY PHONE.
WHAT DO YOU NEED THE PHONE FOR?
I'LL EMAIL YOU THE ADDRESS...SOON AS YOU GIVE ME WHAT I'M OWED, OF COURSE.
EMAIL? I DON'T GOT EMAIL.
WHO DOESN'T HAVE EMAIL?!
ME. COULDN'T YOU JUST WRITE IT DOWN ON A BAR NAPKIN LIKE A NORMAL RAT-FACED SNITCH?
CLIK
SIGH
FINE. YOU GOT THE MONEY?
ONE MILLION YEN, AS AGREED. NOW HAND IT OVER, EITO. AIN'T GOT ALL DAY.

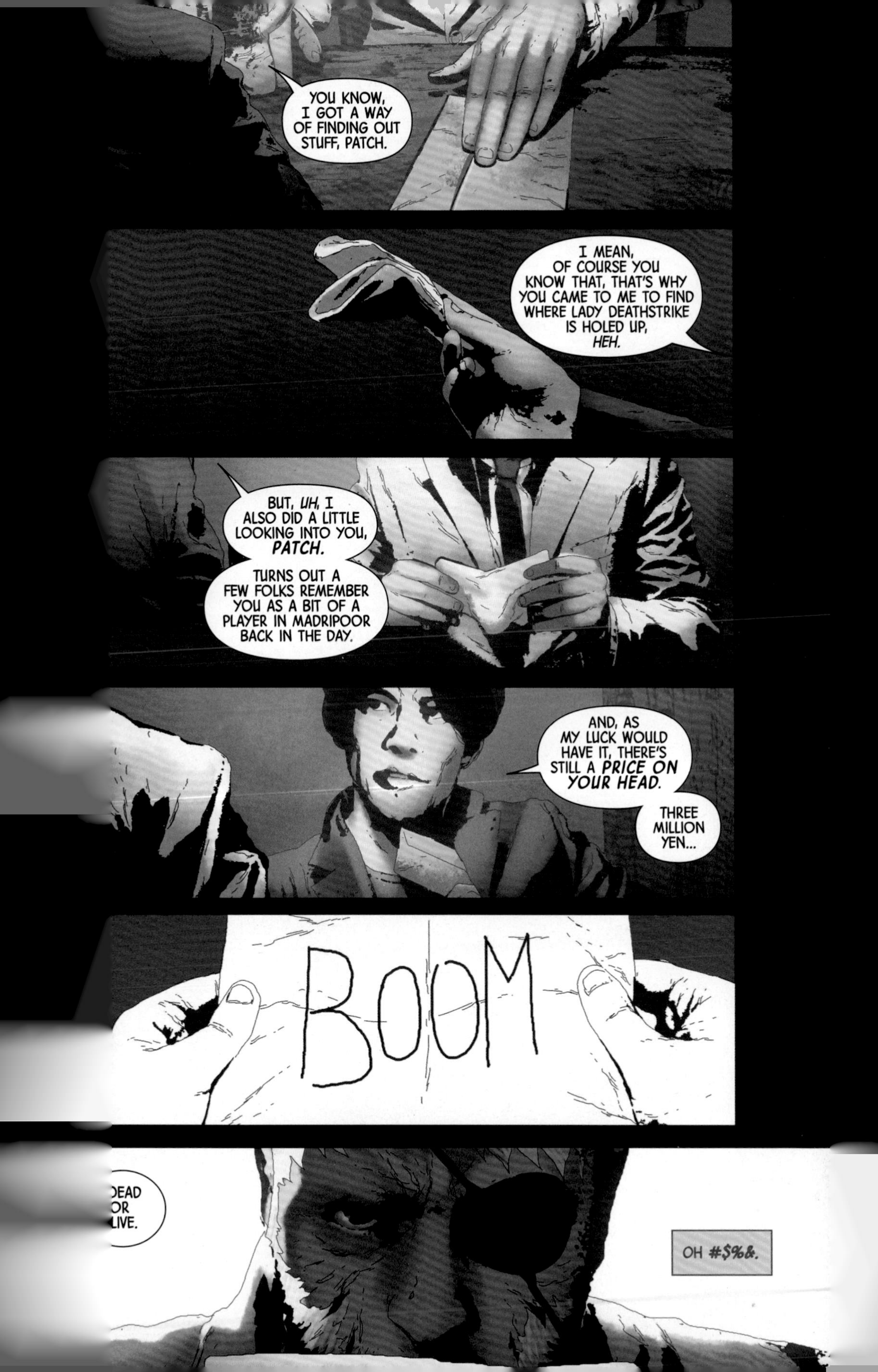
YOU KNOW, I GOT A WAY OF FINDING OUT STUFF, PATCH.
I MEAN, OF COURSE YOU KNOW THAT, THAT'S WHY YOU CAME TO ME TO FIND WHERE LADY DEATHSTRIKE IS HOLED UP, HEH.
BUT, UH, I ALSO DID A LITTLE LOOKING INTO YOU, PATCH.
TURNS OUT A FEW FOLKS REMEMBER YOU AS A BIT OF A PLAYER IN MADRIPOOR BACK IN THE DAY.
AND, AS MY LUCK WOULD HAVE IT, THERE'S STILL A PRICE ON YOUR HEAD.
THREE MILLION YEN...
BOOM
DEAD OR LIVE.
OH #$%&.

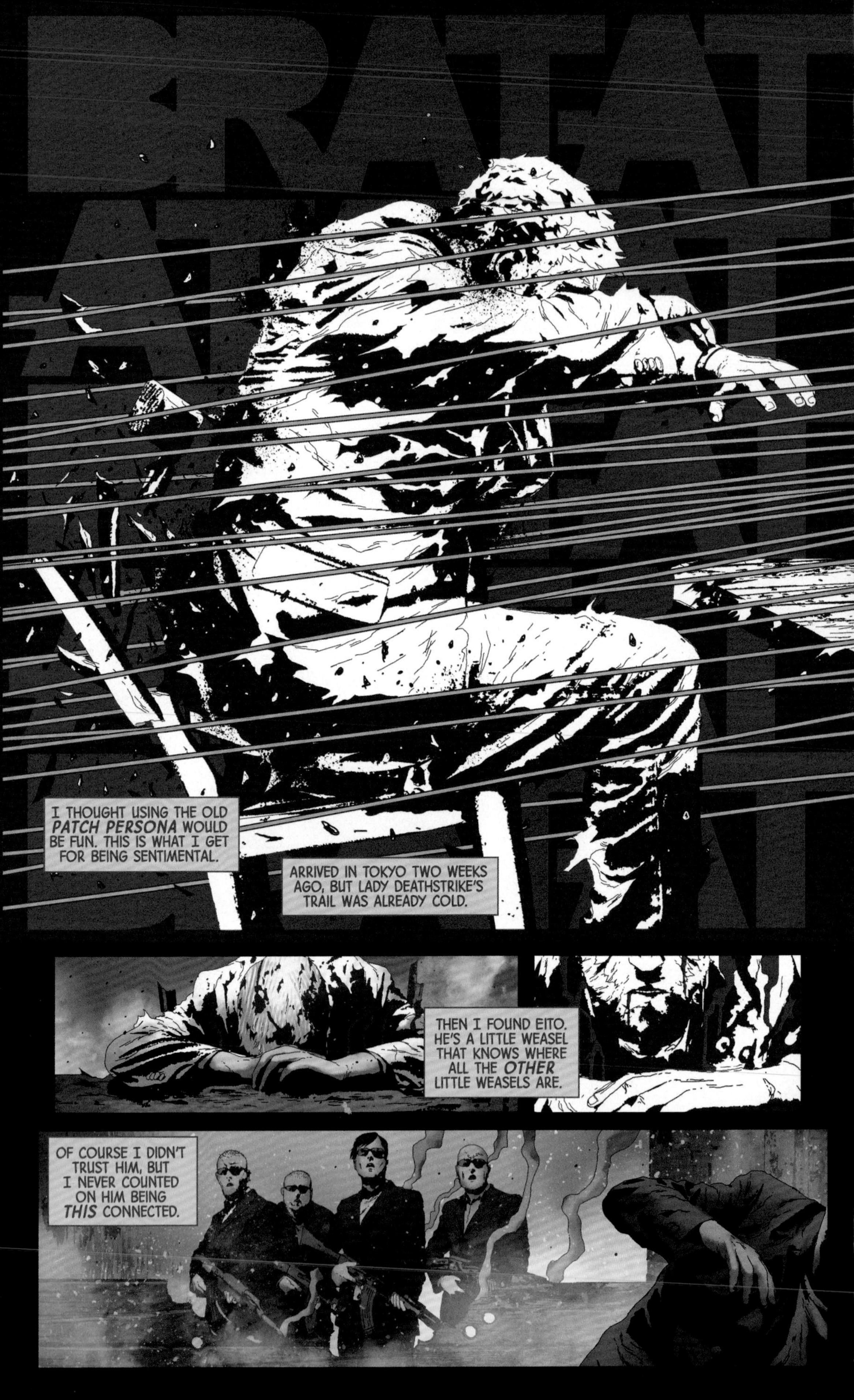
I THOUGHT USING THE OLD PATCH PERSONA WOULD BE FUN. THIS IS WHAT I GET FOR BEING SENTIMENTAL.
ARRIVED IN TOKYO TWO WEEKS AGO, BUT LADY DEATHSTRIKE'S TRAIL WAS ALREADY COLD.
THEN I FOUND EITO. HE'S A LITTLE WEASEL THAT KNOWS WHERE ALL THE OTHER LITTLE WEASELS ARE.
OF COURSE I DIDN'T TRUST HIM, BUT I NEVER COUNTED ON HIM BEING THIS CONNECTED.

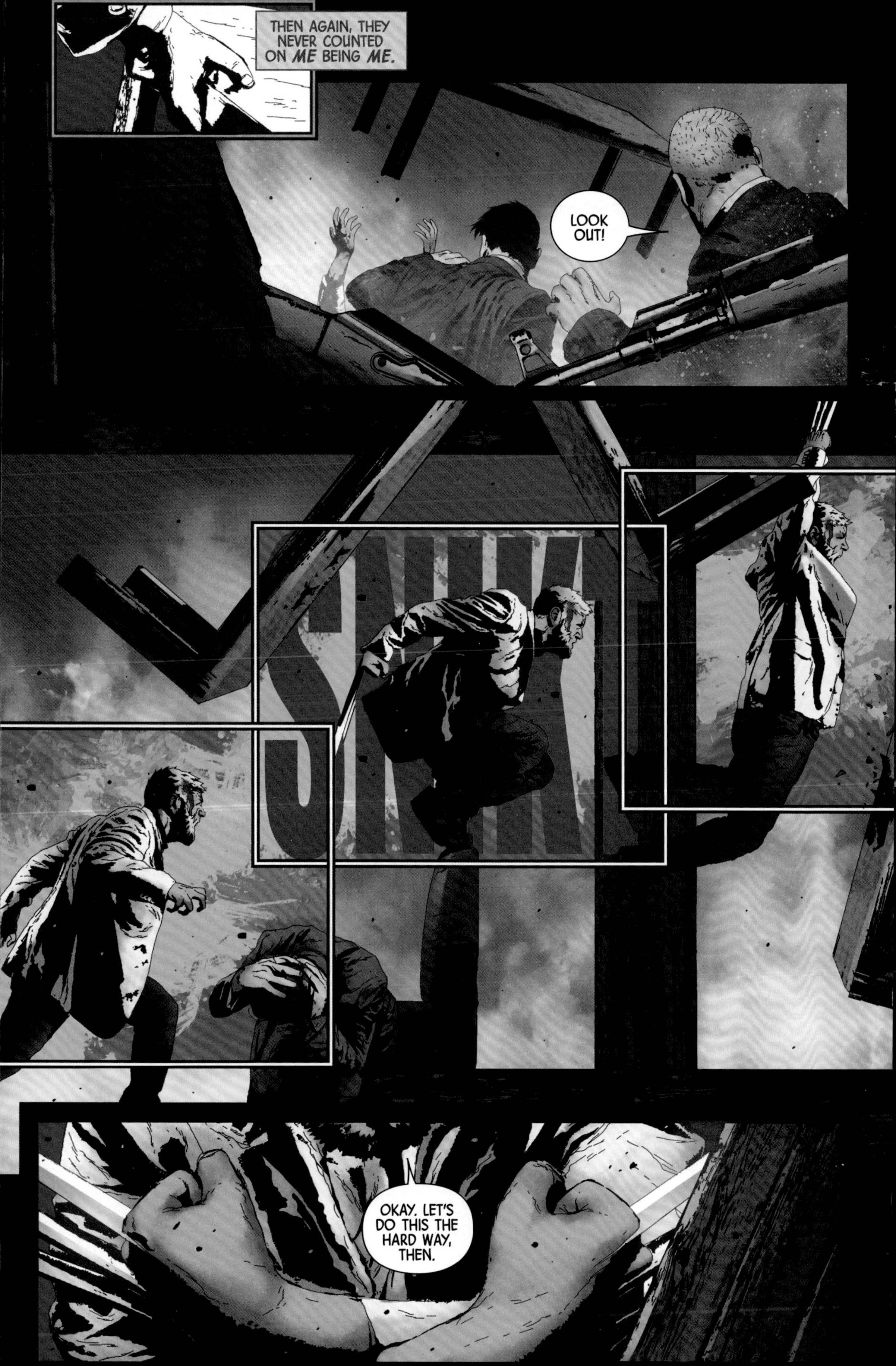
THEN AGAIN, THEY NEVER COUNTED ON *ME* BEING *ME*.
LOOK OUT!
OKAY. LET'S DO THIS THE HARD WAY, THEN.

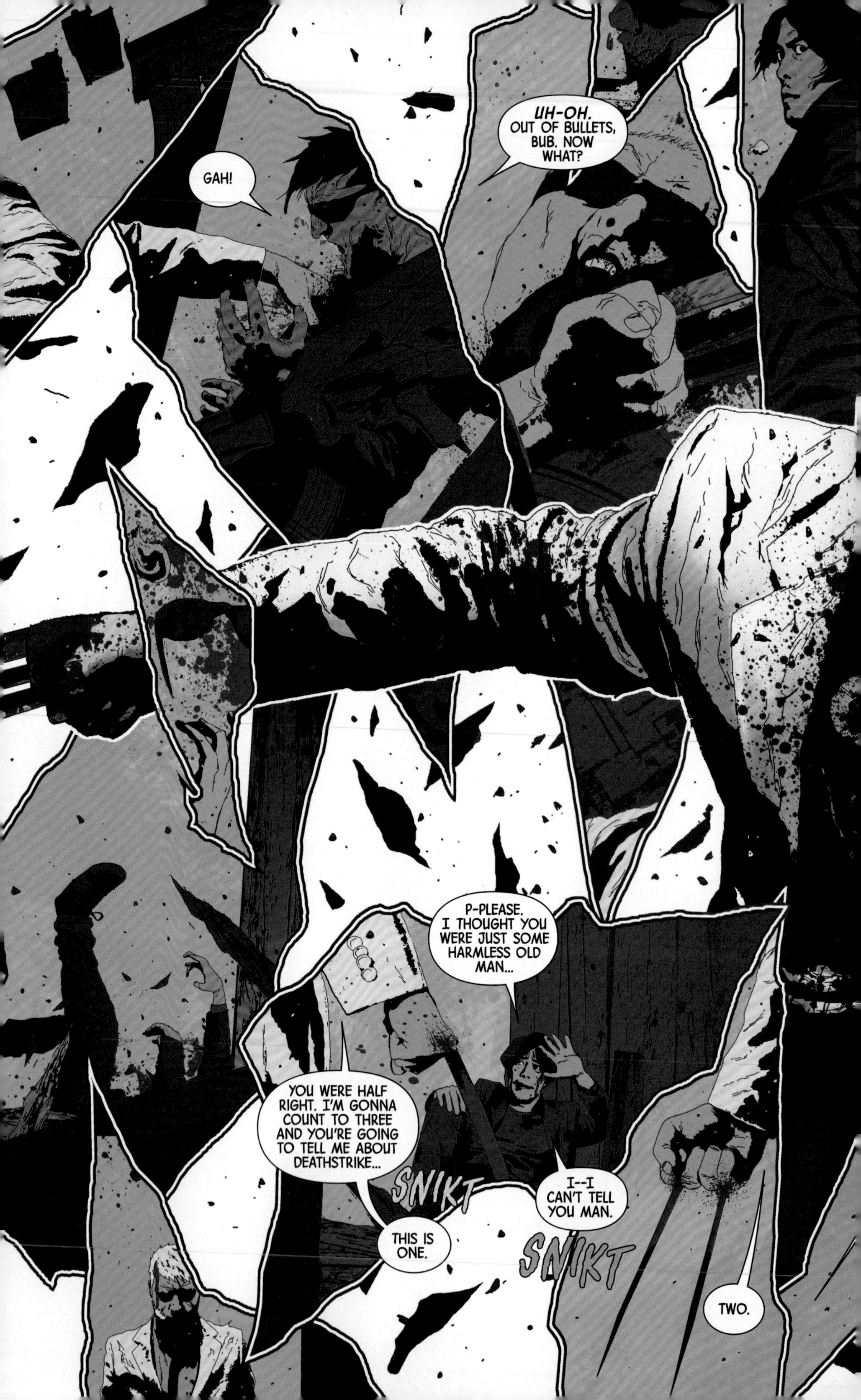
GAH!
UH-OH. OUT OF BULLETS, BUB. NOW WHAT?
P-PLEASE. I THOUGHT YOU WERE JUST SOME HARMLESS OLD MAN...
YOU WERE HALF RIGHT. I'M GONNA COUNT TO THREE AND YOU'RE GOING TO TELL ME ABOUT DEATHSTRIKE...
SNIKT
THIS IS ONE.
I--I CAN'T TELL YOU MAN.
SNIKT
TWO.

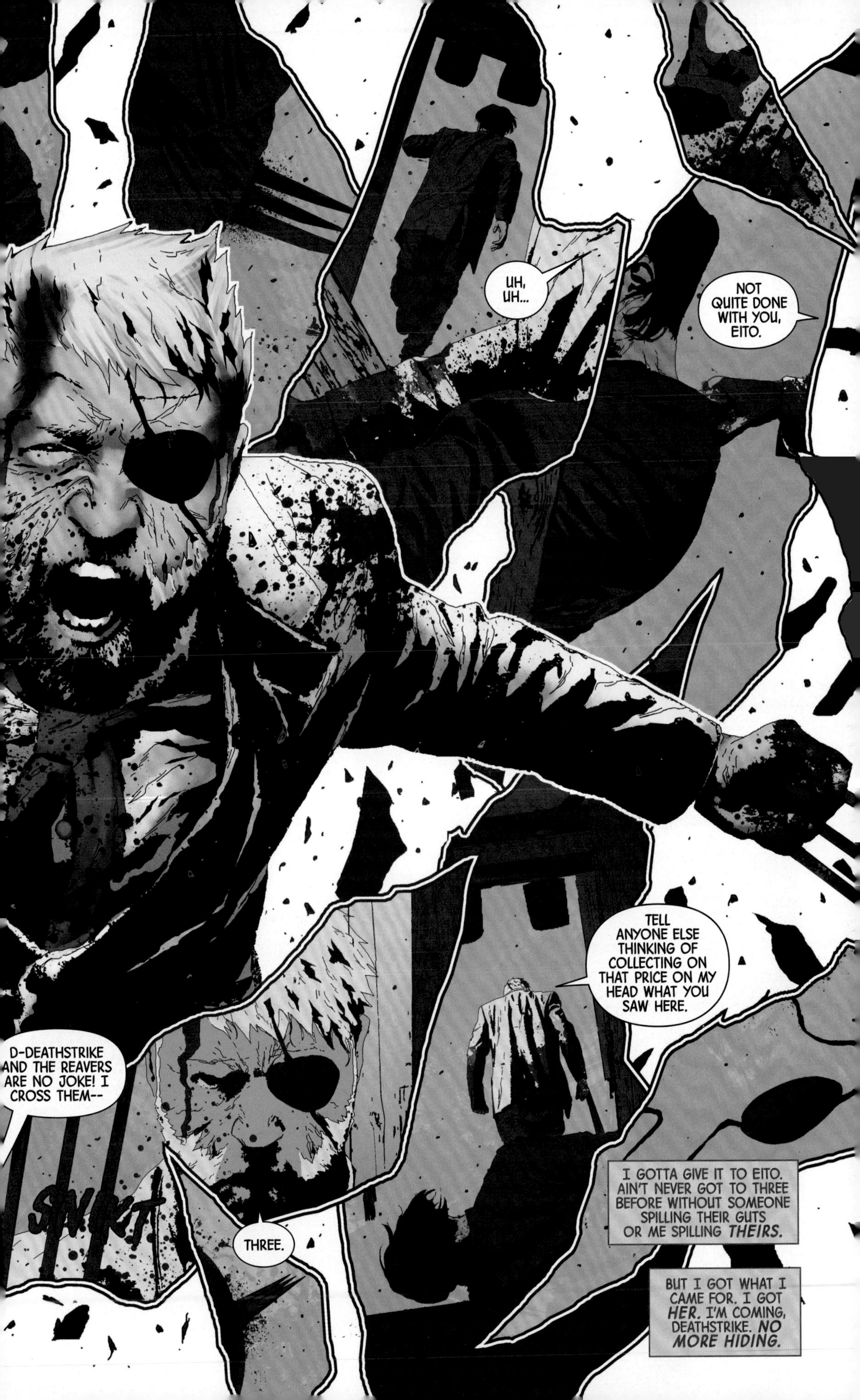
UH, UH...
NOT QUITE DONE WITH YOU, EITO.
TELL ANYONE ELSE THINKING OF COLLECTING ON THAT PRICE ON MY HEAD WHAT YOU SAW HERE.
D-DEATHSTRIKE AND THE REAVERS ARE NO JOKE! I CROSS THEM--
SNIKT
THREE.
I GOTTA GIVE IT TO EITO. AIN'T NEVER GOT TO THREE BEFORE WITHOUT SOMEONE SPILLING THEIR GUTS OR ME SPILLING *THEIRS.*
BUT I GOT WHAT I CAME FOR. I GOT *HER.* I'M COMING, DEATHSTRIKE. *NO MORE HIDING.*

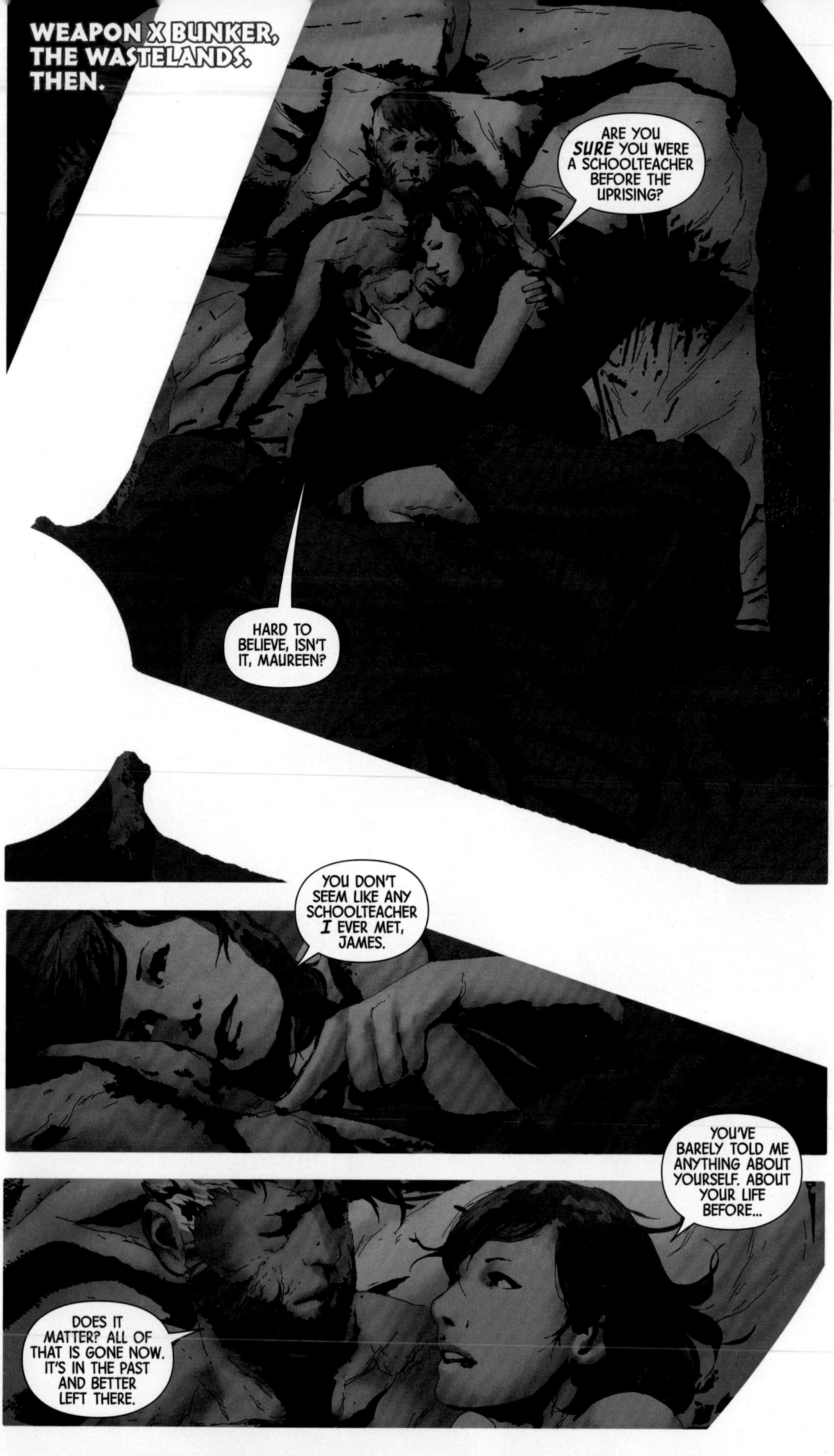
WEAPON X BUNKER, THE WASTELANDS. THEN.
ARE YOU SURE YOU WERE A SCHOOLTEACHER BEFORE THE UPRISING?
HARD TO BELIEVE, ISN'T IT, MAUREEN?
YOU DON'T SEEM LIKE ANY SCHOOLTEACHER I EVER MET, JAMES.
YOU'VE BARELY TOLD ME ANYTHING ABOUT YOURSELF. ABOUT YOUR LIFE BEFORE...
DOES IT MATTER? ALL OF THAT IS GONE NOW. IT'S IN THE PAST AND BETTER LEFT THERE.

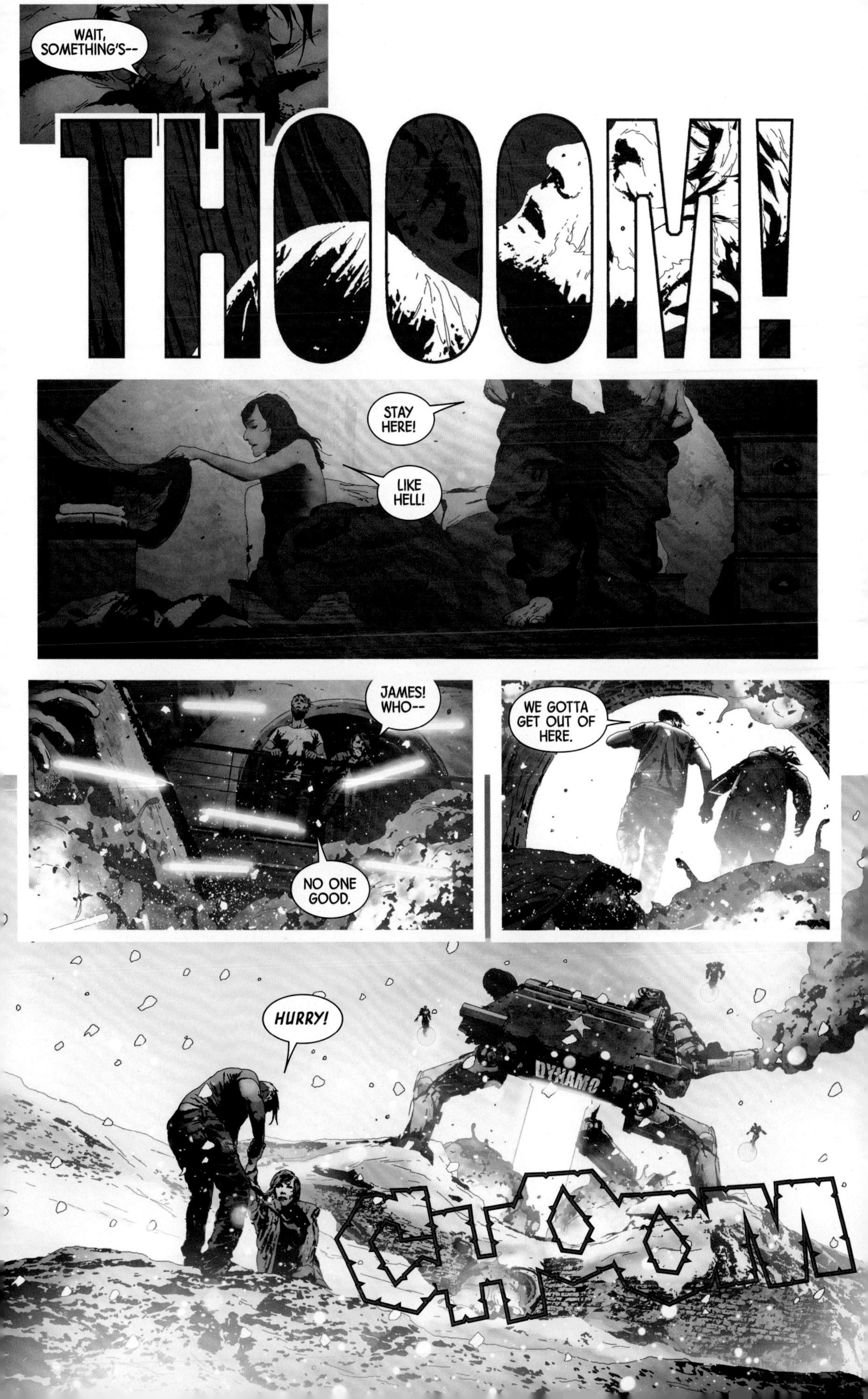
WAIT, SOMETHING'S--
THOOOM!
STAY HERE!
LIKE HELL!
JAMES! WHO--
NO ONE GOOD.
WE GOTTA GET OUT OF HERE.
HURRY!
DYNAMO
CHOOOM

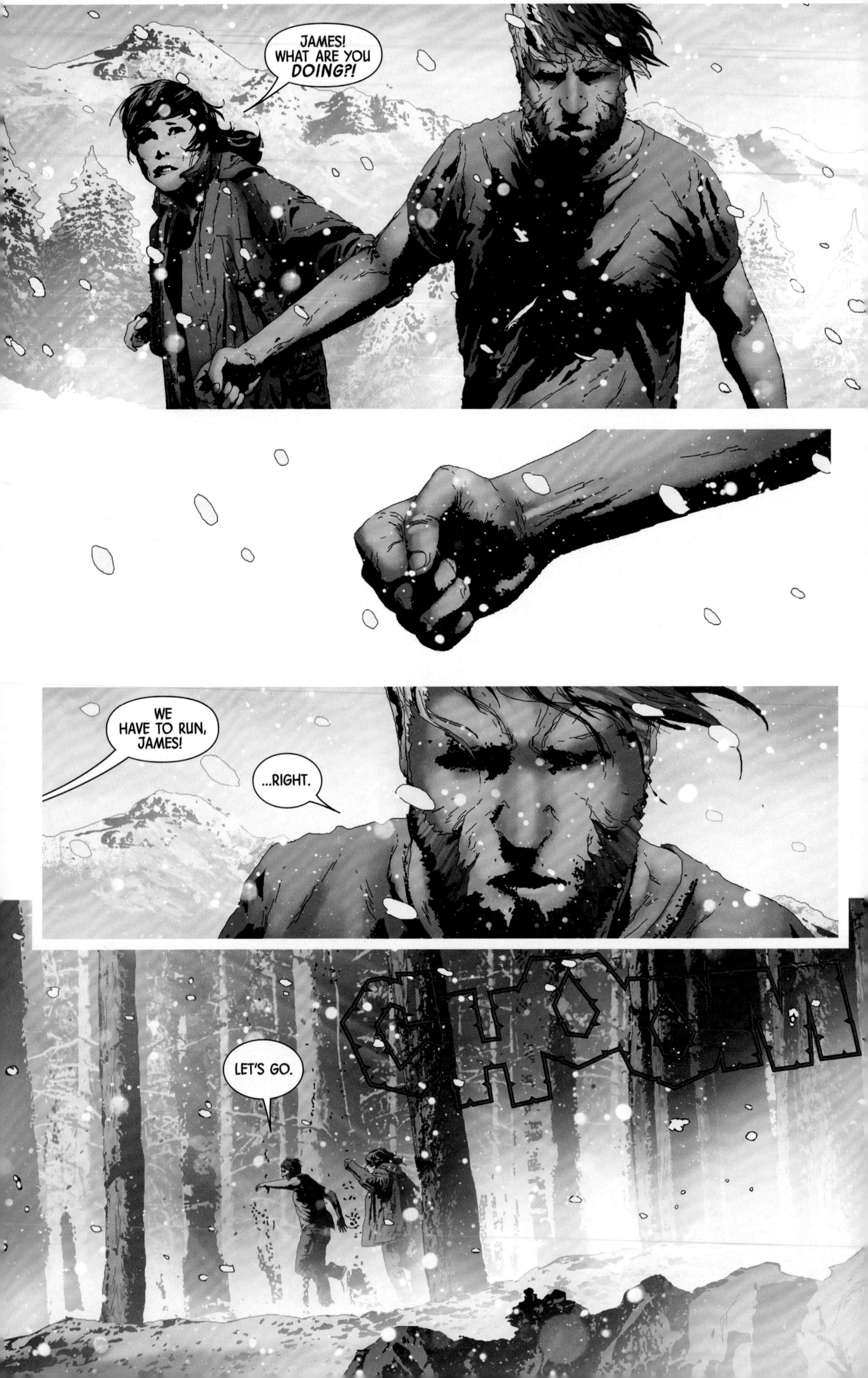
JAMES! WHAT ARE YOU DOING?!
WE HAVE TO RUN, JAMES!
...RIGHT.
LET'S GO.

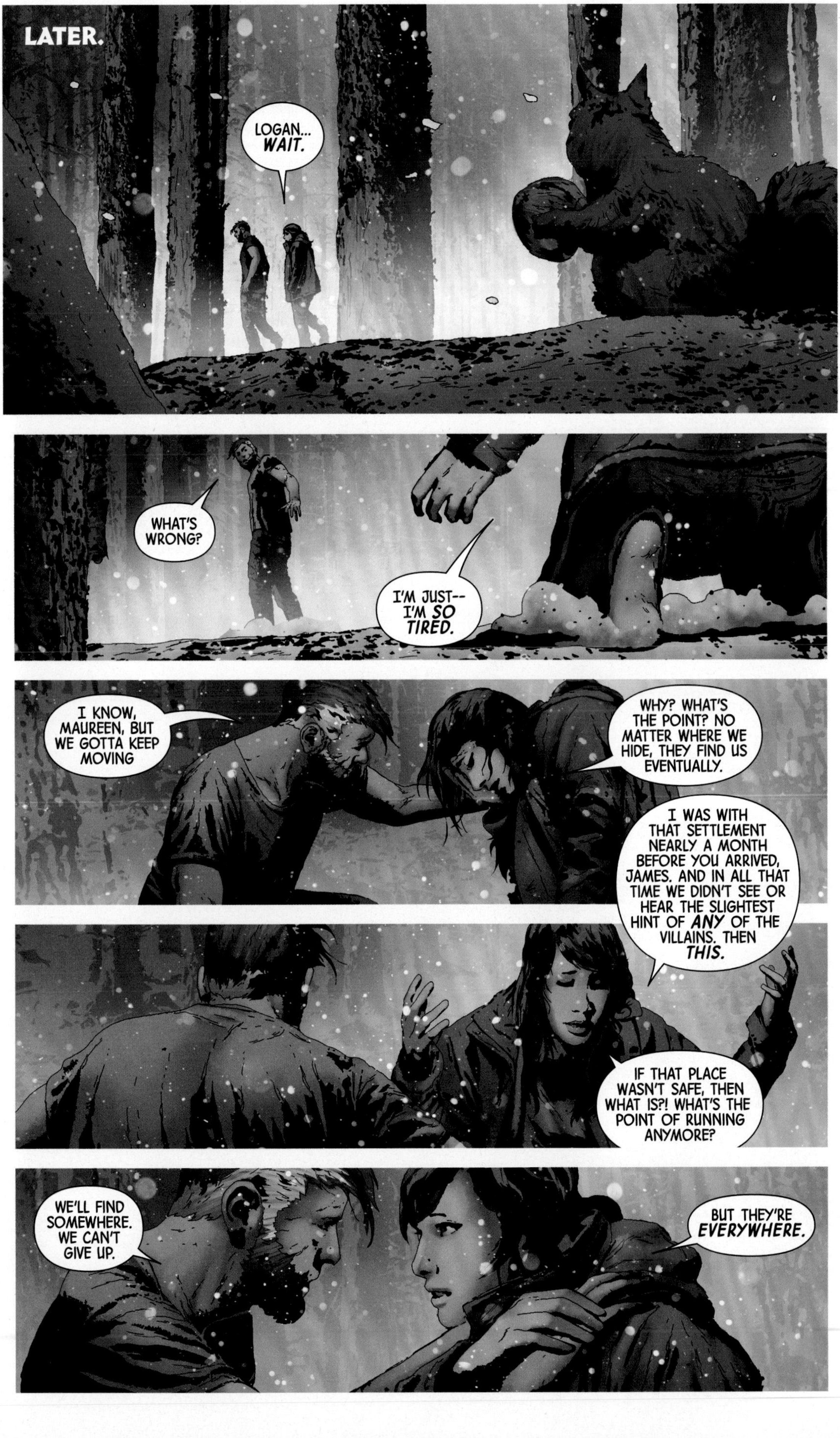
LATER.
LOGAN... WAIT.
WHAT'S WRONG?
I'M JUST-- I'M SO TIRED.
I KNOW, MAUREEN, BUT WE GOTTA KEEP MOVING
WHY? WHAT'S THE POINT? NO MATTER WHERE WE HIDE, THEY FIND US EVENTUALLY.
I WAS WITH THAT SETTLEMENT NEARLY A MONTH BEFORE YOU ARRIVED, JAMES. AND IN ALL THAT TIME WE DIDN'T SEE OR HEAR THE SLIGHTEST HINT OF ANY OF THE VILLAINS. THEN THIS.
IF THAT PLACE WASN'T SAFE, THEN WHAT IS?! WHAT'S THE POINT OF RUNNING ANYMORE?
WE'LL FIND SOMEWHERE. WE CAN'T GIVE UP.
BUT THEY'RE EVERYWHERE.

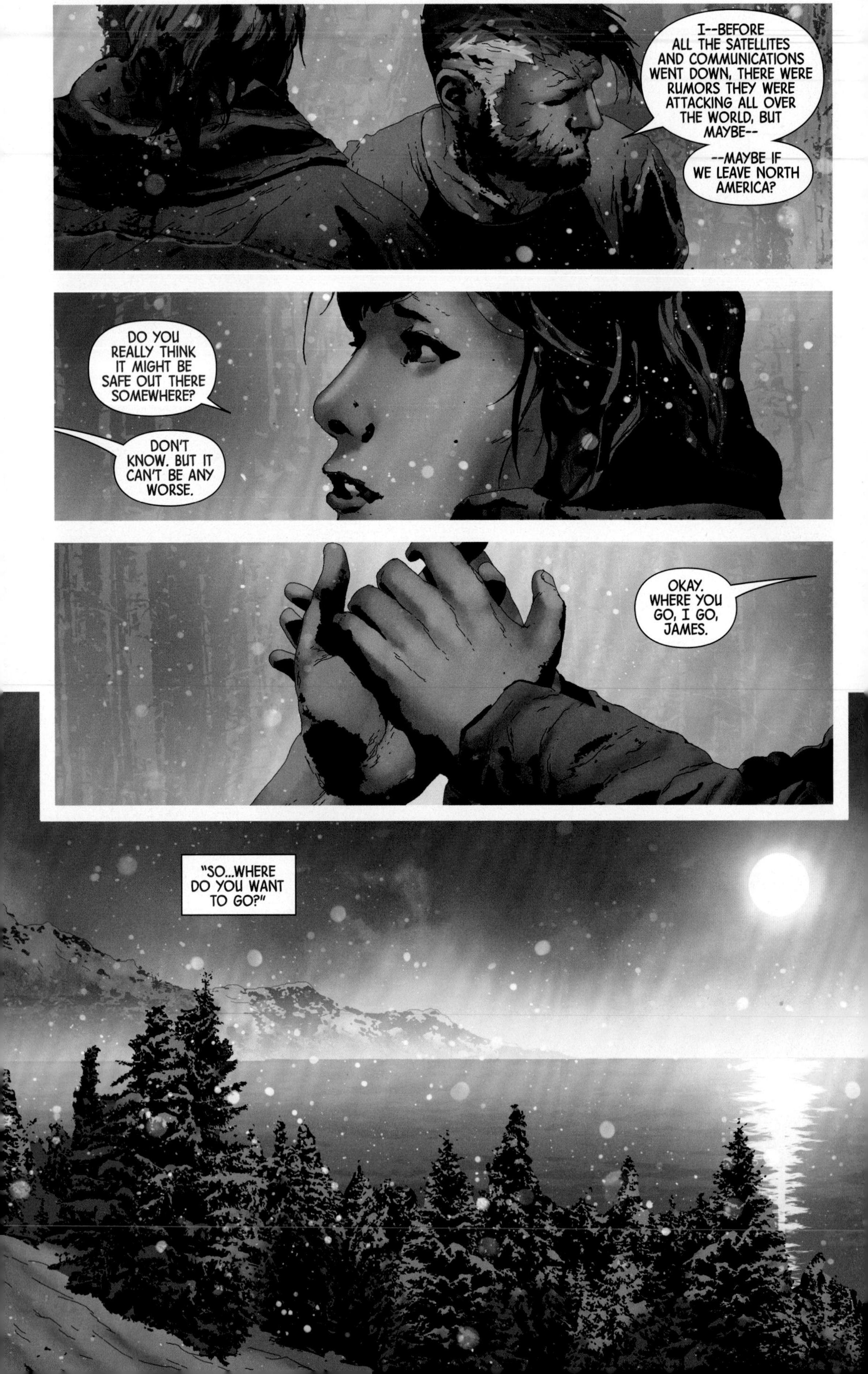
I--BEFORE ALL THE SATELLITES AND COMMUNICATIONS WENT DOWN, THERE WERE RUMORS THEY WERE ATTACKING ALL OVER THE WORLD, BUT MAYBE--
--MAYBE IF WE LEAVE NORTH AMERICA?
DO YOU REALLY THINK IT MIGHT BE SAFE OUT THERE SOMEWHERE?
DON'T KNOW. BUT IT CAN'T BE ANY WORSE.
OKAY. WHERE YOU GO, I GO, JAMES.
"SO...WHERE DO YOU WANT TO GO?"

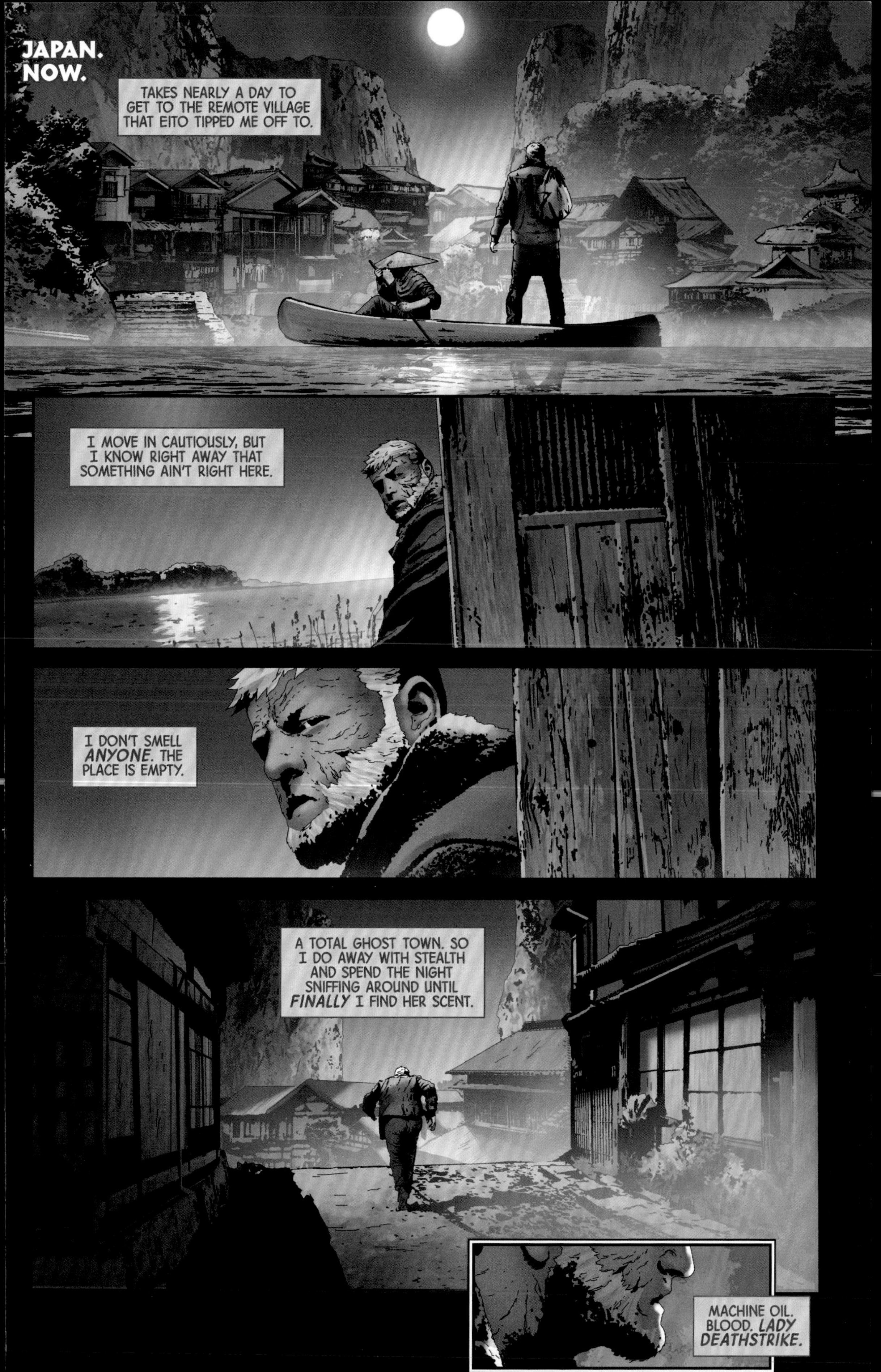
JAPAN.
NOW.
TAKES NEARLY A DAY TO GET TO THE REMOTE VILLAGE THAT EITO TIPPED ME OFF TO.
I MOVE IN CAUTIOUSLY, BUT I KNOW RIGHT AWAY THAT SOMETHING AIN'T RIGHT HERE.
I DON'T SMELL *ANYONE*. THE PLACE IS EMPTY.
A TOTAL GHOST TOWN. SO I DO AWAY WITH STEALTH AND SPEND THE NIGHT SNIFFING AROUND UNTIL *FINALLY* I FIND HER SCENT.
MACHINE OIL. BLOOD. *LADY DEATHSTRIKE.*

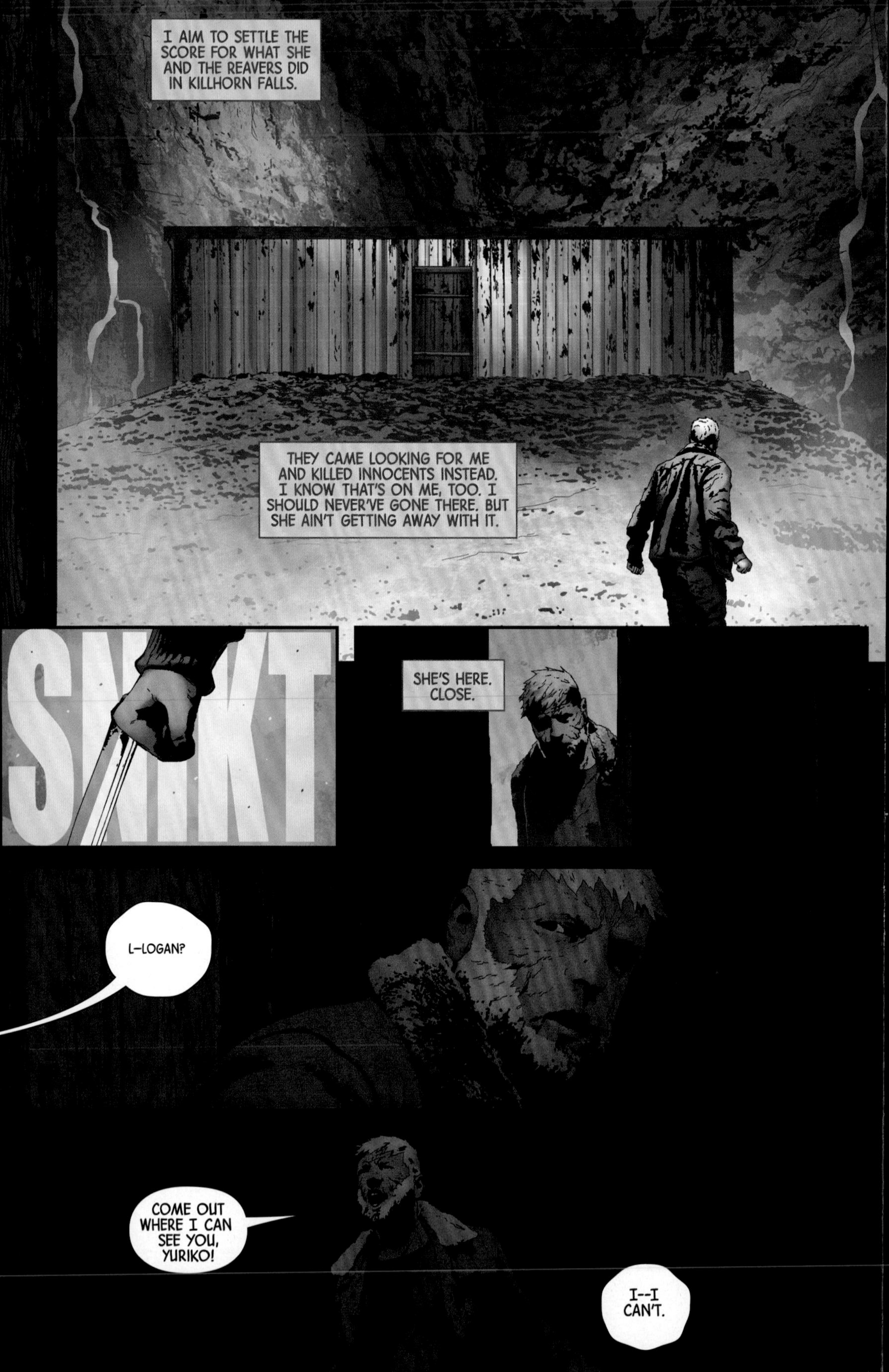
I AIM TO SETTLE THE SCORE FOR WHAT SHE AND THE REAVERS DID IN KILLHORN FALLS.
THEY CAME LOOKING FOR ME AND KILLED INNOCENTS INSTEAD. I KNOW THAT'S ON ME, TOO. I SHOULD NEVER'VE GONE THERE. BUT SHE AIN'T GETTING AWAY WITH IT.
SNIKT
SHE'S HERE. CLOSE.
L--LOGAN?
COME OUT WHERE I CAN SEE YOU, YURIKO!
I--I CAN'T.

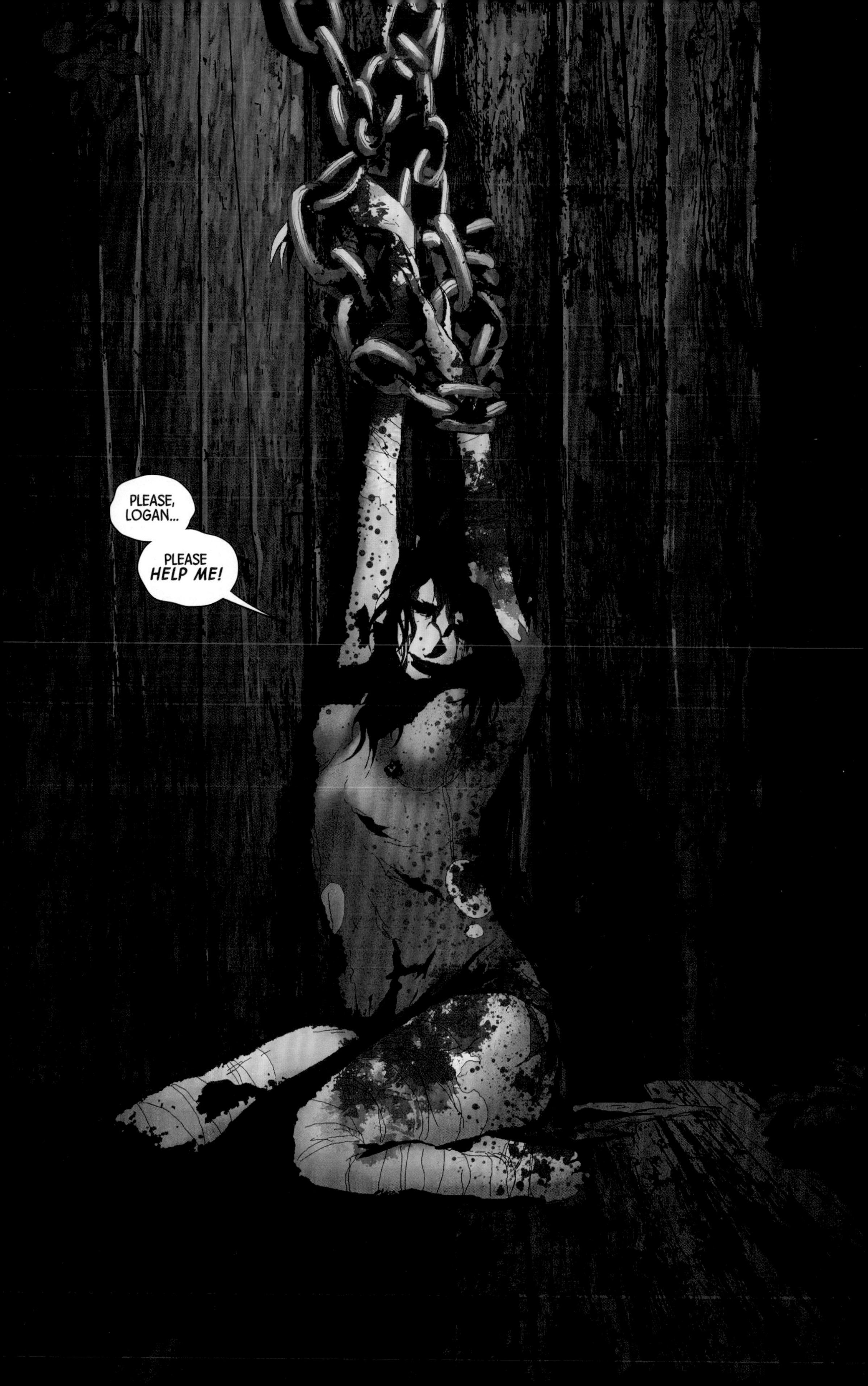
PLEASE, LOGAN...
PLEASE HELP ME!

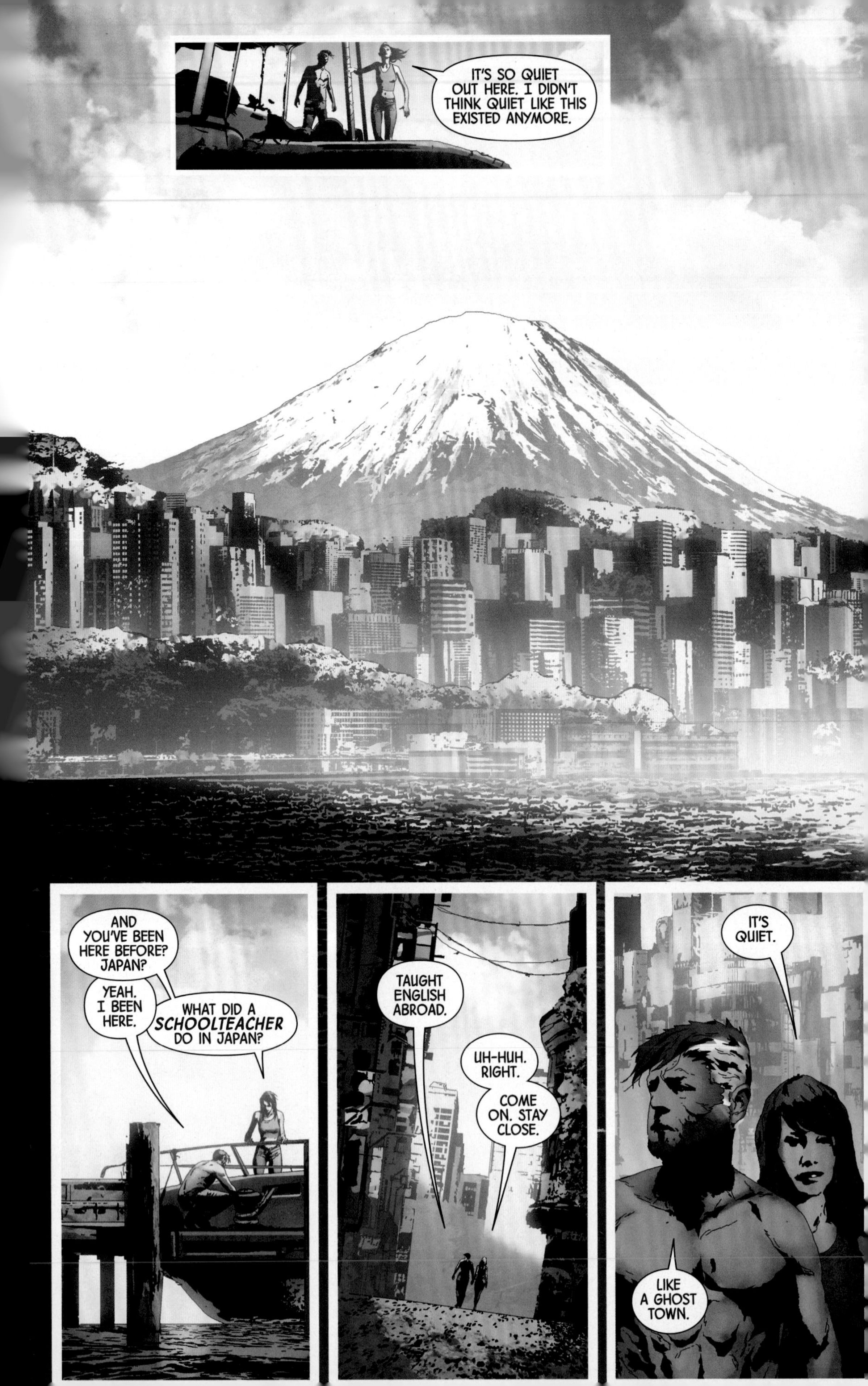
IT'S SO QUIET OUT HERE. I DIDN'T THINK QUIET LIKE THIS EXISTED ANYMORE.
AND YOU'VE BEEN HERE BEFORE? JAPAN?
YEAH. I BEEN HERE.
WHAT DID A *SCHOOLTEACHER* DO IN JAPAN?
TAUGHT ENGLISH ABROAD.
UH-HUH. RIGHT.
COME ON. STAY CLOSE.
IT'S QUIET.
LIKE A GHOST TOWN.

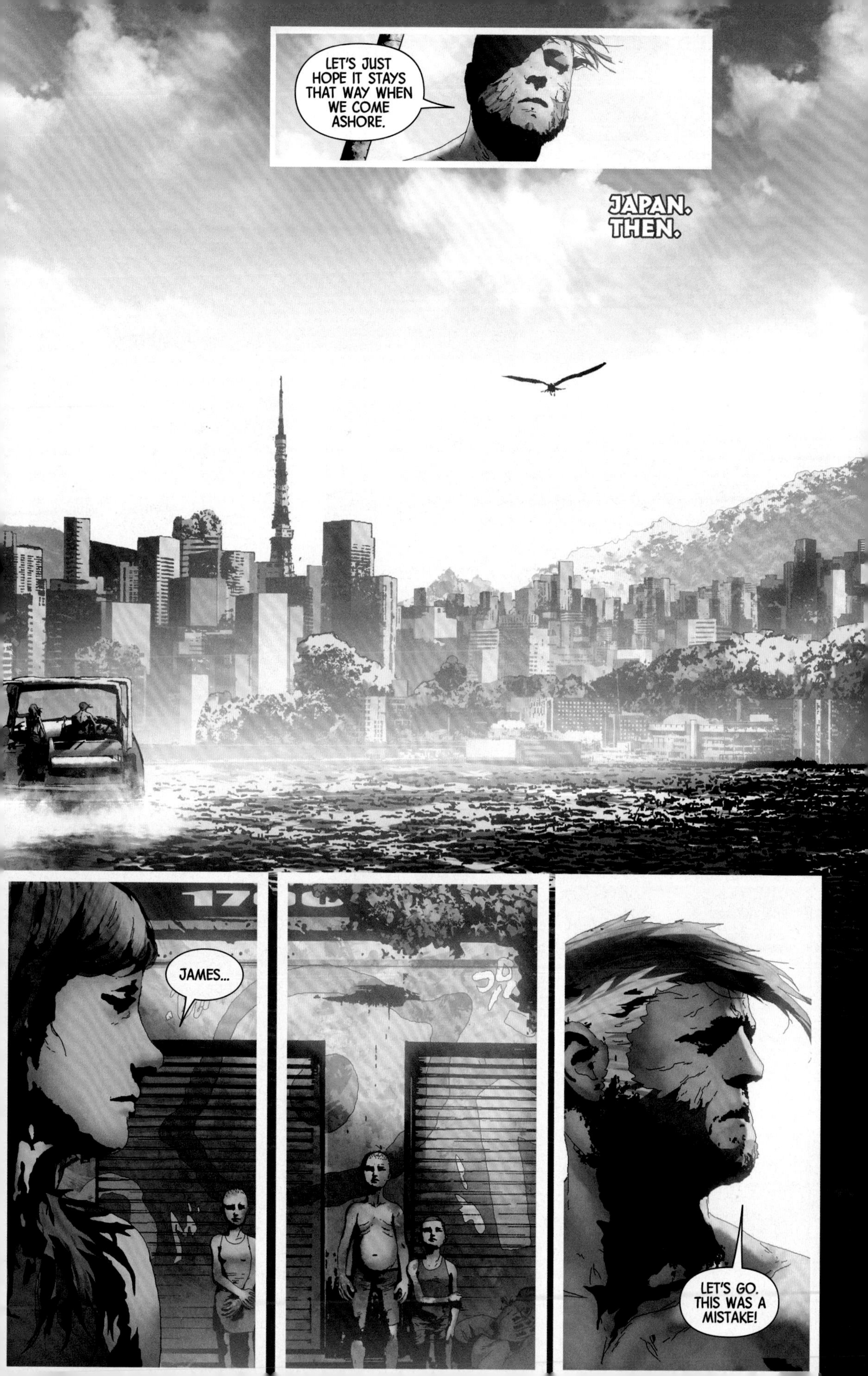
LET'S JUST HOPE IT STAYS THAT WAY WHEN WE COME ASHORE.
JAPAN. THEN.
JAMES...
LET'S GO. THIS WAS A MISTAKE!

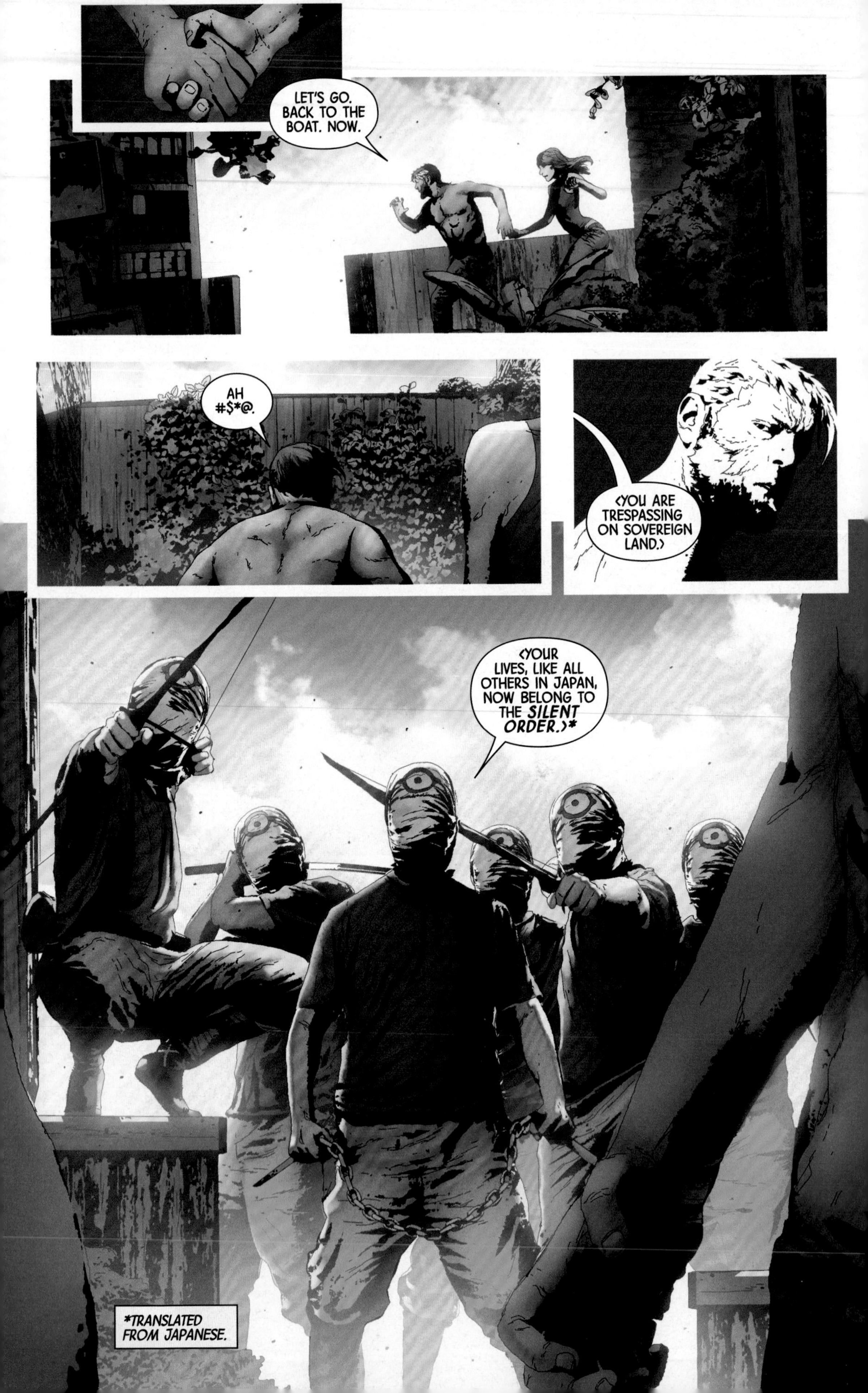
LET'S GO. BACK TO THE BOAT. NOW.
AH #$*@.
<YOU ARE TRESPASSING ON SOVEREIGN LAND.>
<YOUR LIVES, LIKE ALL OTHERS IN JAPAN, NOW BELONG TO THE SILENT ORDER.>*
*TRANSLATED FROM JAPANESE.

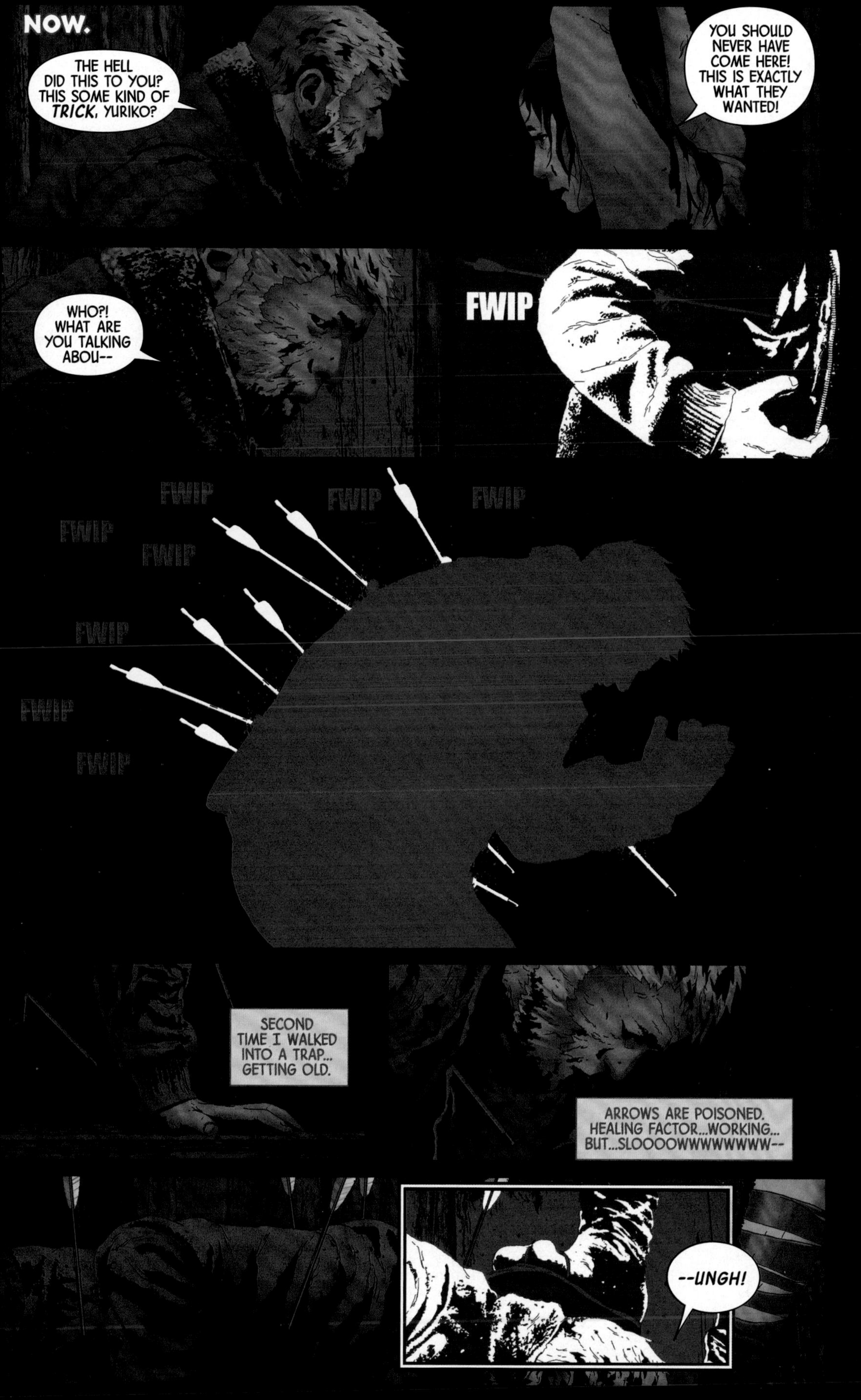
NOW.
THE HELL DID THIS TO YOU? THIS SOME KIND OF TRICK, YURIKO?
YOU SHOULD NEVER HAVE COME HERE! THIS IS EXACTLY WHAT THEY WANTED!
WHO?! WHAT ARE YOU TALKING ABOU--
FWIP
FWIP
FWIP
FWIP
FWIP
FWIP
FWIP
FWIP
SECOND TIME I WALKED INTO A TRAP... GETTING OLD.
ARROWS ARE POISONED. HEALING FACTOR...WORKING... BUT...SLOOOOWWWWWWWW--
--UNGH!

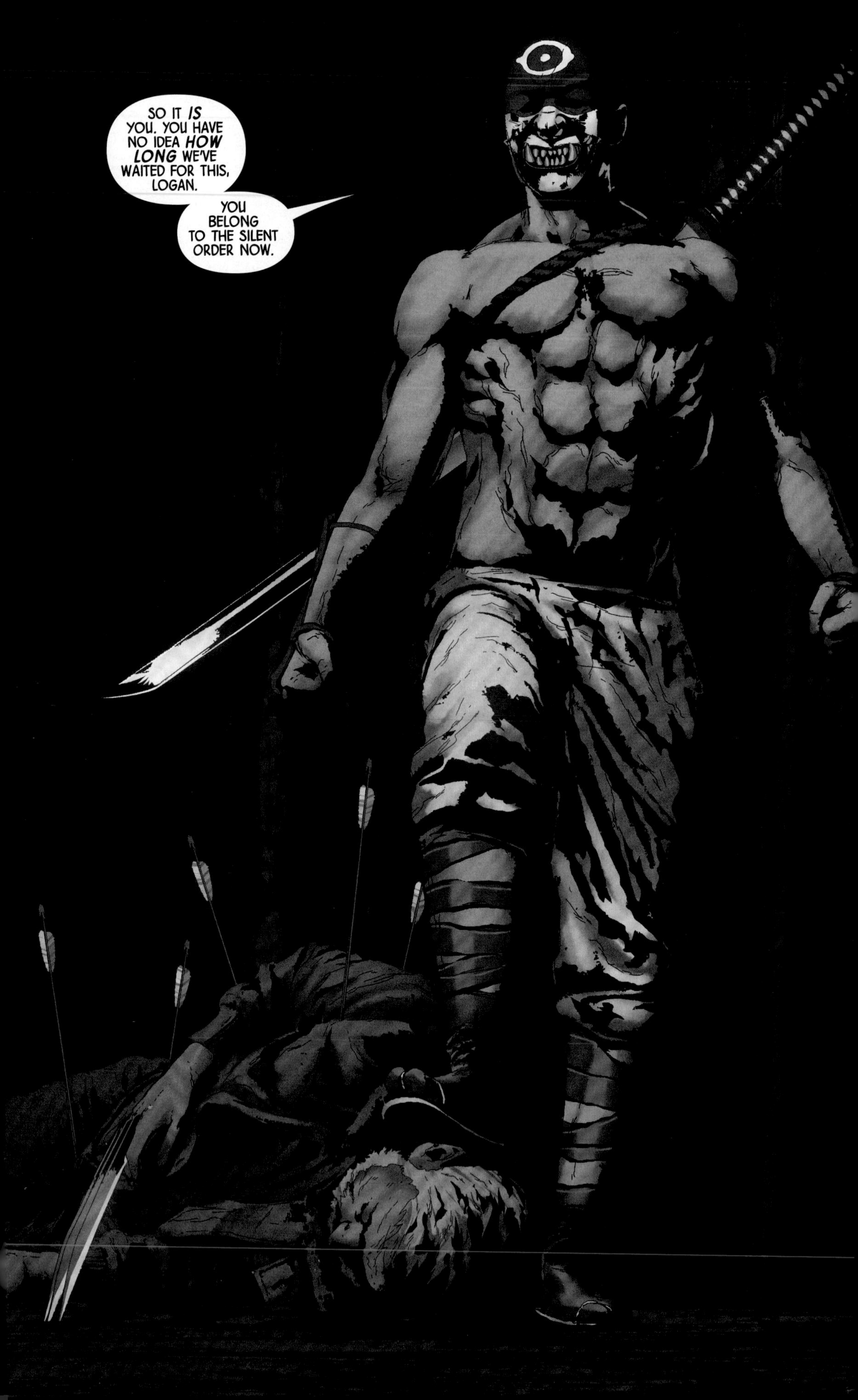
SO IT IS YOU. YOU HAVE NO IDEA HOW LONG WE'VE WAITED FOR THIS, LOGAN.
YOU BELONG TO THE SILENT ORDER NOW.

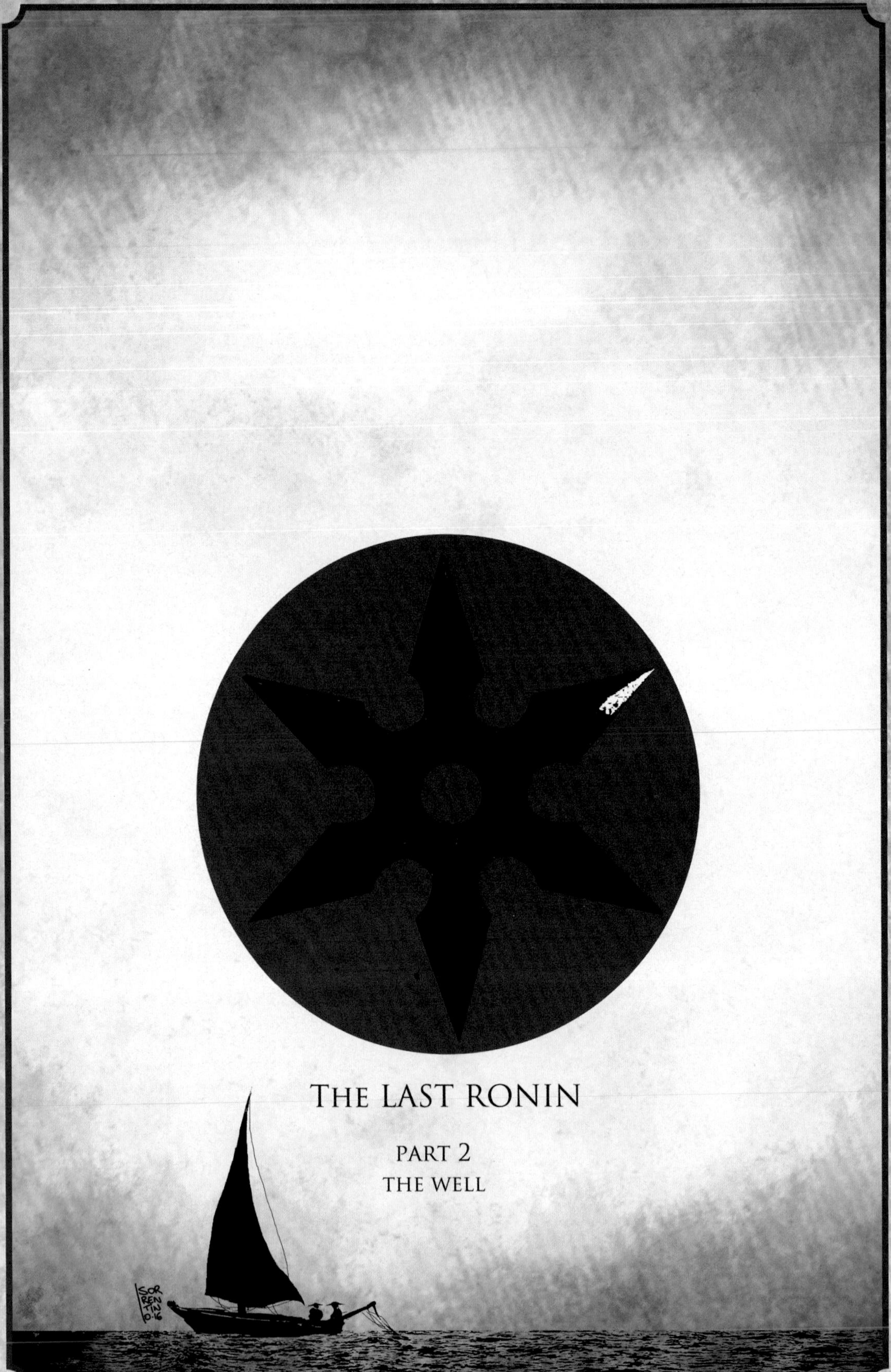

THE LAST RONIN
PART 2
THE WELL

10

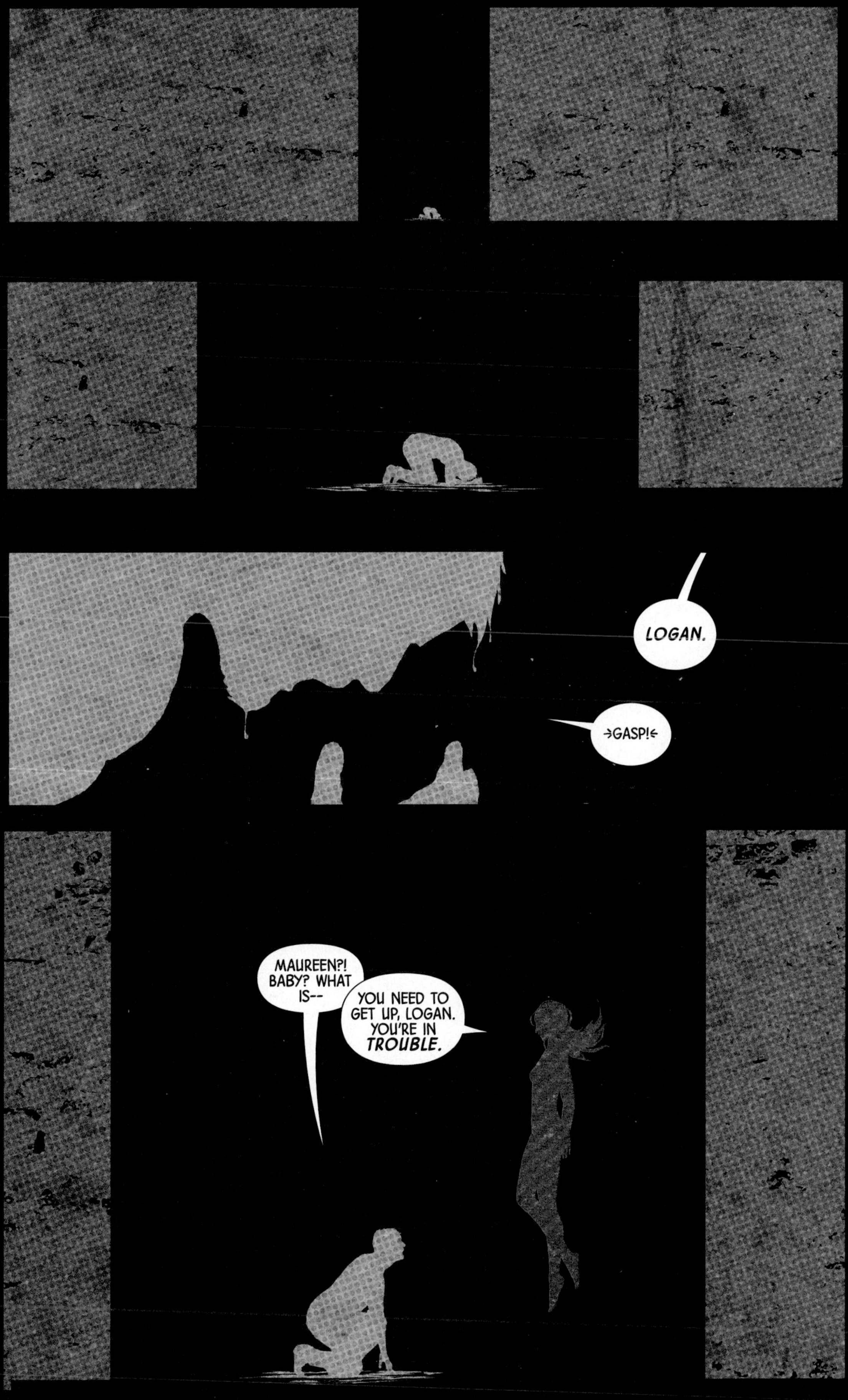
LOGAN.
>GASP!<
MAUREEN?! BABY? WHAT IS--
YOU NEED TO GET UP, LOGAN. YOU'RE IN TROUBLE.

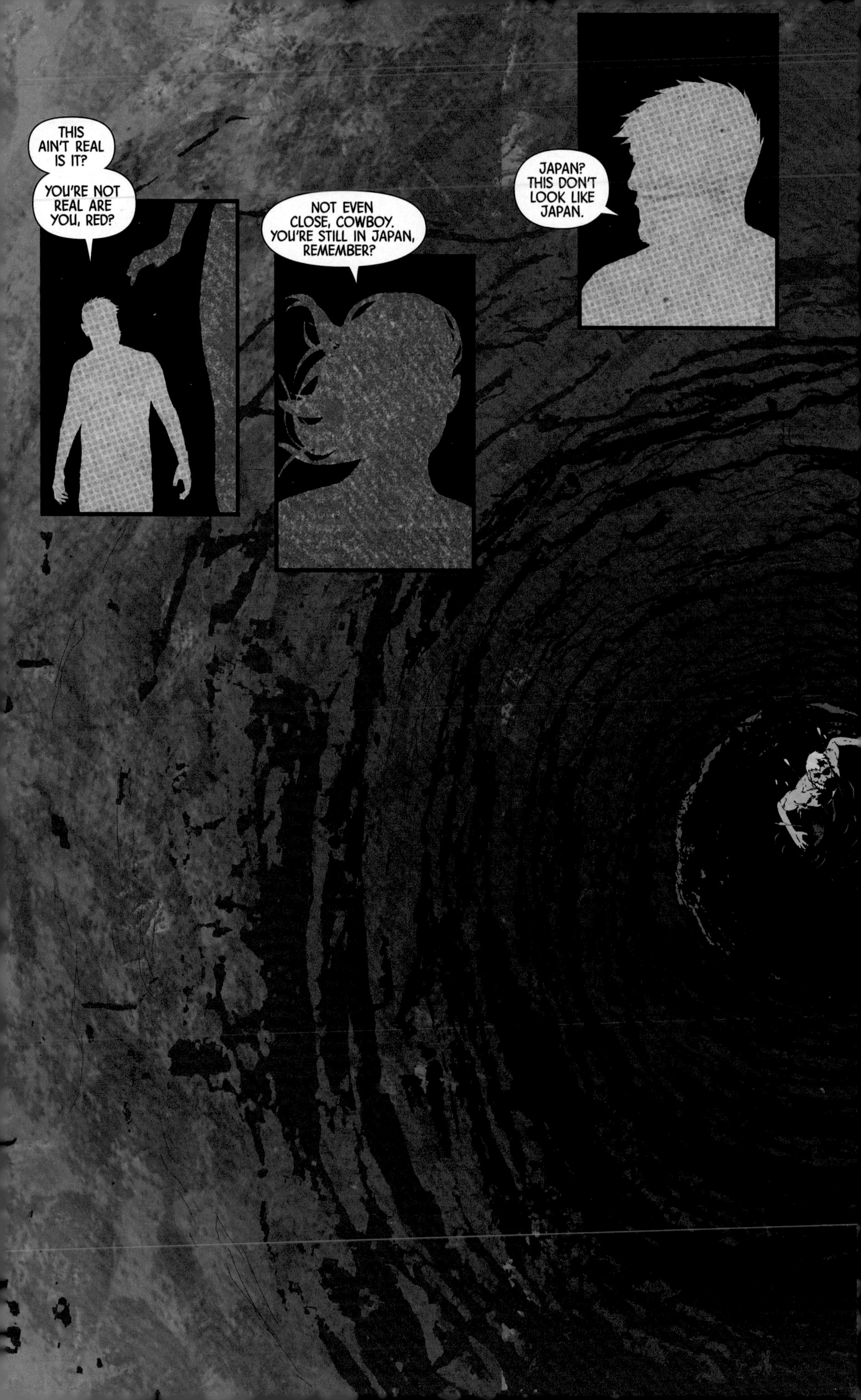
THIS AIN'T REAL IS IT?
YOU'RE NOT REAL ARE YOU, RED?
NOT EVEN CLOSE, COWBOY. YOU'RE STILL IN JAPAN, REMEMBER?
JAPAN? THIS DON'T LOOK LIKE JAPAN.

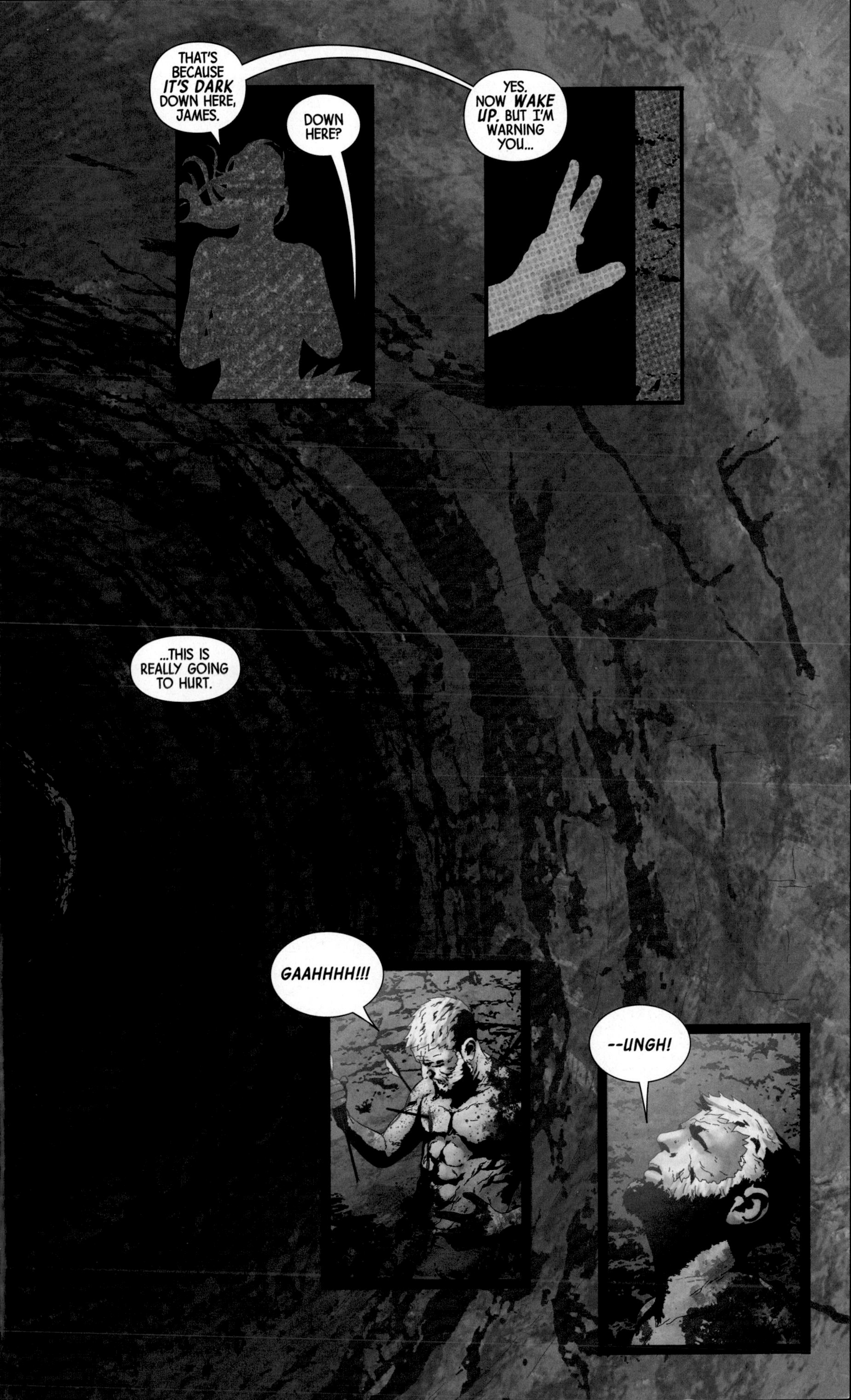
THAT'S BECAUSE *IT'S DARK* DOWN HERE, JAMES.
DOWN HERE?
YES. NOW *WAKE UP*. BUT I'M WARNING YOU...
...THIS IS REALLY GOING TO HURT.
GAAHHHH!!!
--UNGH!

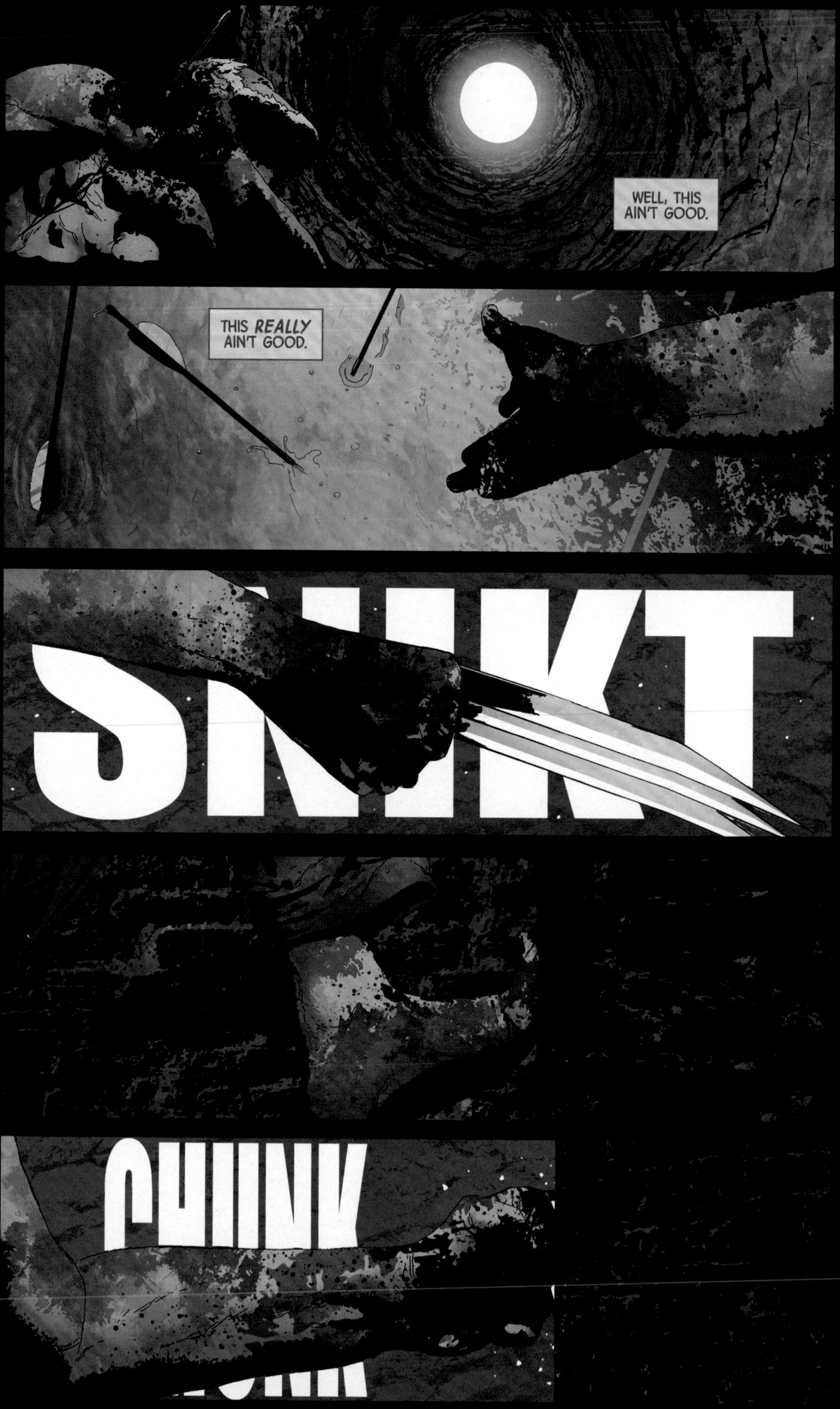
WELL, THIS AIN'T GOOD.
THIS *REALLY* AIN'T GOOD.
SNIKT
CHUNK

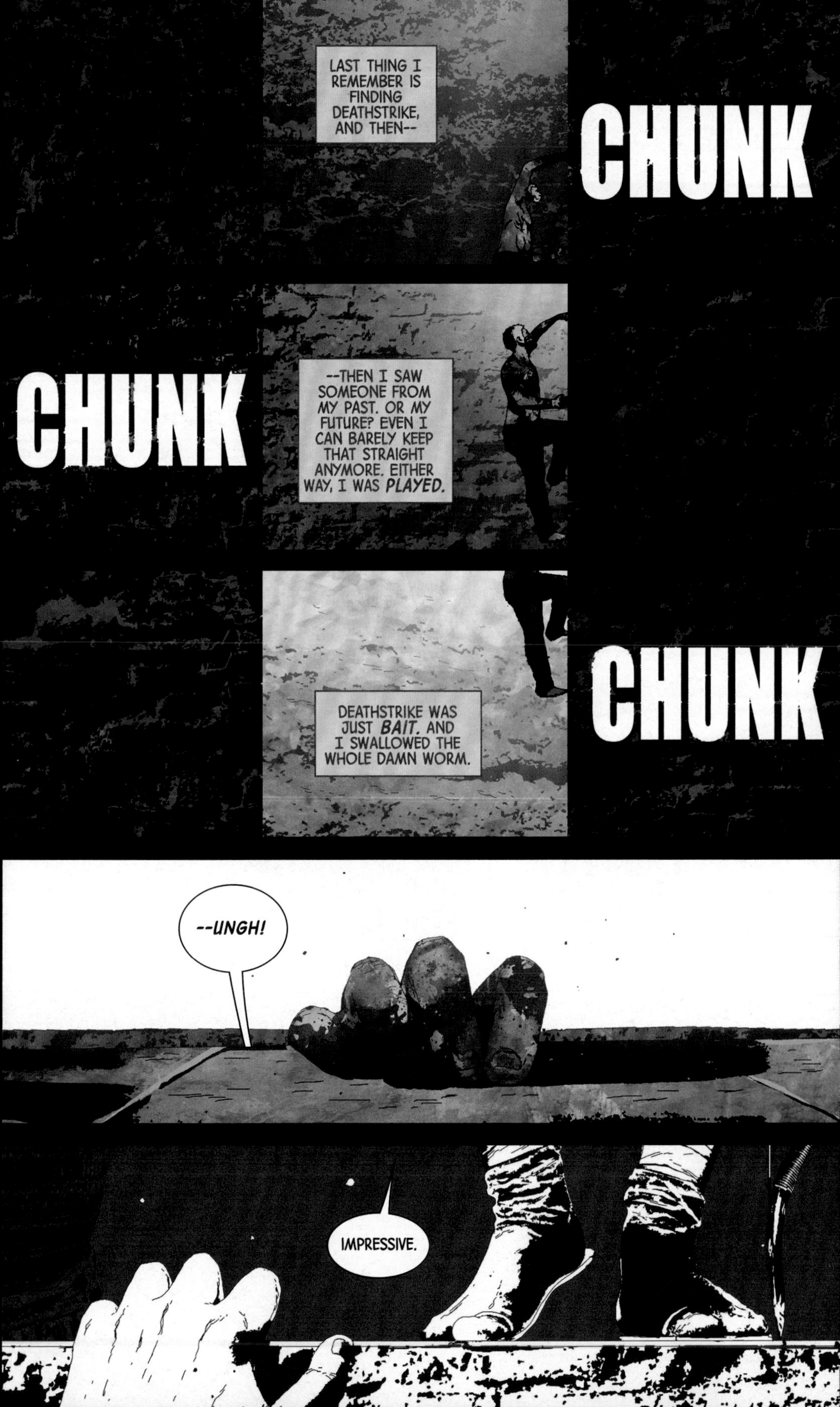
LAST THING I REMEMBER IS FINDING DEATHSTRIKE, AND THEN--
CHUNK
CHUNK
--THEN I SAW SOMEONE FROM MY PAST. OR MY FUTURE? EVEN I CAN BARELY KEEP THAT STRAIGHT ANYMORE. EITHER WAY, I WAS PLAYED.
CHUNK
DEATHSTRIKE WAS JUST BAIT. AND I SWALLOWED THE WHOLE DAMN WORM.
--UNGH!
IMPRESSIVE.

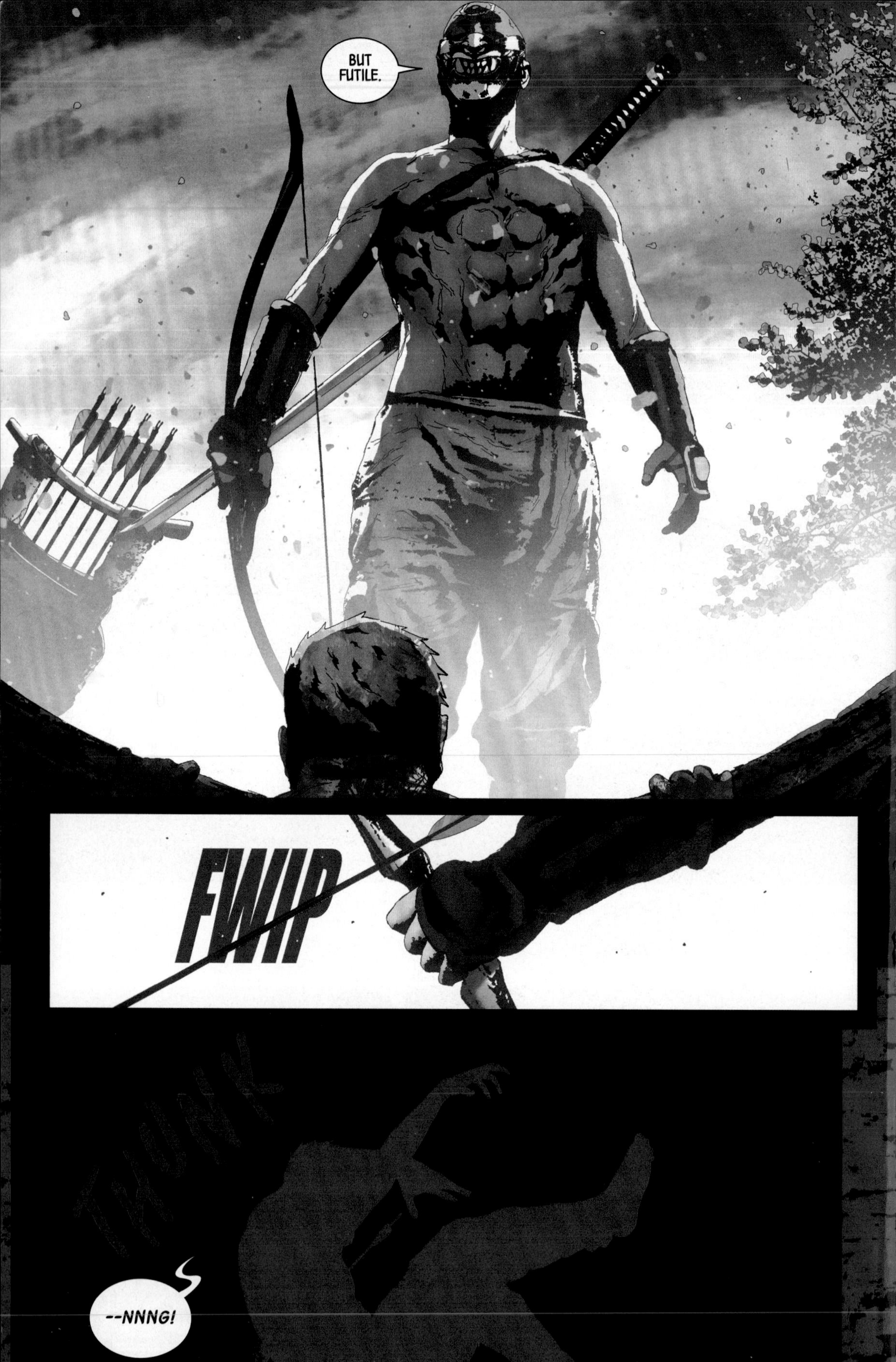
BUT FUTILE.
FWIP
THUNK
--NNNG!

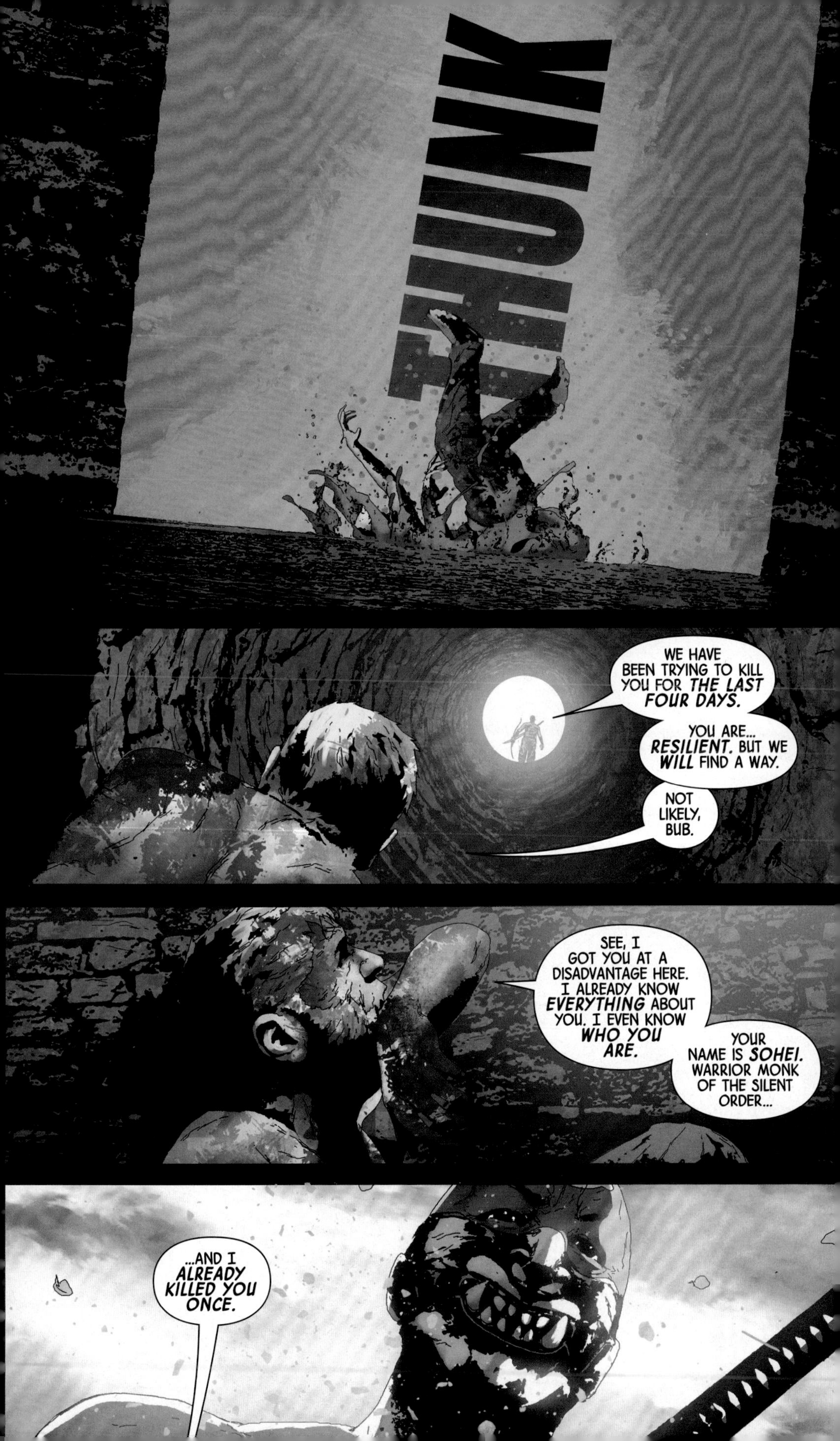
THUNK
WE HAVE BEEN TRYING TO KILL YOU FOR THE LAST FOUR DAYS.
YOU ARE... RESILIENT. BUT WE WILL FIND A WAY.
NOT LIKELY, BUB.
SEE, I GOT YOU AT A DISADVANTAGE HERE. I ALREADY KNOW EVERYTHING ABOUT YOU. I EVEN KNOW WHO YOU ARE.
YOUR NAME IS SOHEI. WARRIOR MONK OF THE SILENT ORDER...
...AND I ALREADY KILLED YOU ONCE.

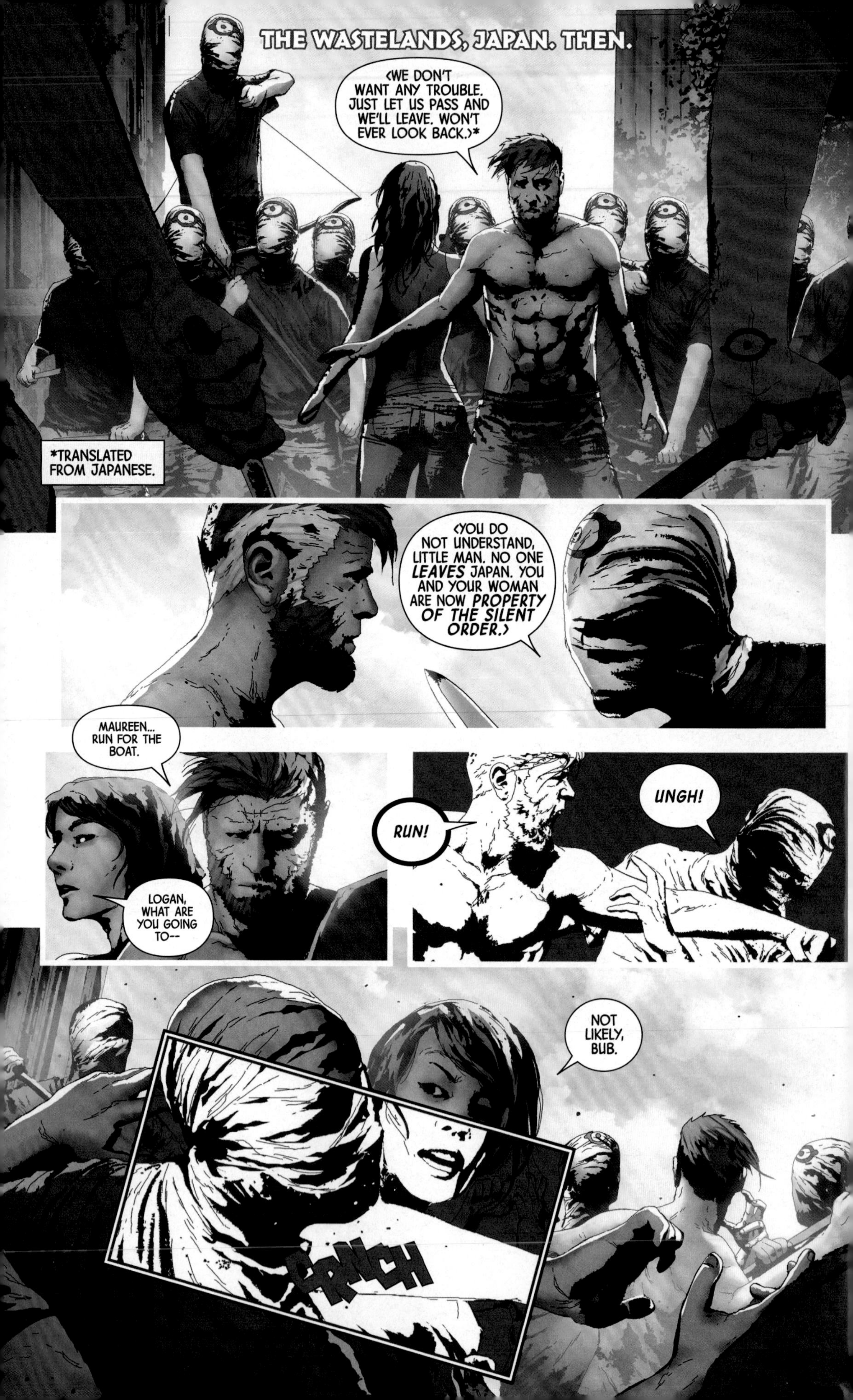
THE WASTELANDS, JAPAN. THEN.
<WE DON'T WANT ANY TROUBLE. JUST LET US PASS AND WE'LL LEAVE. WON'T EVER LOOK BACK.>*
*TRANSLATED FROM JAPANESE.
<YOU DO NOT UNDERSTAND, LITTLE MAN. NO ONE LEAVES JAPAN. YOU AND YOUR WOMAN ARE NOW PROPERTY OF THE SILENT ORDER.>
MAUREEN... RUN FOR THE BOAT.
LOGAN, WHAT ARE YOU GOING TO--
RUN!
UNGH!
NOT LIKELY, BUB.
CRNCH

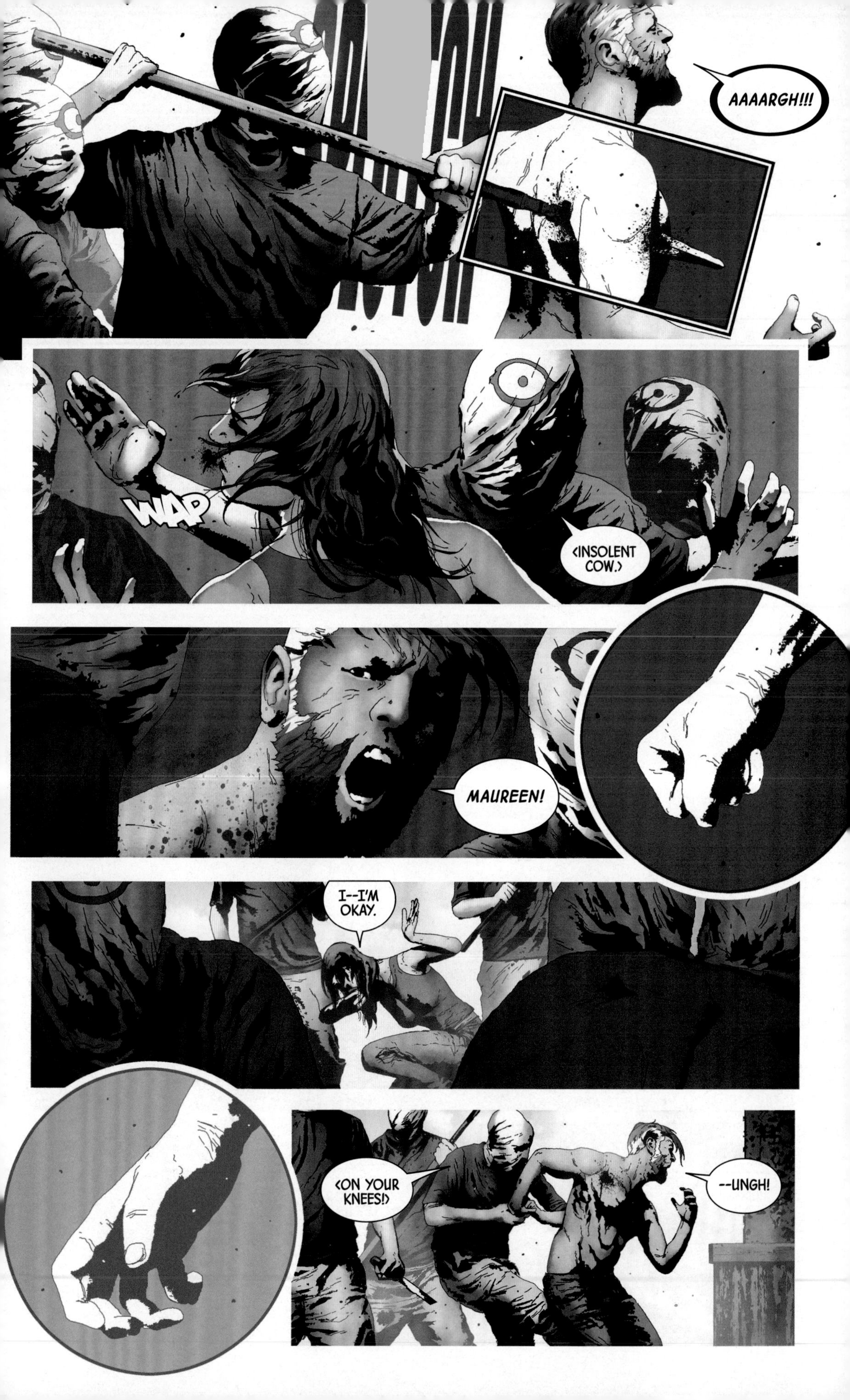
AAAARGH!!!
WAP
<INSOLENT COW.>
MAUREEN!
I--I'M OKAY.
<ON YOUR KNEES!>
--UNGH!

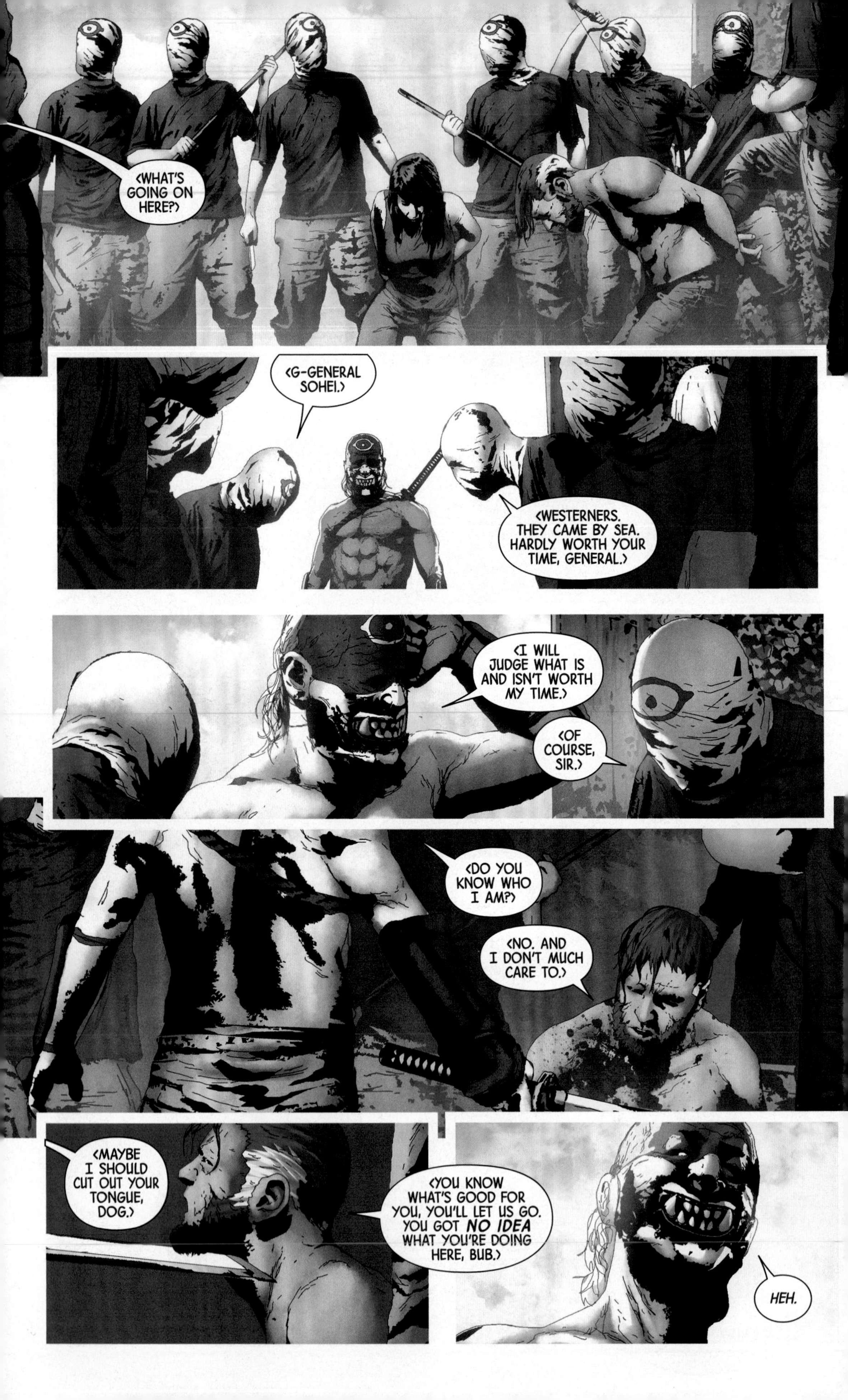

<WHAT'S GOING ON HERE?>
<G-GENERAL SOHEI.>
<WESTERNERS. THEY CAME BY SEA. HARDLY WORTH YOUR TIME, GENERAL.>
<I WILL JUDGE WHAT IS AND ISN'T WORTH MY TIME.>
<OF COURSE, SIR.>
<DO YOU KNOW WHO I AM?>
<NO. AND I DON'T MUCH CARE TO.>
<MAYBE I SHOULD CUT OUT YOUR TONGUE, DOG.>
<YOU KNOW WHAT'S GOOD FOR YOU, YOU'LL LET US GO. YOU GOT NO IDEA WHAT YOU'RE DOING HERE, BUB.>
HEH.

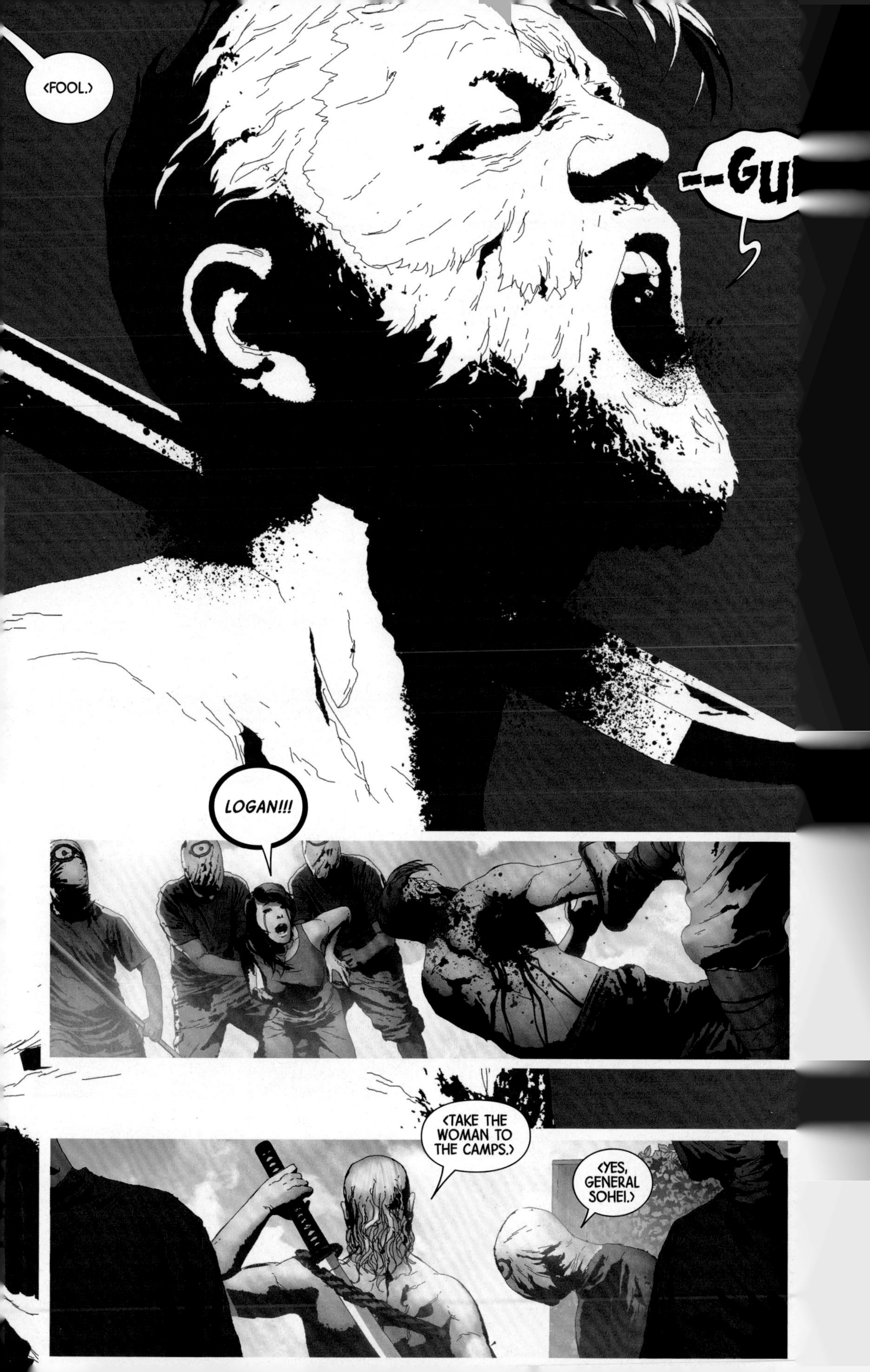
<FOOL.>
--GU
LOGAN!!!
<TAKE THE WOMAN TO THE CAMPS.>
<YES, GENERAL SOHEI.>

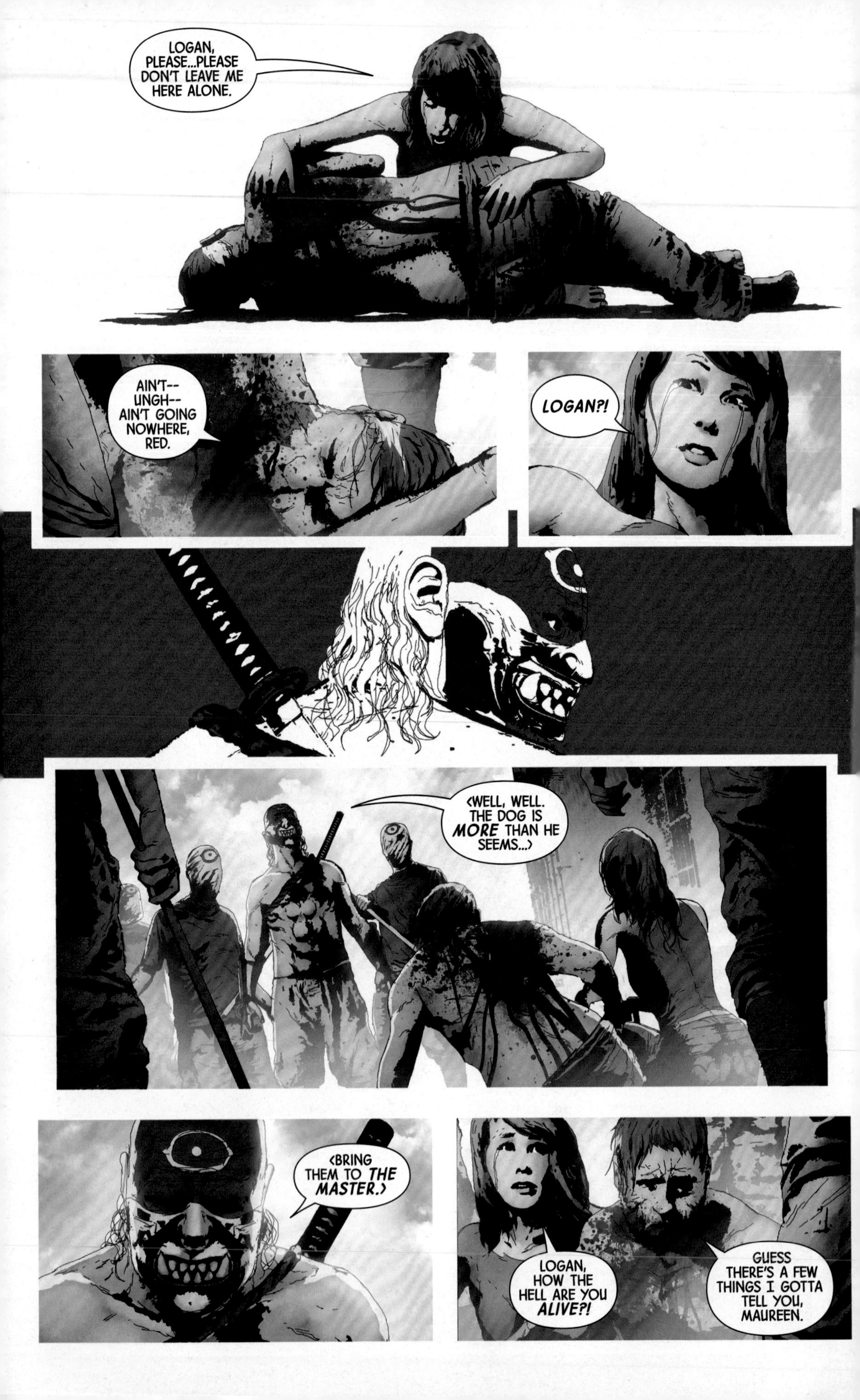
LOGAN, PLEASE...PLEASE DON'T LEAVE ME HERE ALONE.
AIN'T-- UNGH-- AIN'T GOING NOWHERE, RED.
LOGAN?!
<WELL, WELL. THE DOG IS MORE THAN HE SEEMS...>
<BRING THEM TO THE MASTER.>
LOGAN, HOW THE HELL ARE YOU ALIVE?!
GUESS THERE'S A FEW THINGS I GOTTA TELL YOU, MAUREEN.

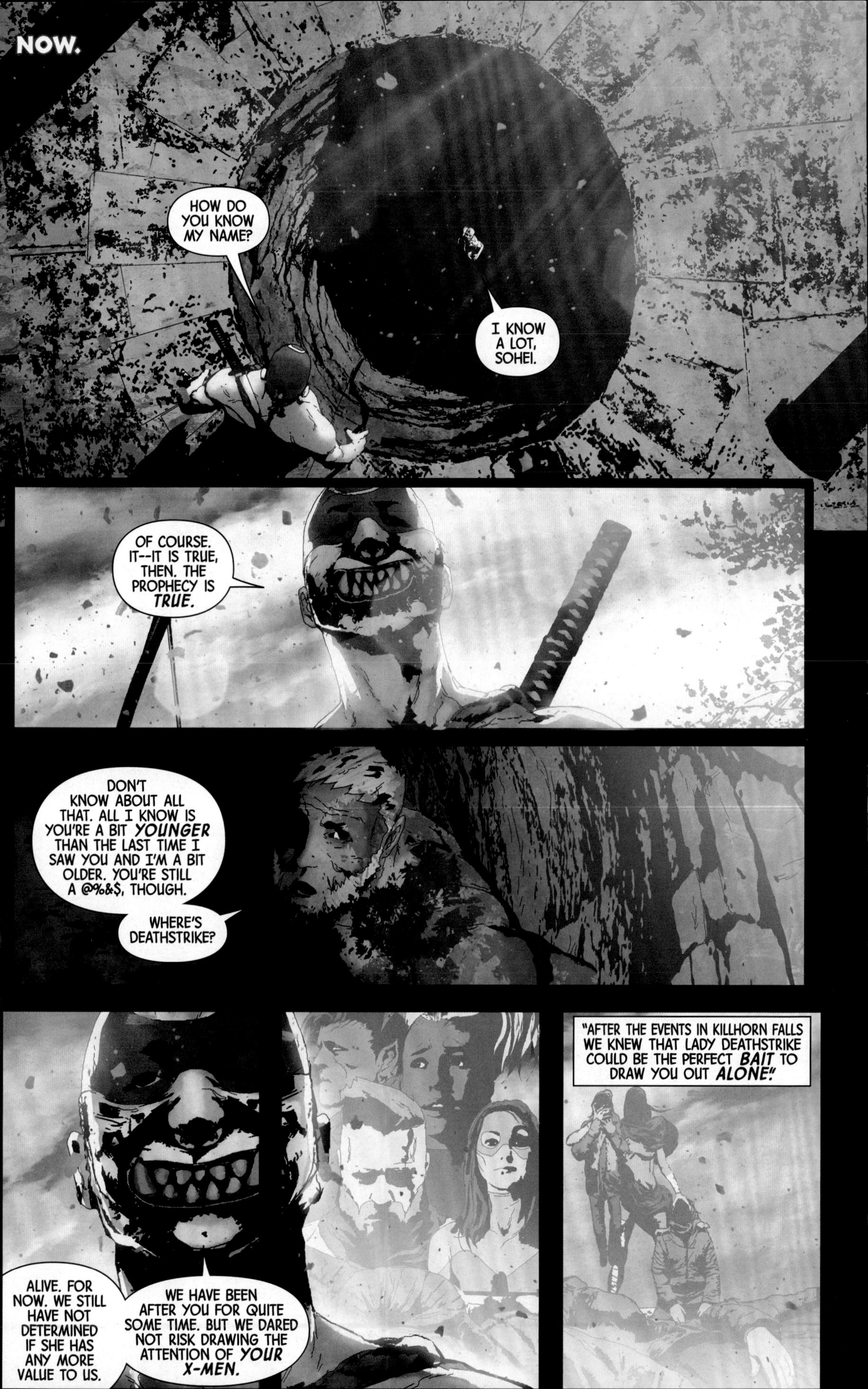
NOW.
HOW DO YOU KNOW MY NAME?
I KNOW A LOT, SOHEI.
OF COURSE. IT--IT IS TRUE, THEN. THE PROPHECY IS TRUE.
DON'T KNOW ABOUT ALL THAT. ALL I KNOW IS YOU'RE A BIT YOUNGER THAN THE LAST TIME I SAW YOU AND I'M A BIT OLDER. YOU'RE STILL A @%&$, THOUGH.
WHERE'S DEATHSTRIKE?
"AFTER THE EVENTS IN KILLHORN FALLS WE KNEW THAT LADY DEATHSTRIKE COULD BE THE PERFECT BAIT TO DRAW YOU OUT ALONE!"
WE HAVE BEEN AFTER YOU FOR QUITE SOME TIME. BUT WE DARED NOT RISK DRAWING THE ATTENTION OF YOUR X-MEN.
ALIVE. FOR NOW. WE STILL HAVE NOT DETERMINED IF SHE HAS ANY MORE VALUE TO US.

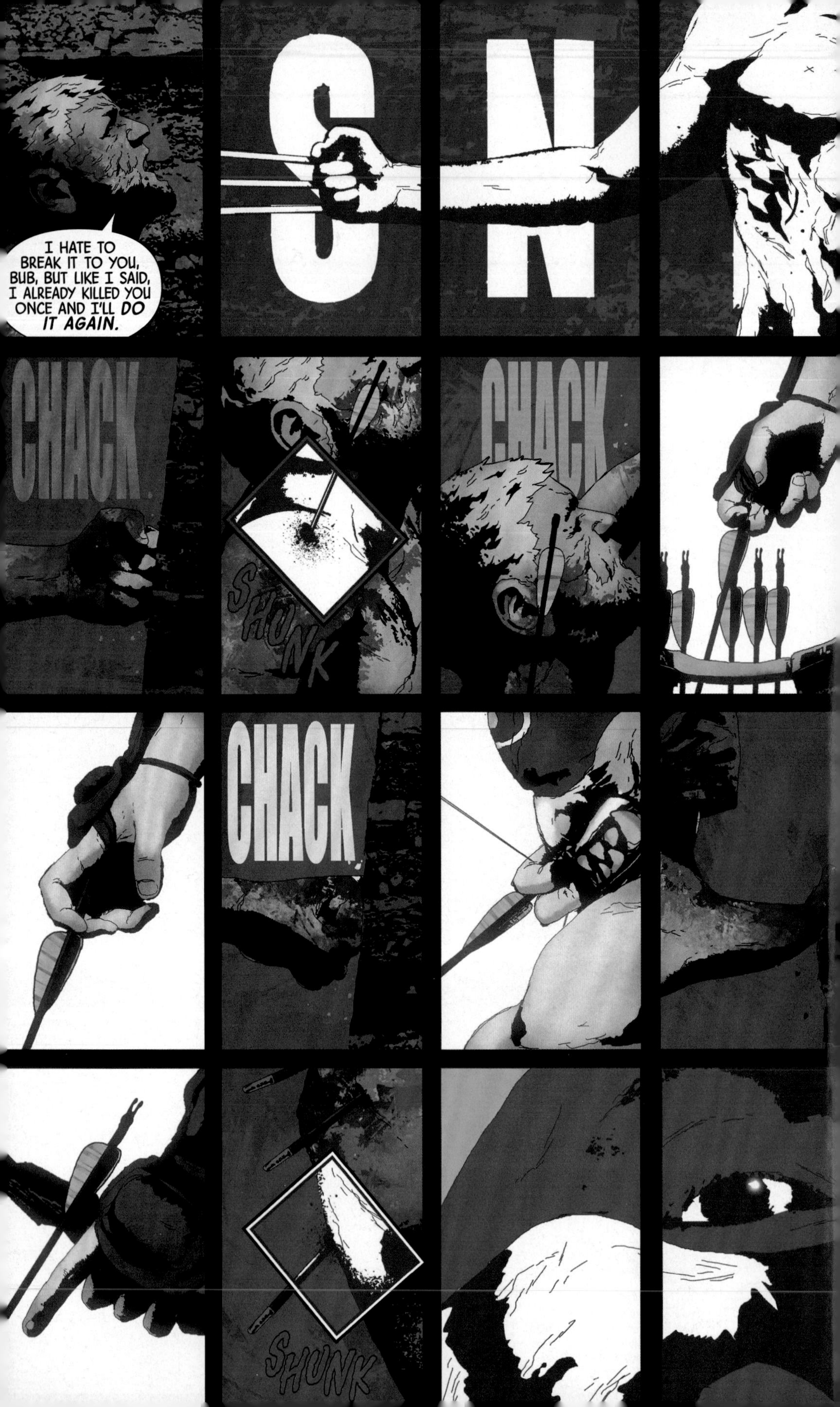
I HATE TO BREAK IT TO YOU, BUB, BUT LIKE I SAID, I ALREADY KILLED YOU ONCE AND I'LL DO IT AGAIN.
CHACK
SHUNK
CHACK
CHACK
SHUNK

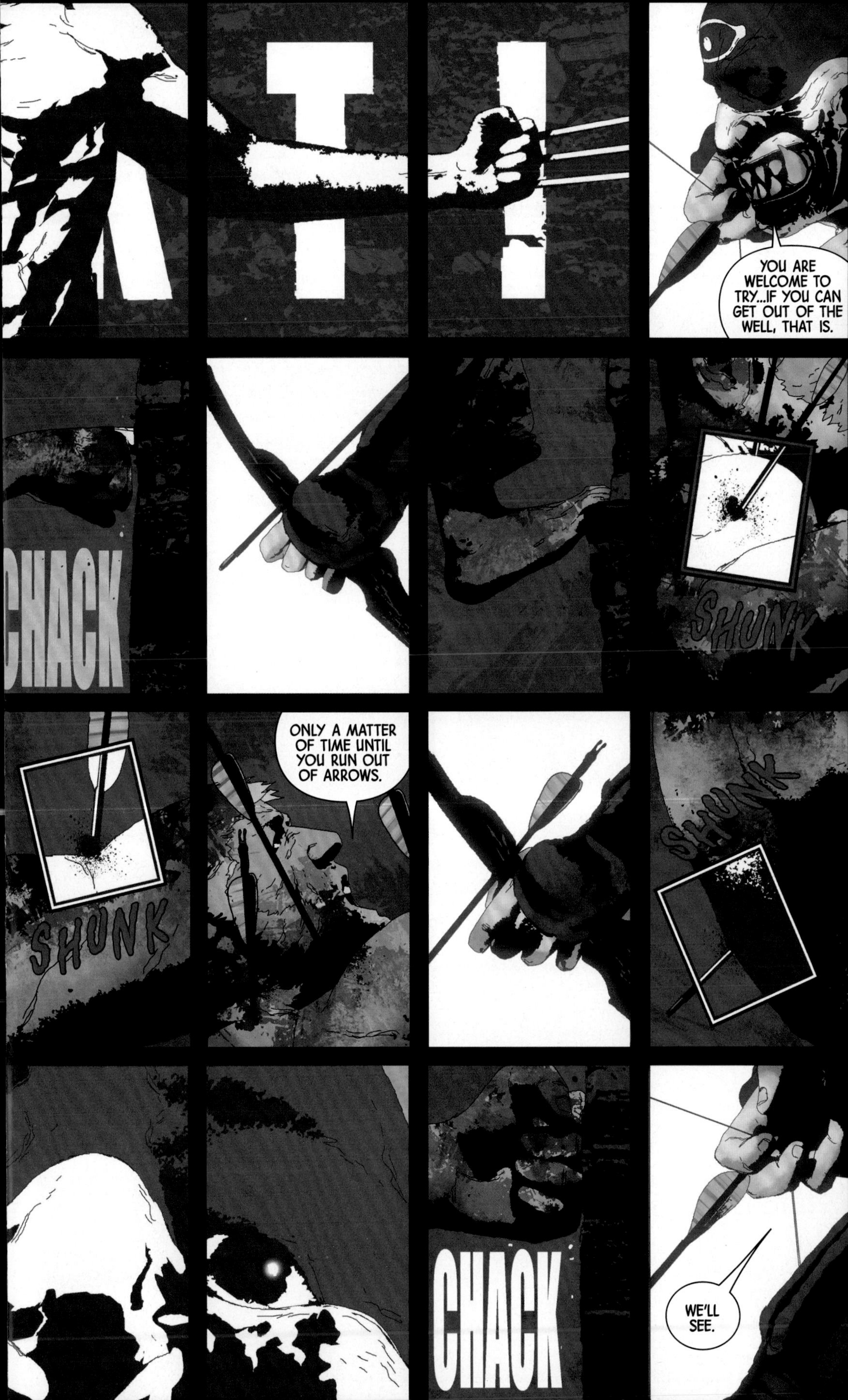
YOU ARE WELCOME TO TRY...IF YOU CAN GET OUT OF THE WELL, THAT IS.
CHACK
SHUNK
SHUNK
ONLY A MATTER OF TIME UNTIL YOU RUN OUT OF ARROWS.
SHUNK
CHACK
WE'LL SEE.

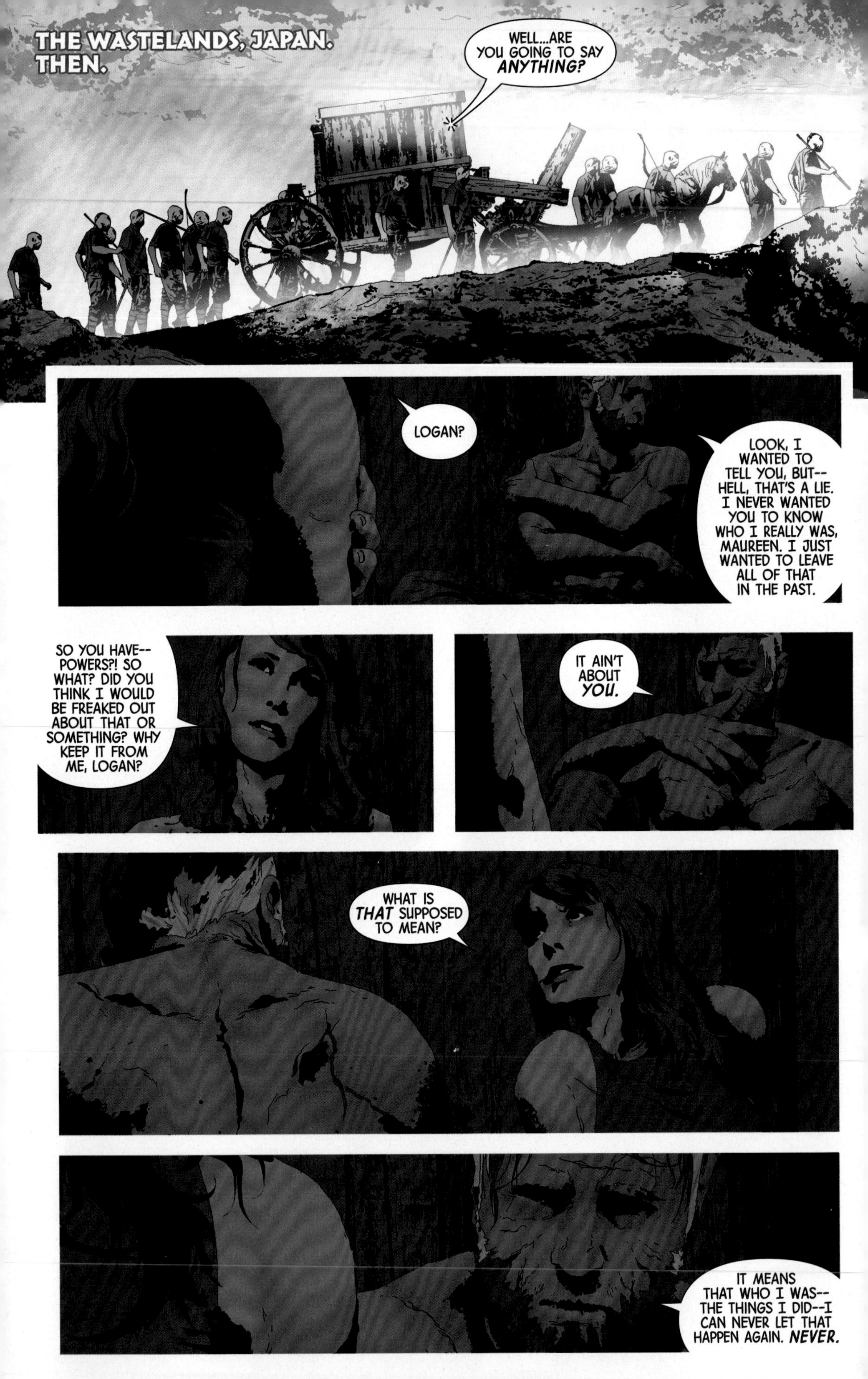
THE WASTELANDS, JAPAN. THEN.
WELL...ARE YOU GOING TO SAY ANYTHING?
LOGAN?
LOOK, I WANTED TO TELL YOU, BUT-- HELL, THAT'S A LIE. I NEVER WANTED YOU TO KNOW WHO I REALLY WAS, MAUREEN. I JUST WANTED TO LEAVE ALL OF THAT IN THE PAST.
SO YOU HAVE-- POWERS?! SO WHAT? DID YOU THINK I WOULD BE FREAKED OUT ABOUT THAT OR SOMETHING? WHY KEEP IT FROM ME, LOGAN?
IT AIN'T ABOUT YOU.
WHAT IS THAT SUPPOSED TO MEAN?
IT MEANS THAT WHO I WAS-- THE THINGS I DID--I CAN NEVER LET THAT HAPPEN AGAIN. NEVER.

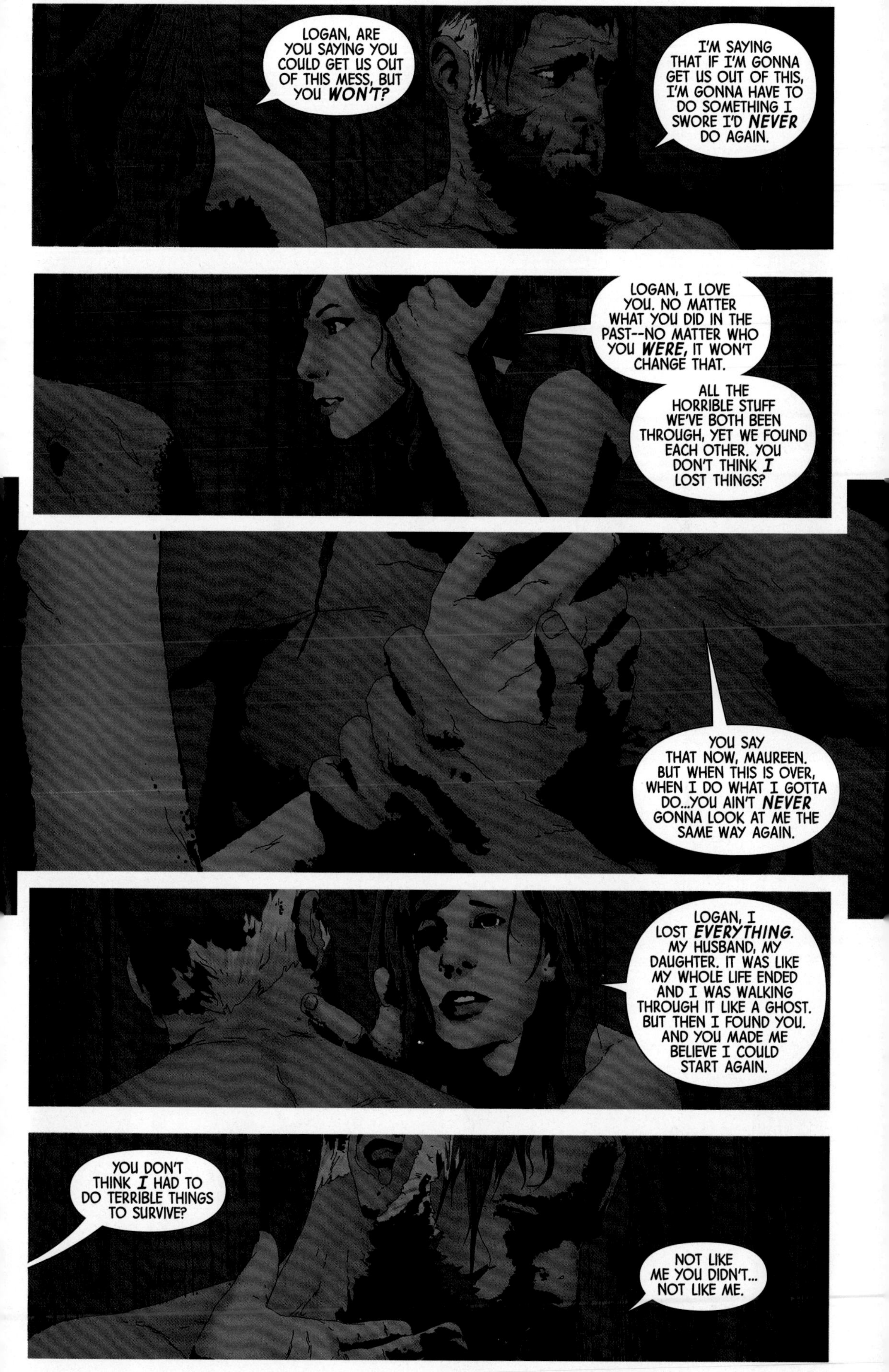
LOGAN, ARE YOU SAYING YOU COULD GET US OUT OF THIS MESS, BUT YOU WON'T?
I'M SAYING THAT IF I'M GONNA GET US OUT OF THIS, I'M GONNA HAVE TO DO SOMETHING I SWORE I'D NEVER DO AGAIN.
LOGAN, I LOVE YOU. NO MATTER WHAT YOU DID IN THE PAST--NO MATTER WHO YOU WERE, IT WON'T CHANGE THAT.
ALL THE HORRIBLE STUFF WE'VE BOTH BEEN THROUGH, YET WE FOUND EACH OTHER. YOU DON'T THINK I LOST THINGS?
YOU SAY THAT NOW, MAUREEN. BUT WHEN THIS IS OVER, WHEN I DO WHAT I GOTTA DO...YOU AIN'T NEVER GONNA LOOK AT ME THE SAME WAY AGAIN.
LOGAN, I LOST EVERYTHING. MY HUSBAND, MY DAUGHTER. IT WAS LIKE MY WHOLE LIFE ENDED AND I WAS WALKING THROUGH IT LIKE A GHOST. BUT THEN I FOUND YOU. AND YOU MADE ME BELIEVE I COULD START AGAIN.
YOU DON'T THINK I HAD TO DO TERRIBLE THINGS TO SURVIVE?
NOT LIKE ME YOU DIDN'T... NOT LIKE ME.

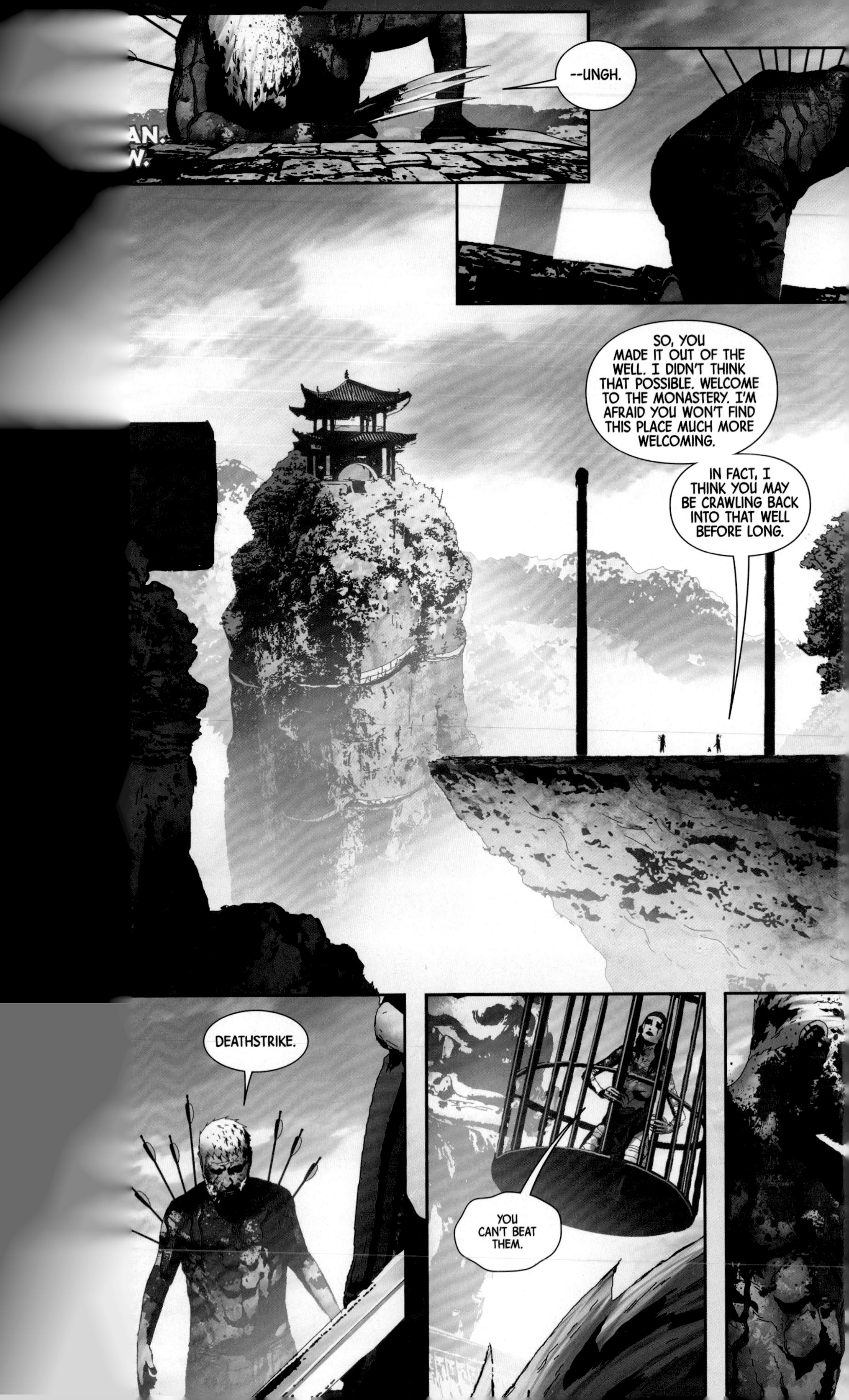
--UNGH.
SO, YOU MADE IT OUT OF THE WELL. I DIDN'T THINK THAT POSSIBLE. WELCOME TO THE MONASTERY. I'M AFRAID YOU WON'T FIND THIS PLACE MUCH MORE WELCOMING.
IN FACT, I THINK YOU MAY BE CRAWLING BACK INTO THAT WELL BEFORE LONG.
DEATHSTRIKE.
YOU CAN'T BEAT THEM.

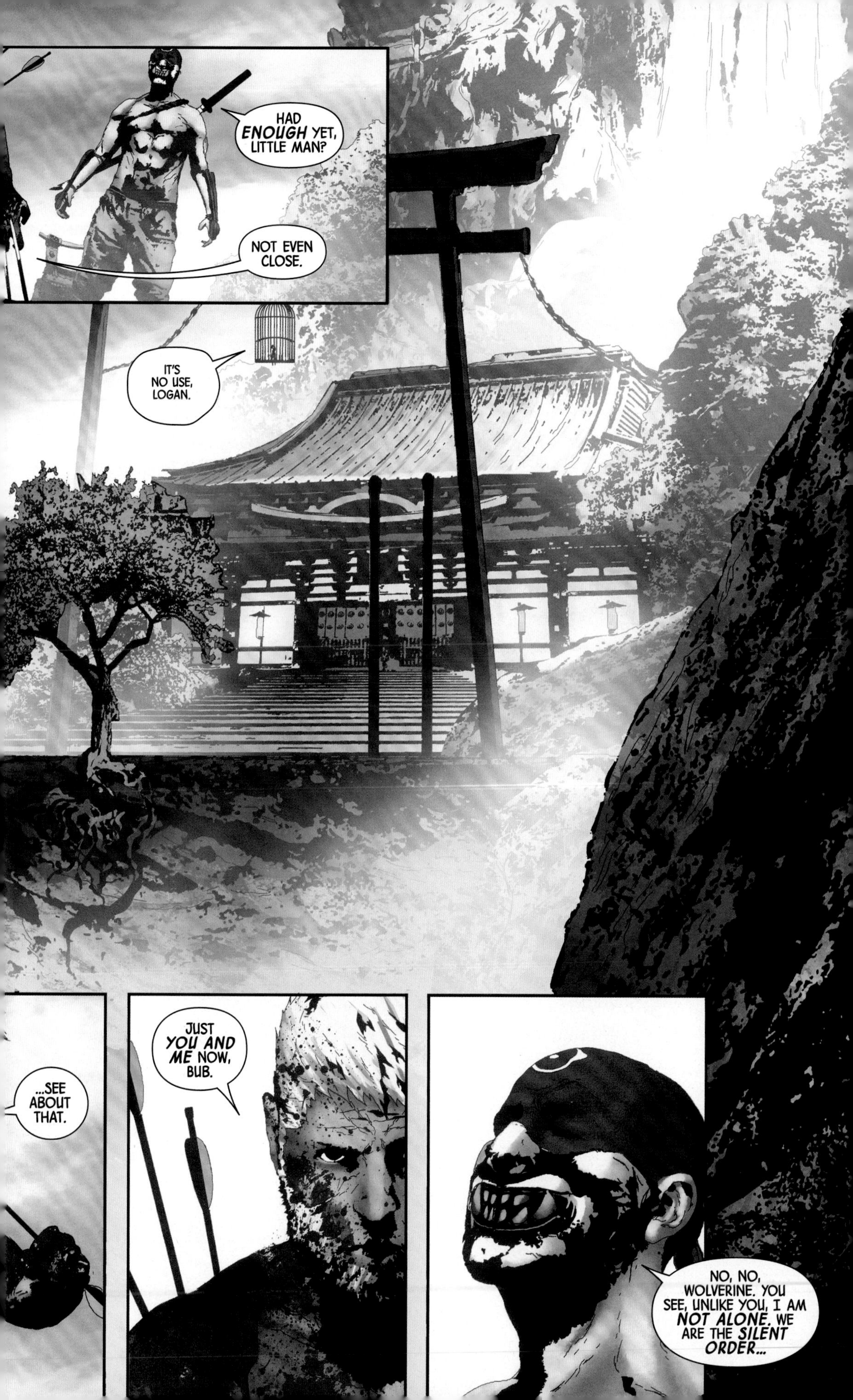
HAD ENOUGH YET, LITTLE MAN?
NOT EVEN CLOSE.
IT'S NO USE, LOGAN.
...SEE ABOUT THAT.
JUST YOU AND ME NOW, BUB.
NO, NO, WOLVERINE. YOU SEE, UNLIKE YOU, I AM NOT ALONE. WE ARE THE SILENT ORDER...

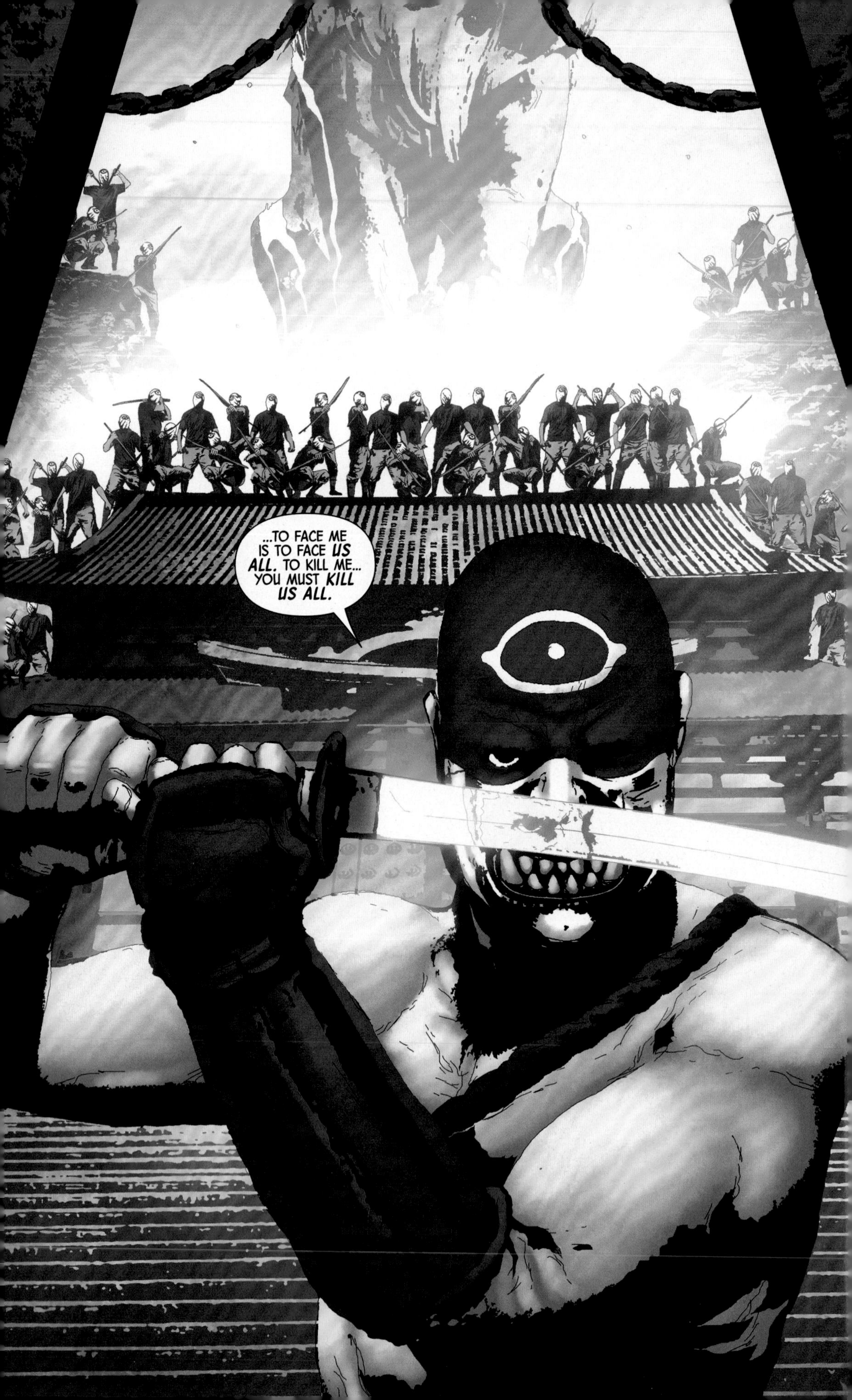
...TO FACE ME IS TO FACE US ALL. TO KILL ME... YOU MUST KILL US ALL.

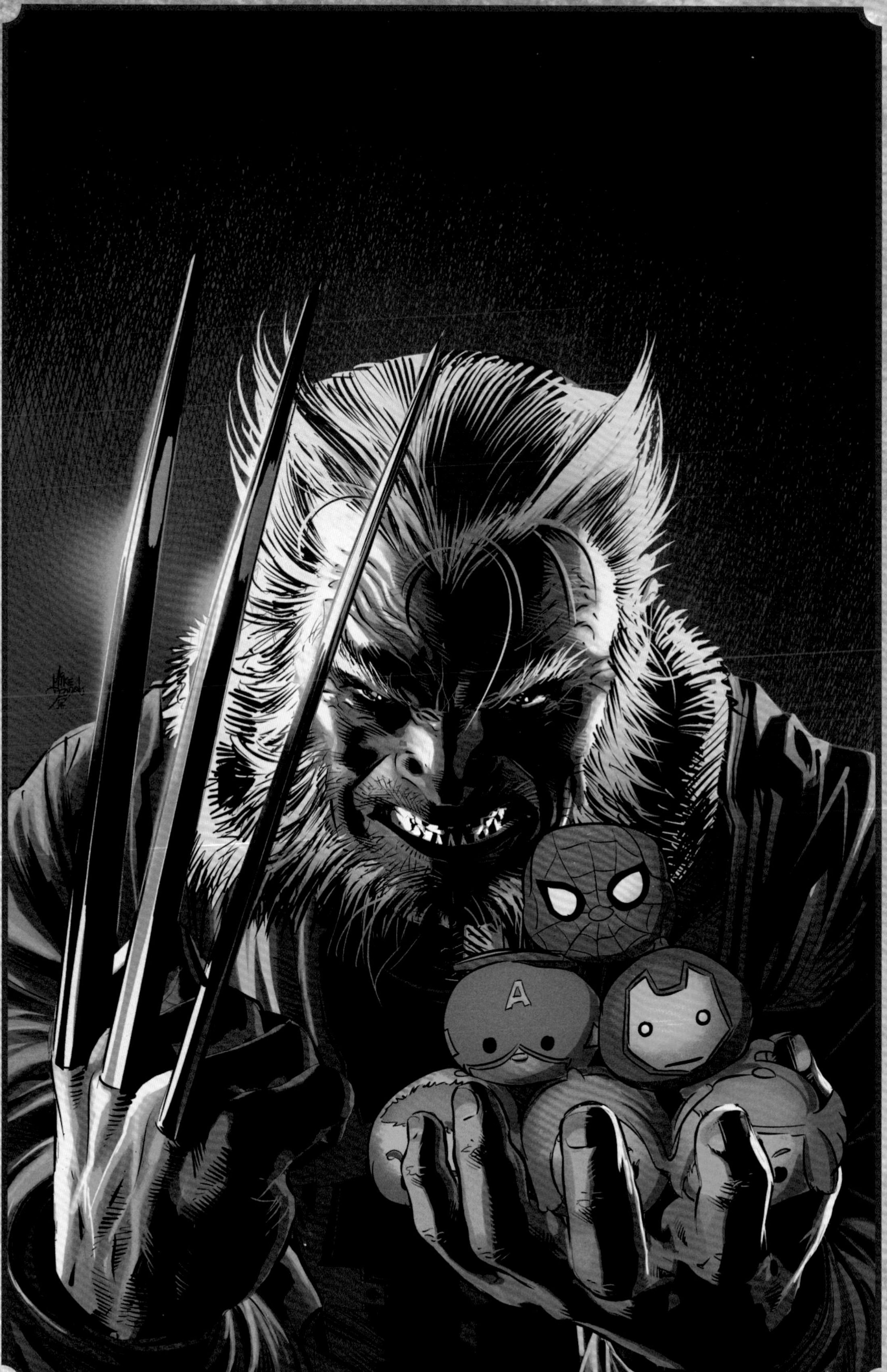

#10 TSUM TSUM TAKEOVER VARIANT BY
MIKE DEODATO & FRANK MARTIN

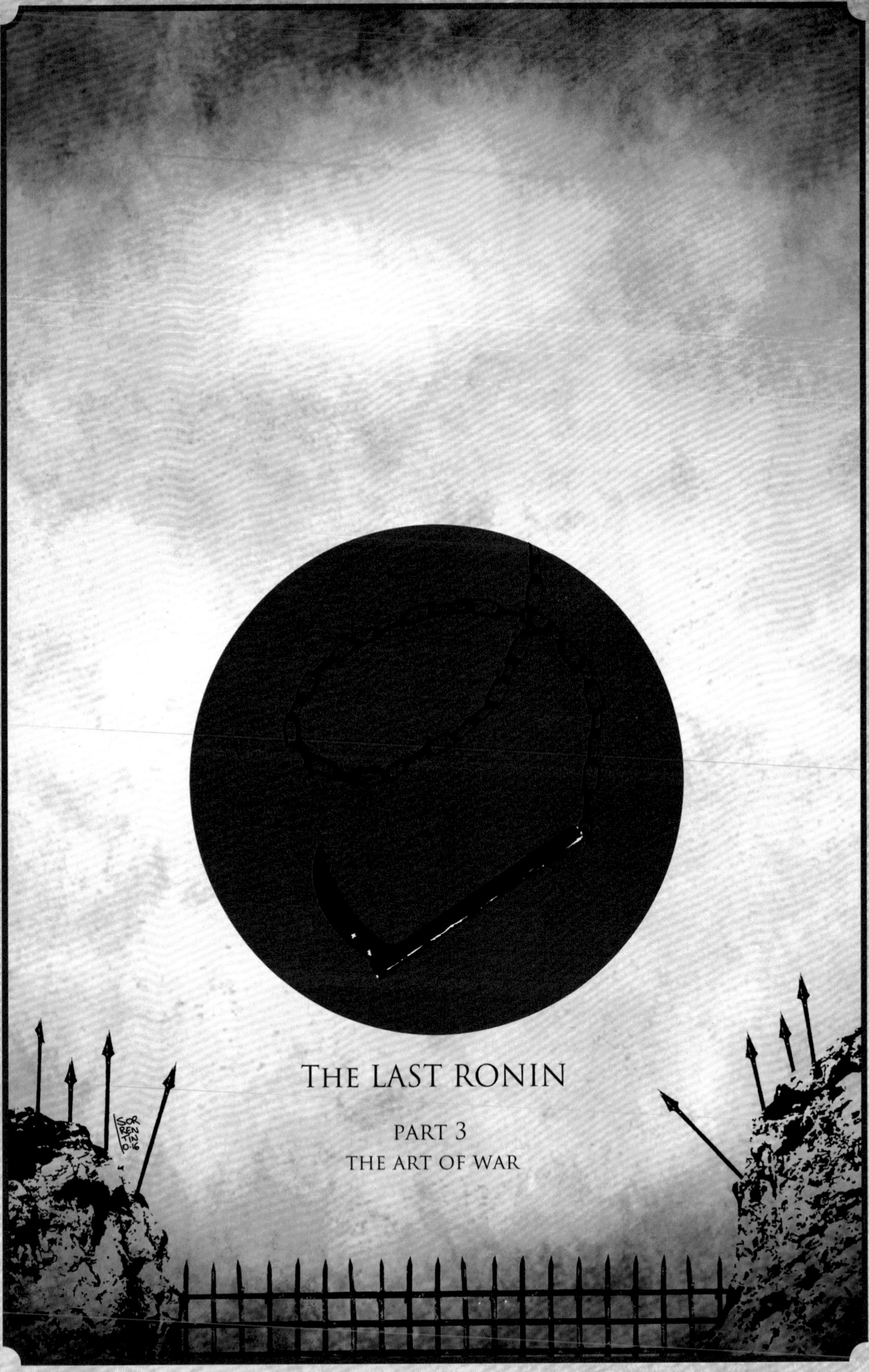
THE LAST RONIN
PART 3
THE ART OF WAR

11

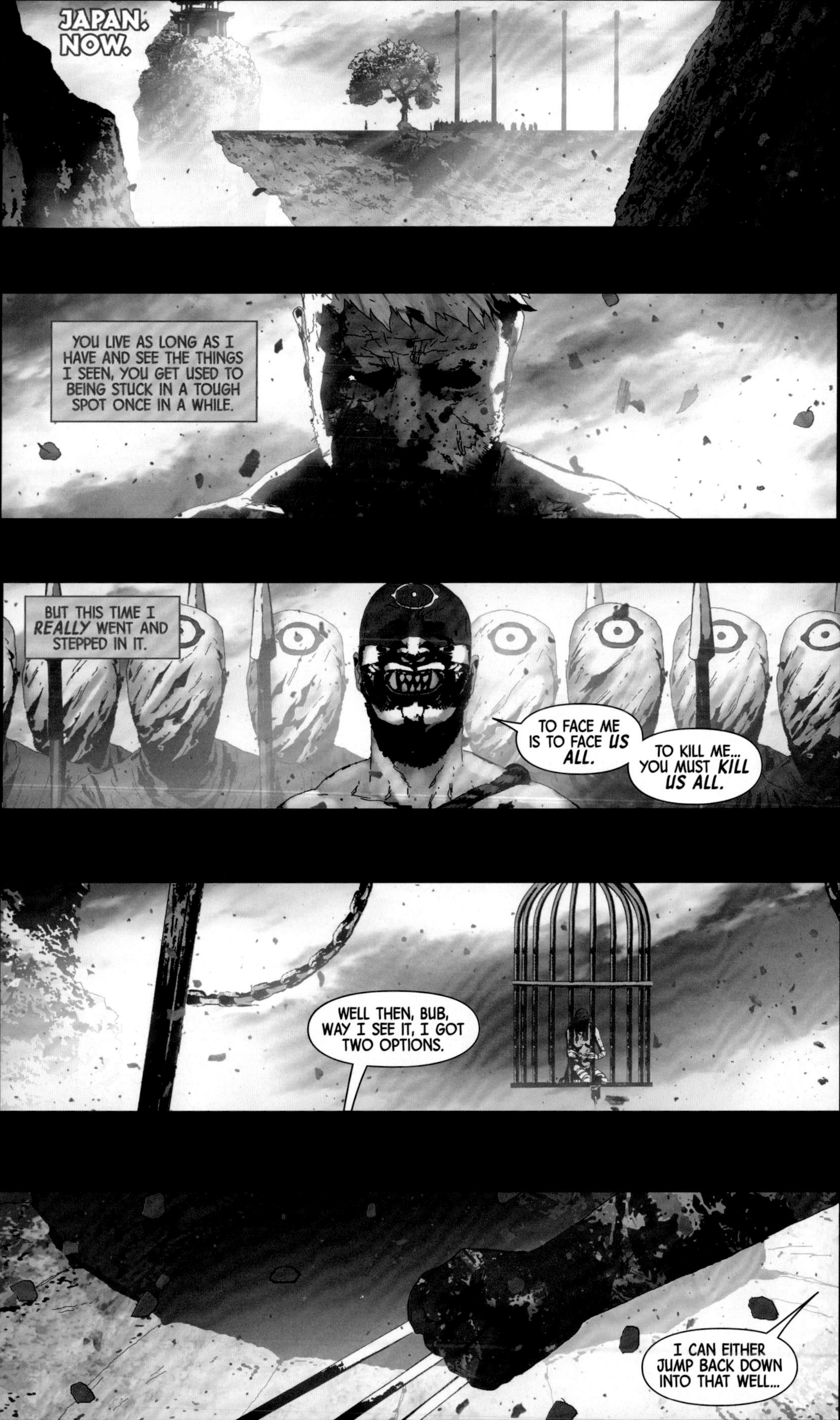
JAPAN. NOW.
YOU LIVE AS LONG AS I HAVE AND SEE THE THINGS I SEEN, YOU GET USED TO BEING STUCK IN A TOUGH SPOT ONCE IN A WHILE.
BUT THIS TIME I *REALLY* WENT AND STEPPED IN IT.
TO FACE ME IS TO FACE *US ALL.*
TO KILL ME... YOU MUST *KILL US ALL.*
WELL THEN, BUB, WAY I SEE IT, I GOT TWO OPTIONS.
I CAN EITHER JUMP BACK DOWN INTO THAT WELL...

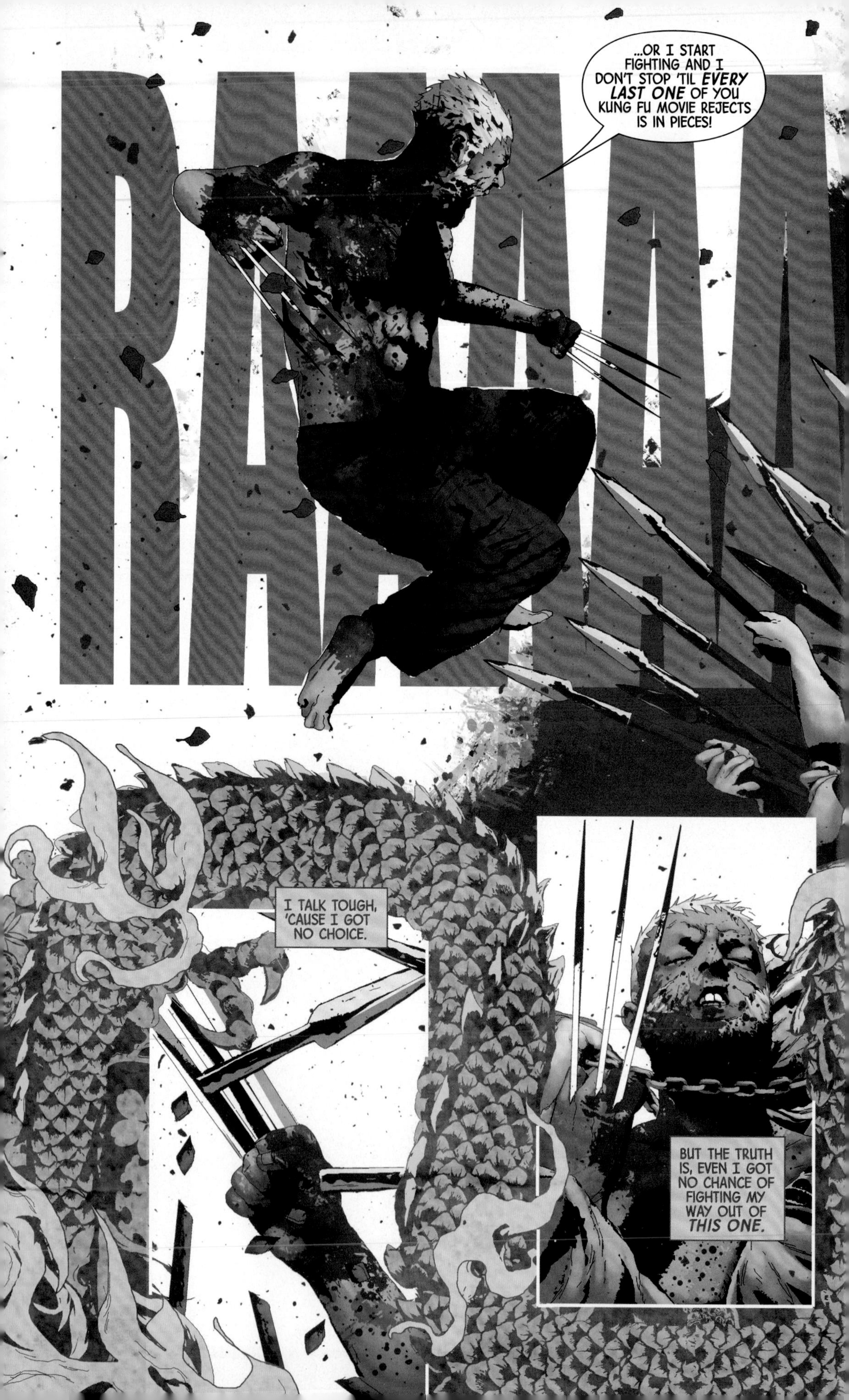

...OR I START FIGHTING AND I DON'T STOP 'TIL EVERY LAST ONE OF YOU KUNG FU MOVIE REJECTS IS IN PIECES!
RAAAA
I TALK TOUGH, 'CAUSE I GOT NO CHOICE.
BUT THE TRUTH IS, EVEN I GOT NO CHANCE OF FIGHTING MY WAY OUT OF THIS ONE.

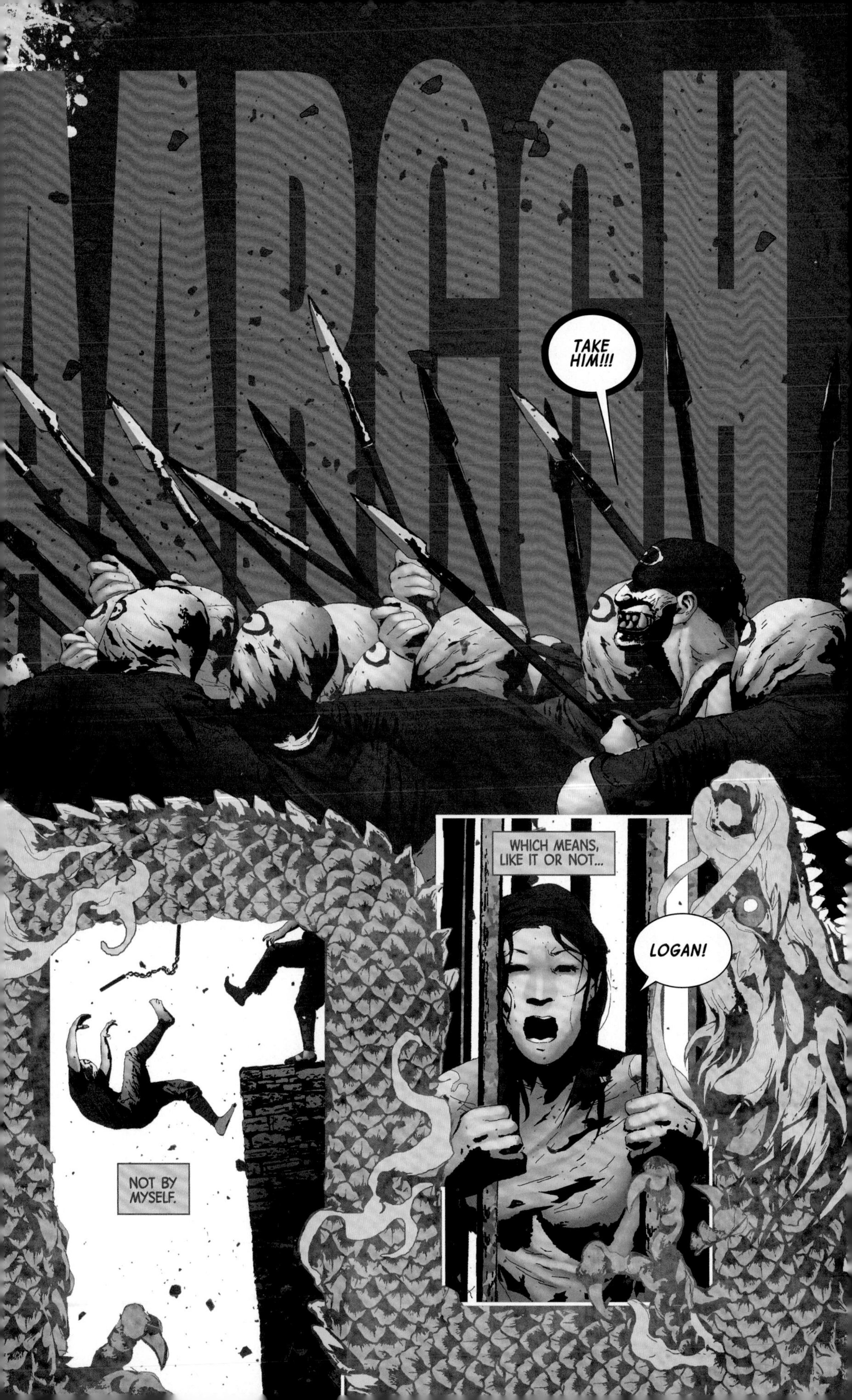
NARGGH
TAKE HIM!!!
WHICH MEANS, LIKE IT OR NOT...
LOGAN!
NOT BY MYSELF.

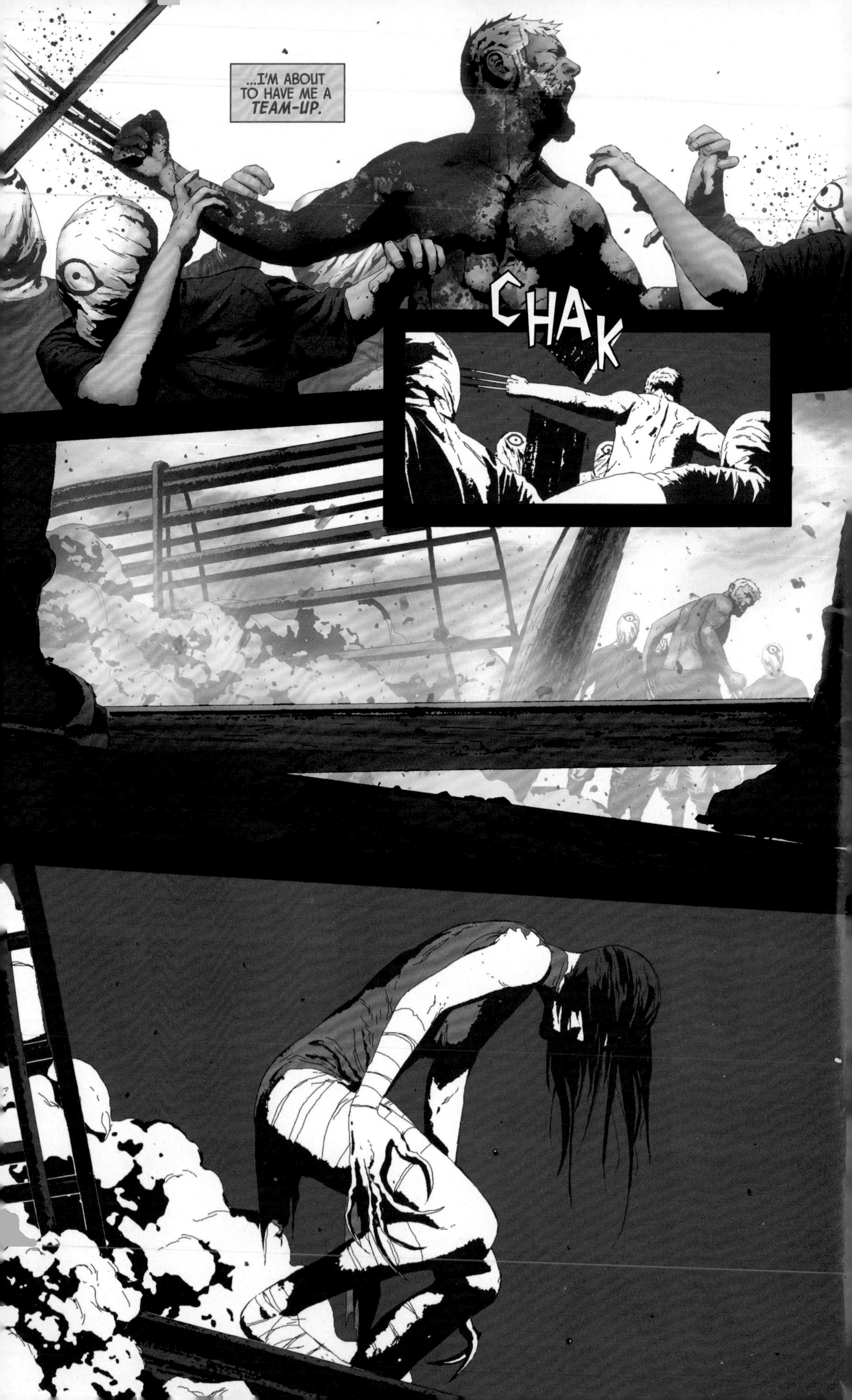
...I'M ABOUT TO HAVE ME A *TEAM-UP*.
CHAK

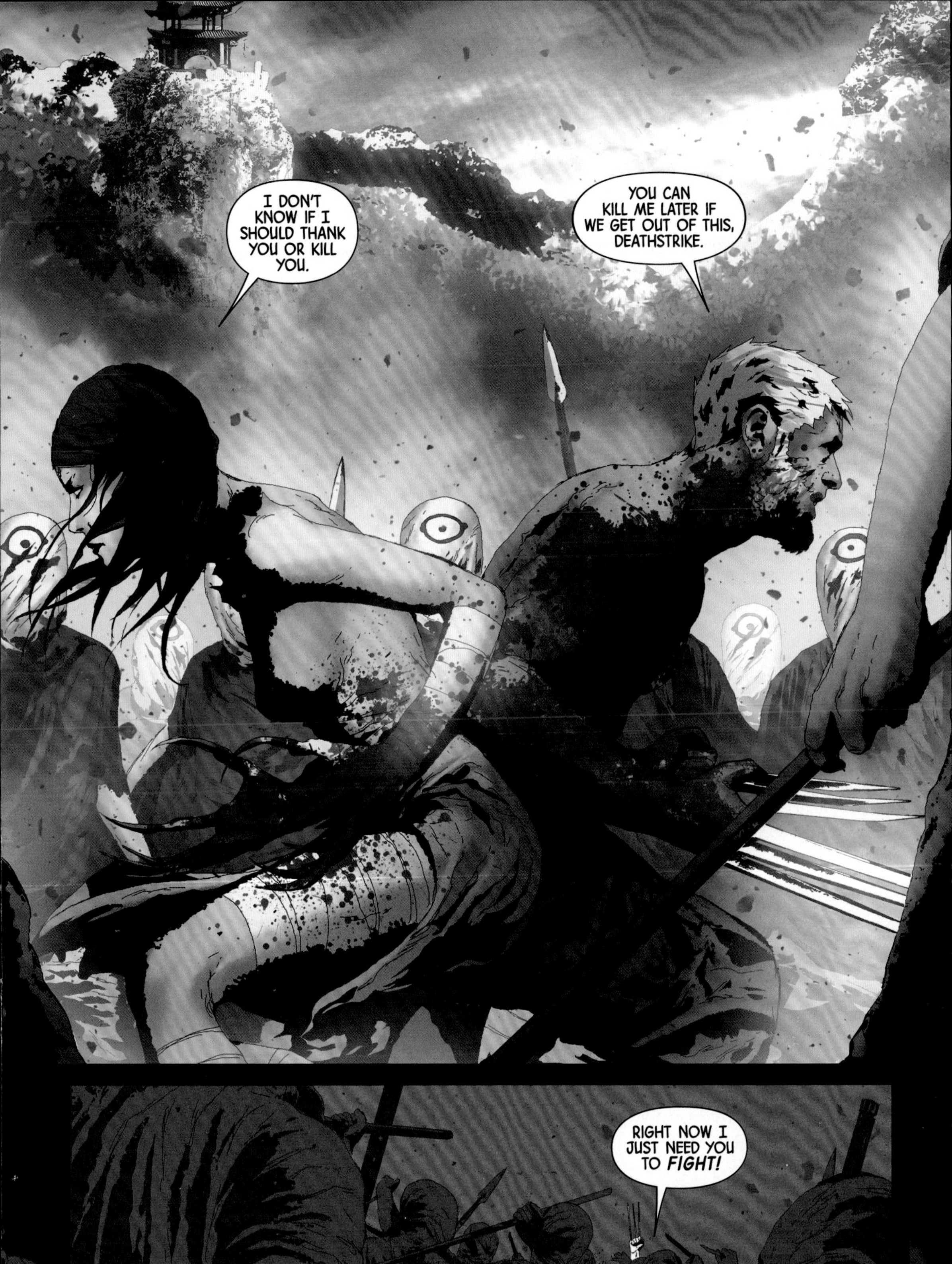
I DON'T KNOW IF I SHOULD THANK YOU OR KILL YOU.
YOU CAN KILL ME LATER IF WE GET OUT OF THIS, DEATHSTRIKE.
RIGHT NOW I JUST NEED YOU TO *FIGHT!*

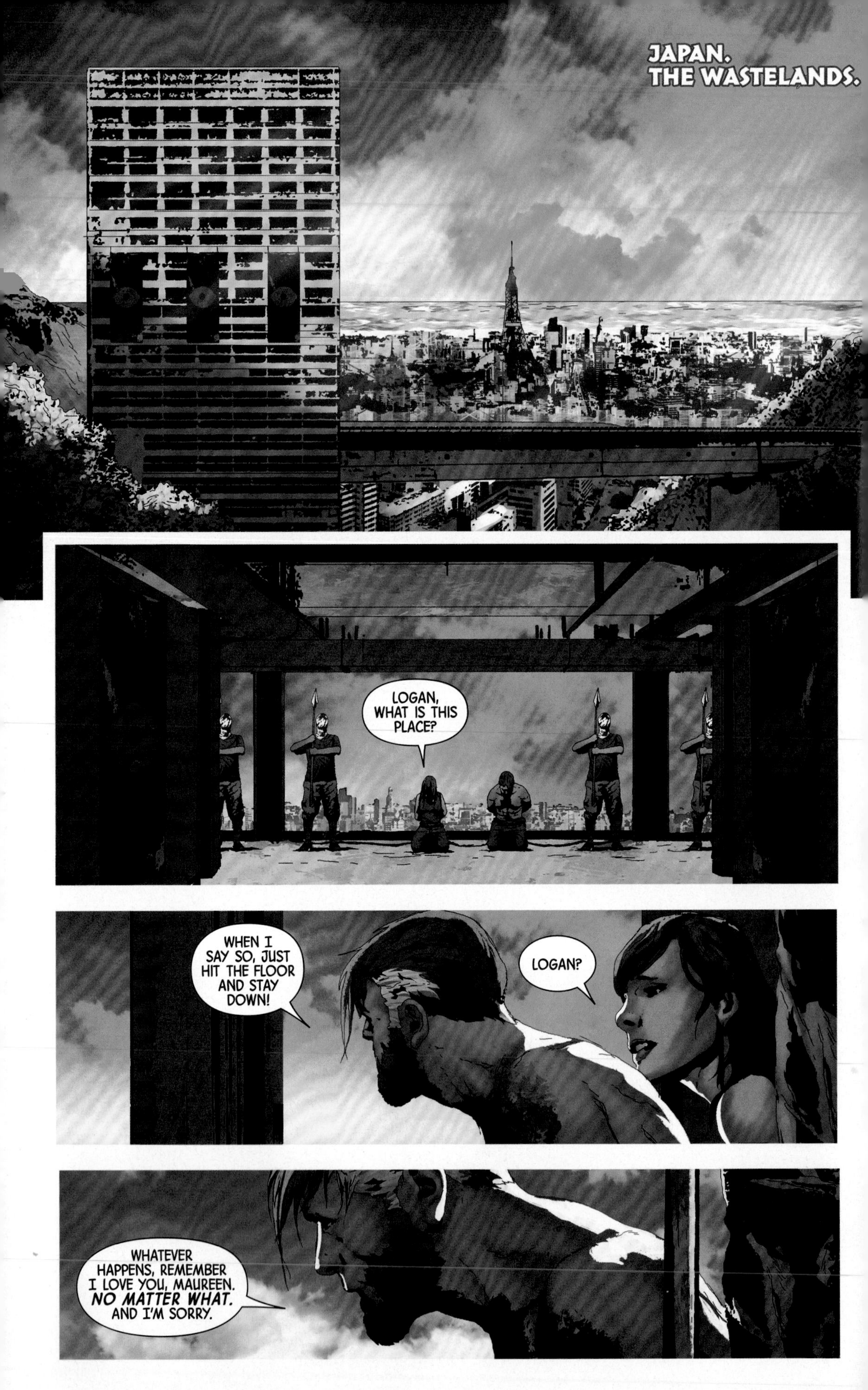
JAPAN.
THE WASTELANDS.
LOGAN, WHAT IS THIS PLACE?
WHEN I SAY SO, JUST HIT THE FLOOR AND STAY DOWN!
LOGAN?
WHATEVER HAPPENS, REMEMBER I LOVE YOU, MAUREEN. *NO MATTER WHAT.* AND I'M SORRY.

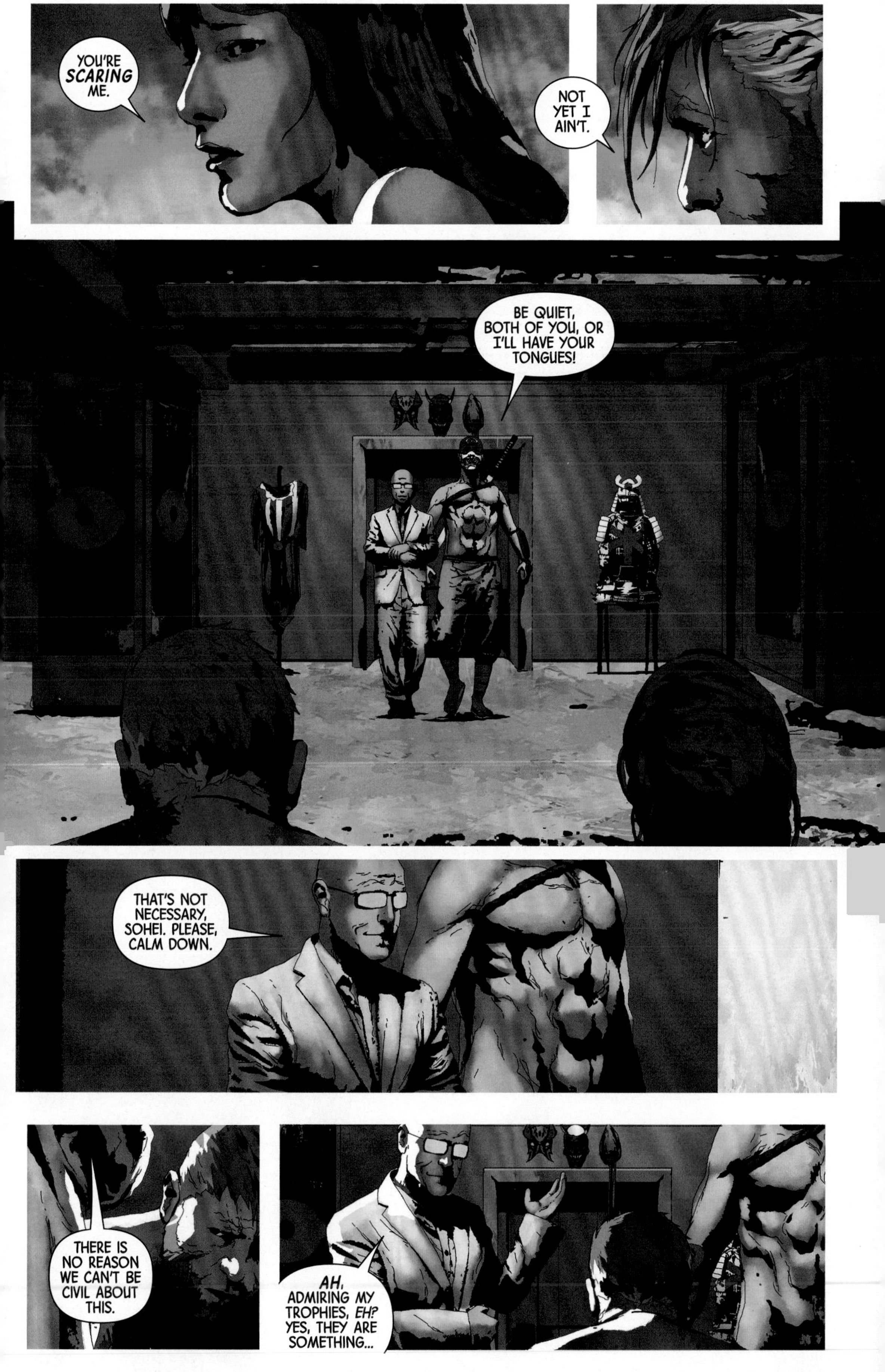

YOU'RE SCARING ME.
NOT YET I AIN'T.
BE QUIET, BOTH OF YOU, OR I'LL HAVE YOUR TONGUES!
THAT'S NOT NECESSARY, SOHEI. PLEASE, CALM DOWN.
THERE IS NO REASON WE CAN'T BE CIVIL ABOUT THIS.
AH, ADMIRING MY TROPHIES, EH? YES, THEY ARE SOMETHING...

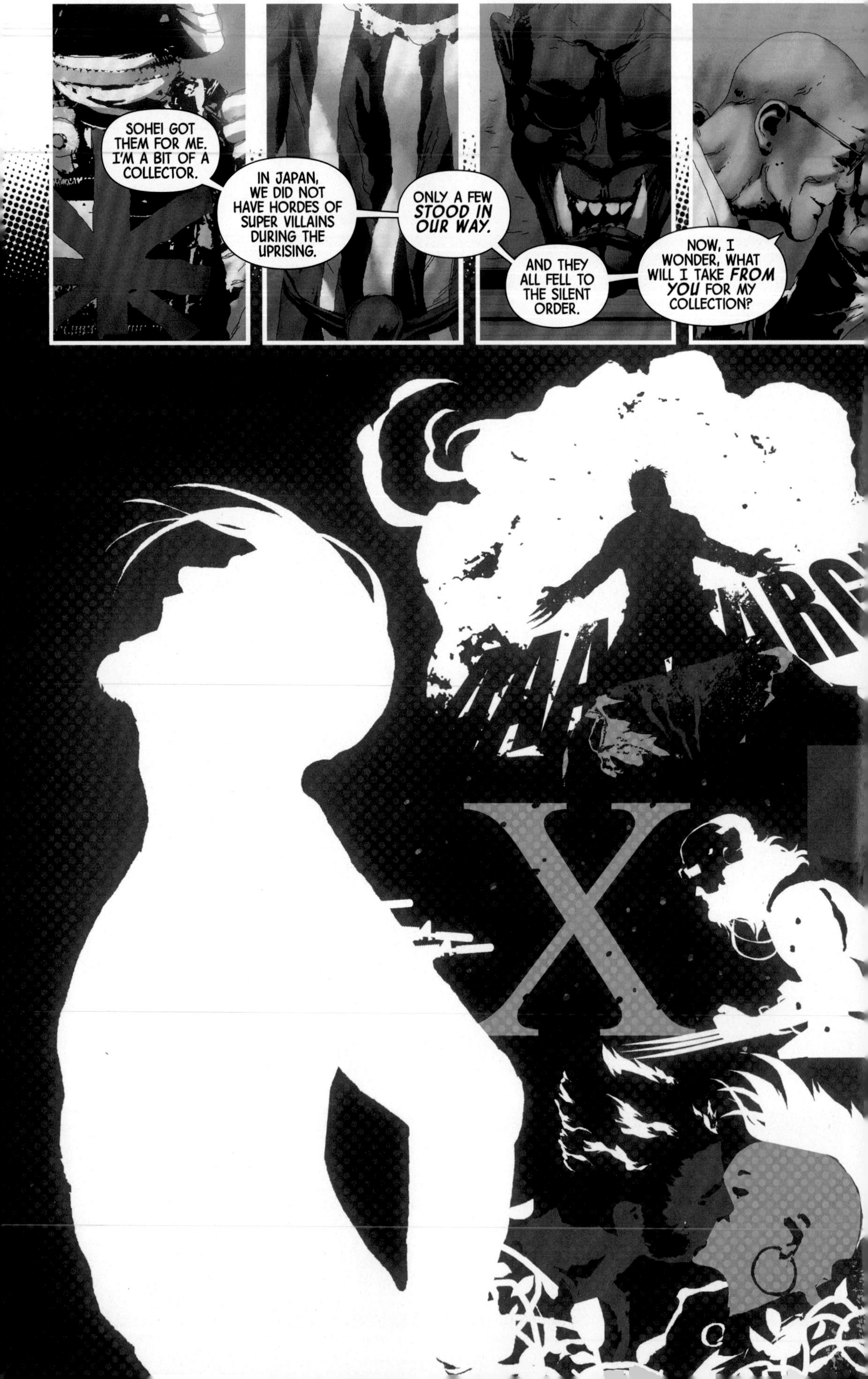
SOHEI GOT THEM FOR ME. I'M A BIT OF A COLLECTOR.
IN JAPAN, WE DID NOT HAVE HORDES OF SUPER VILLAINS DURING THE UPRISING.
ONLY A FEW *STOOD IN OUR WAY.*
AND THEY ALL FELL TO THE SILENT ORDER.
NOW, I WONDER, WHAT WILL I TAKE *FROM YOU* FOR MY COLLECTION?

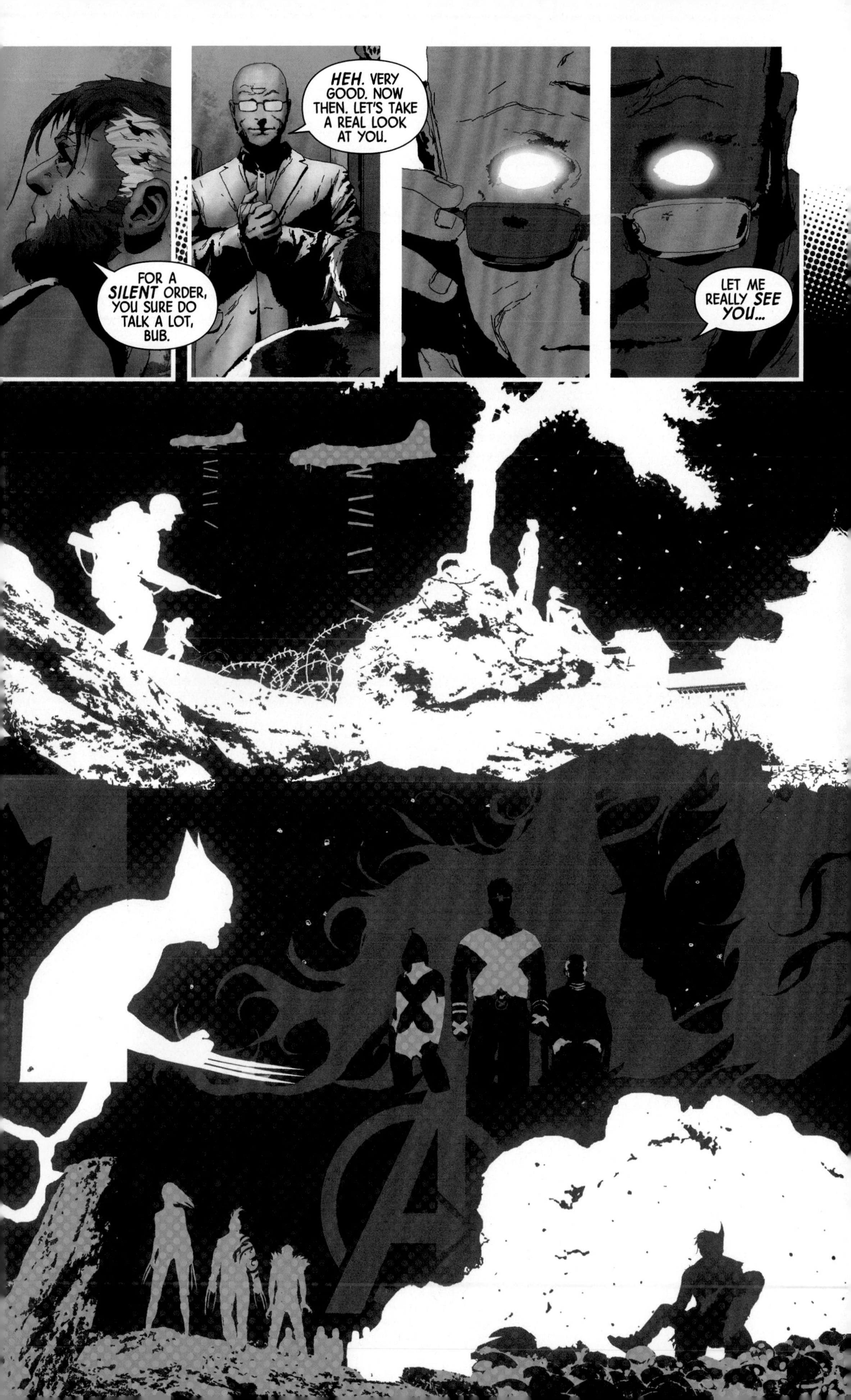
FOR A SILENT ORDER, YOU SURE DO TALK A LOT, BUB.
HEH. VERY GOOD. NOW THEN. LET'S TAKE A REAL LOOK AT YOU.
LET ME REALLY SEE YOU...

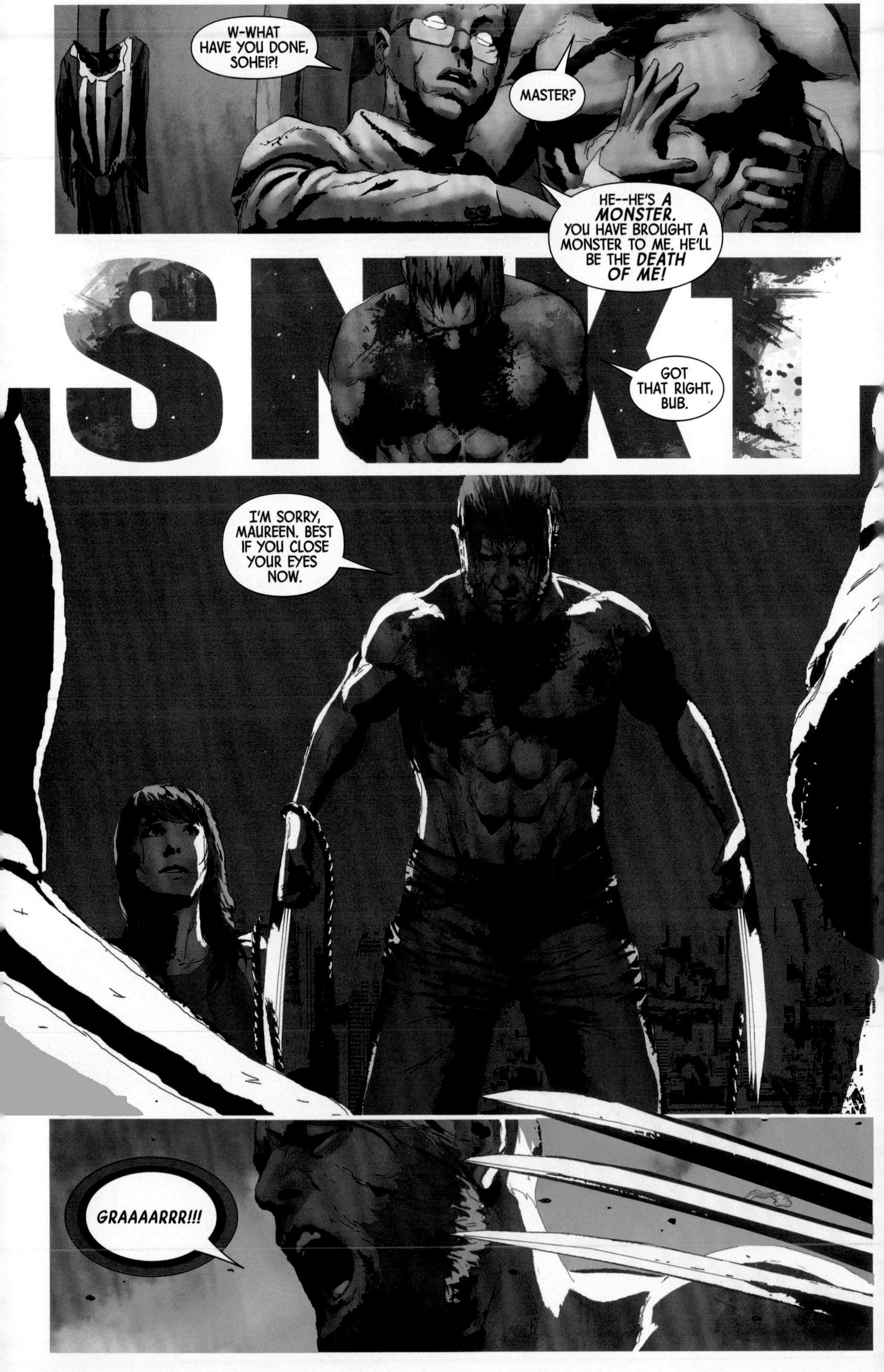
W-WHAT HAVE YOU DONE, SOHEI?!
MASTER?
HE--HE'S *A MONSTER.* YOU HAVE BROUGHT A MONSTER TO ME. HE'LL BE THE *DEATH OF ME!*
SNIKT
GOT THAT RIGHT, BUB.
I'M SORRY, MAUREEN. BEST IF YOU CLOSE YOUR EYES NOW.
GRAAAARRR!!!

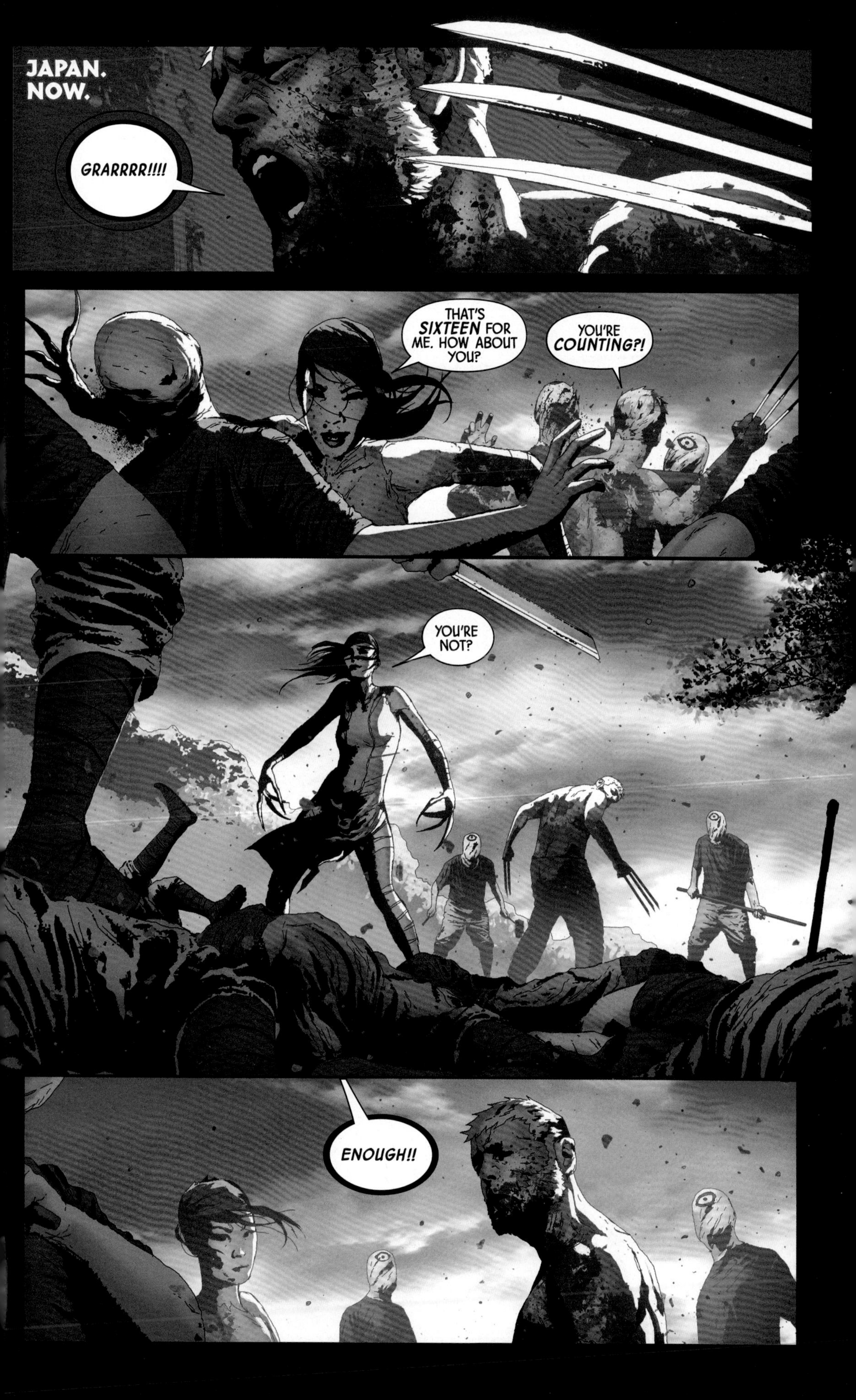
JAPAN.
NOW.
GRARRRR!!!!
THAT'S SIXTEEN FOR ME. HOW ABOUT YOU?
YOU'RE COUNTING?!
YOU'RE NOT?
ENOUGH!!

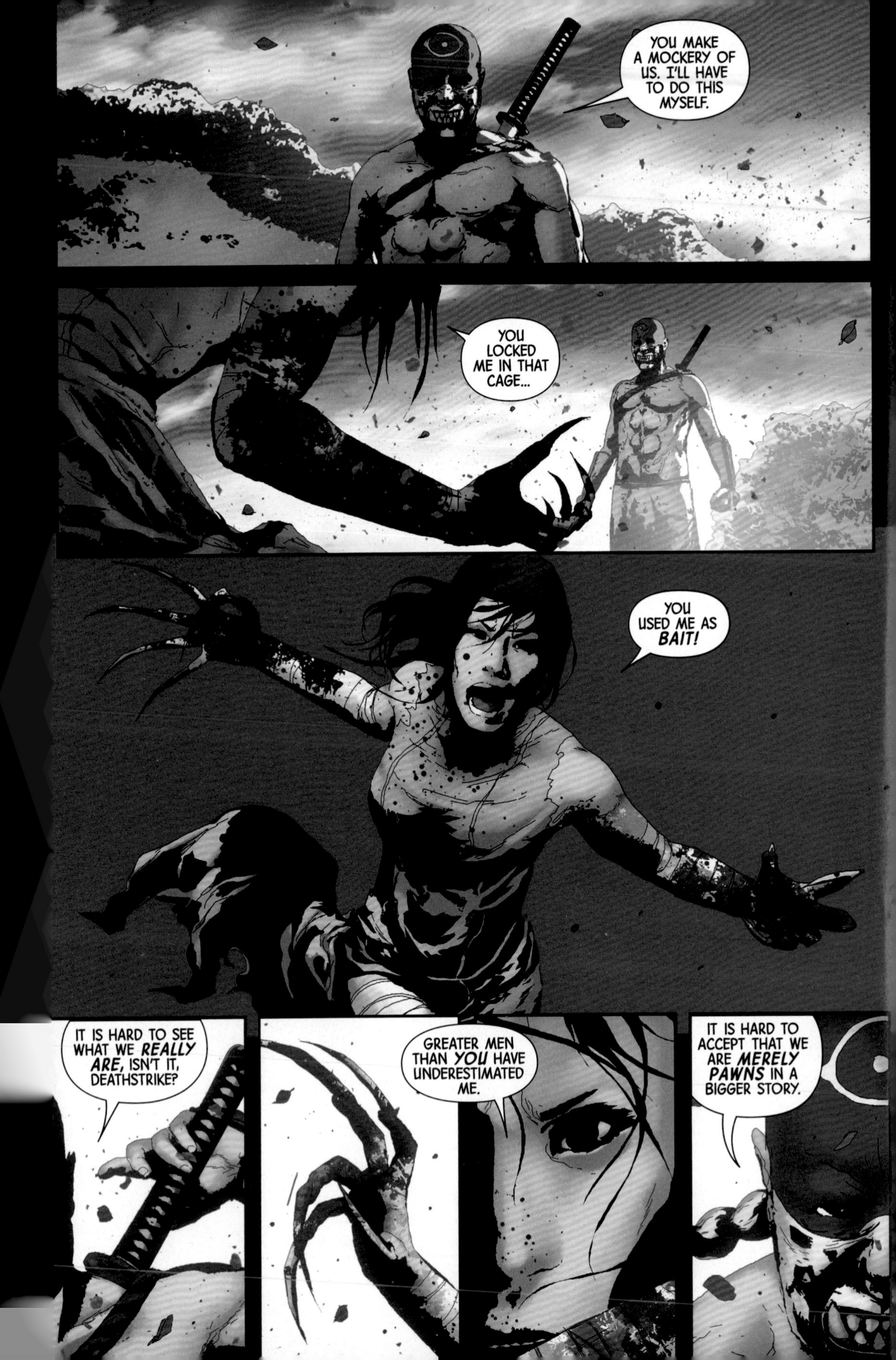
YOU MAKE A MOCKERY OF US. I'LL HAVE TO DO THIS MYSELF.
YOU LOCKED ME IN THAT CAGE...
YOU USED ME AS BAIT!
IT IS HARD TO SEE WHAT WE REALLY ARE, ISN'T IT, DEATHSTRIKE?
GREATER MEN THAN YOU HAVE UNDERESTIMATED ME.
IT IS HARD TO ACCEPT THAT WE ARE MERELY PAWNS IN A BIGGER STORY.

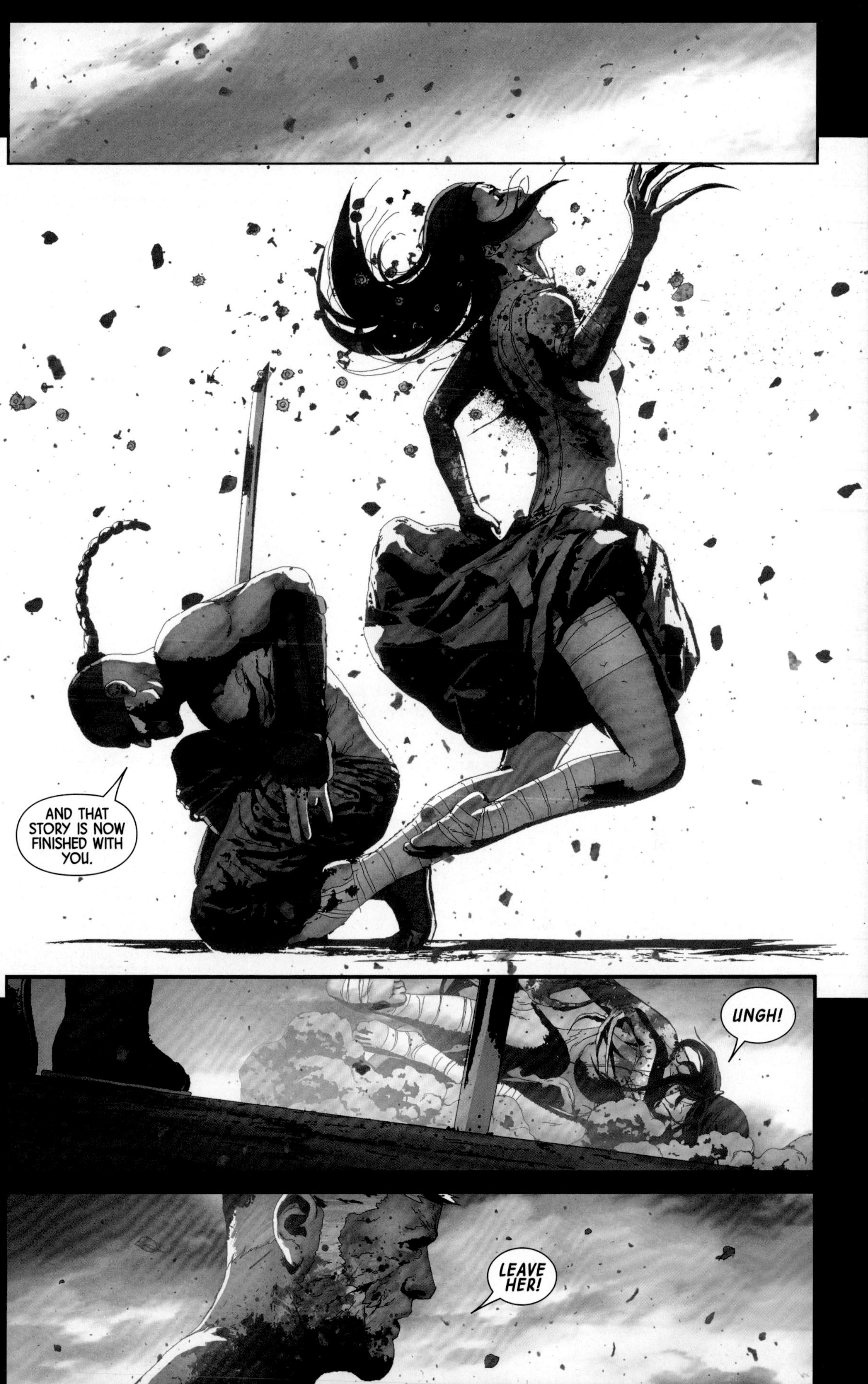
AND THAT STORY IS NOW FINISHED WITH YOU.
UNGH!
LEAVE HER!

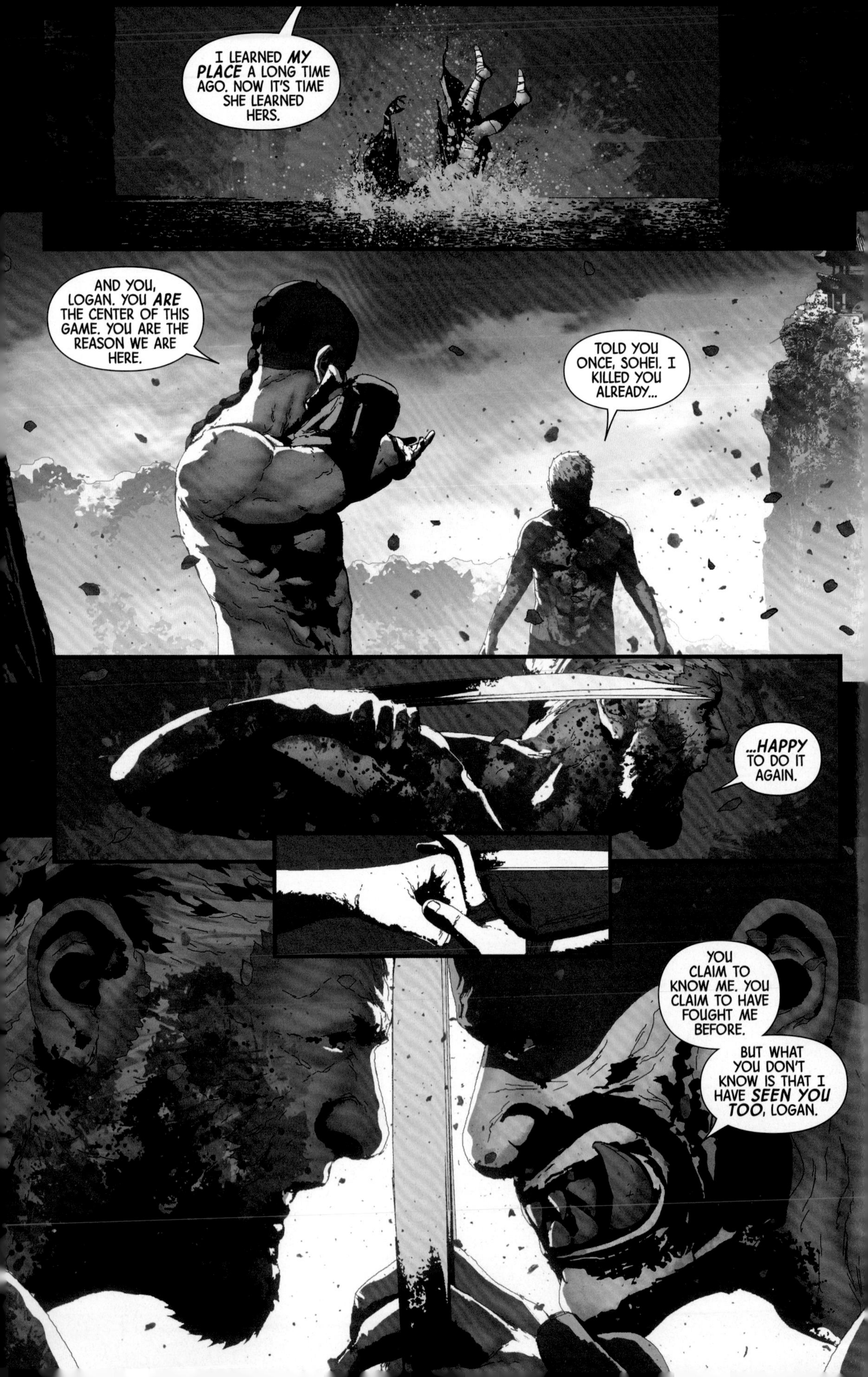
I LEARNED MY PLACE A LONG TIME AGO. NOW IT'S TIME SHE LEARNED HERS.
AND YOU, LOGAN. YOU ARE THE CENTER OF THIS GAME. YOU ARE THE REASON WE ARE HERE.
TOLD YOU ONCE, SOHEI. I KILLED YOU ALREADY...
...HAPPY TO DO IT AGAIN.
YOU CLAIM TO KNOW ME. YOU CLAIM TO HAVE FOUGHT ME BEFORE.
BUT WHAT YOU DON'T KNOW IS THAT I HAVE SEEN YOU TOO, LOGAN.

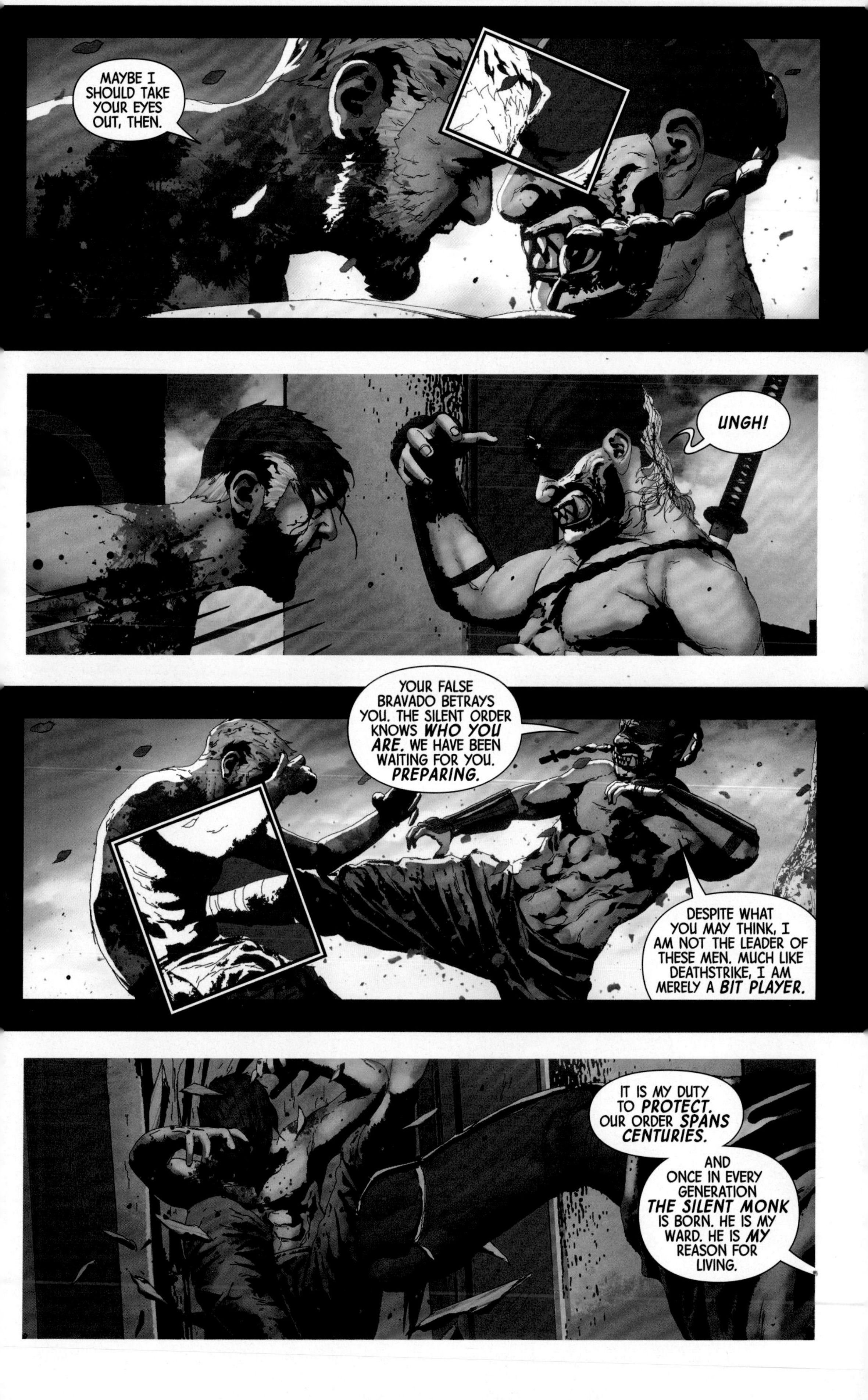
MAYBE I SHOULD TAKE YOUR EYES OUT, THEN.
UNGH!
YOUR FALSE BRAVADO BETRAYS YOU. THE SILENT ORDER KNOWS WHO YOU ARE. WE HAVE BEEN WAITING FOR YOU. PREPARING.
DESPITE WHAT YOU MAY THINK, I AM NOT THE LEADER OF THESE MEN. MUCH LIKE DEATHSTRIKE, I AM MERELY A BIT PLAYER.
IT IS MY DUTY TO PROTECT. OUR ORDER SPANS CENTURIES.
AND ONCE IN EVERY GENERATION THE SILENT MONK IS BORN. HE IS MY WARD. HE IS MY REASON FOR LIVING.

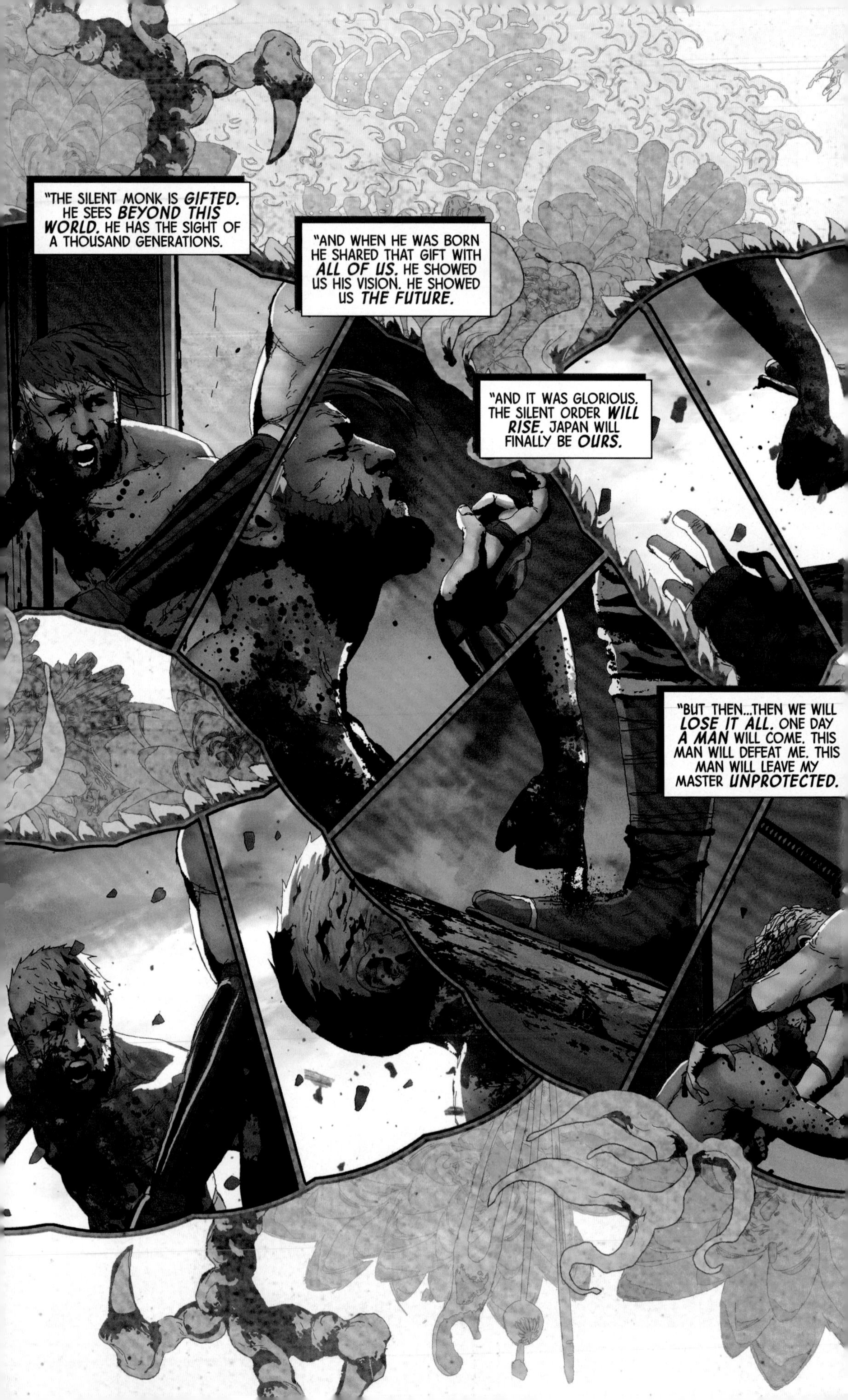
"THE SILENT MONK IS GIFTED. HE SEES BEYOND THIS WORLD. HE HAS THE SIGHT OF A THOUSAND GENERATIONS.
"AND WHEN HE WAS BORN HE SHARED THAT GIFT WITH ALL OF US. HE SHOWED US HIS VISION. HE SHOWED US THE FUTURE.
"AND IT WAS GLORIOUS. THE SILENT ORDER WILL RISE. JAPAN WILL FINALLY BE OURS.
"BUT THEN...THEN WE WILL LOSE IT ALL. ONE DAY A MAN WILL COME. THIS MAN WILL DEFEAT ME. THIS MAN WILL LEAVE MY MASTER UNPROTECTED.

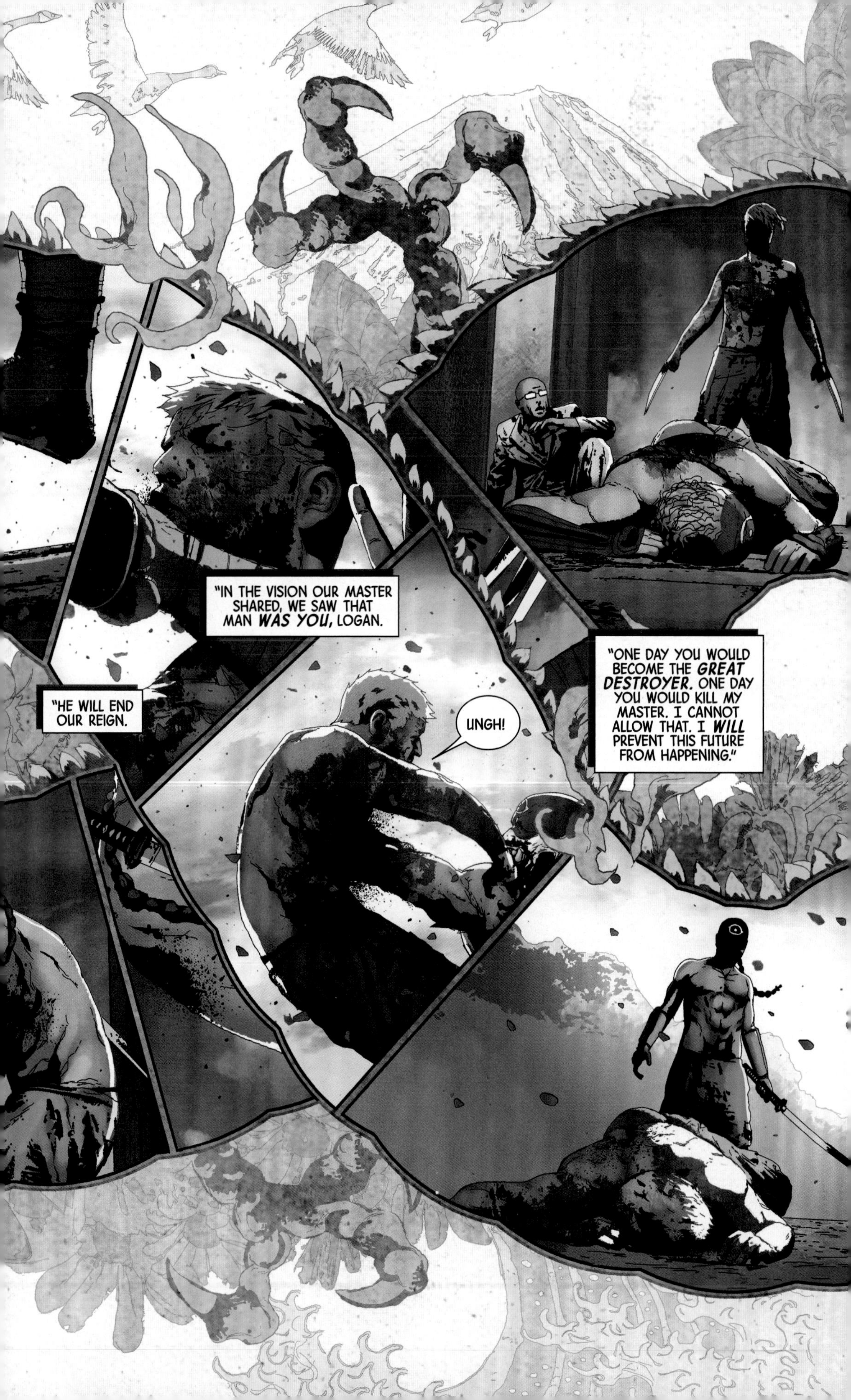
"IN THE VISION OUR MASTER SHARED, WE SAW THAT MAN WAS YOU, LOGAN.
"ONE DAY YOU WOULD BECOME THE GREAT DESTROYER. ONE DAY YOU WOULD KILL MY MASTER. I CANNOT ALLOW THAT. I WILL PREVENT THIS FUTURE FROM HAPPENING."
"HE WILL END OUR REIGN.
UNGH!

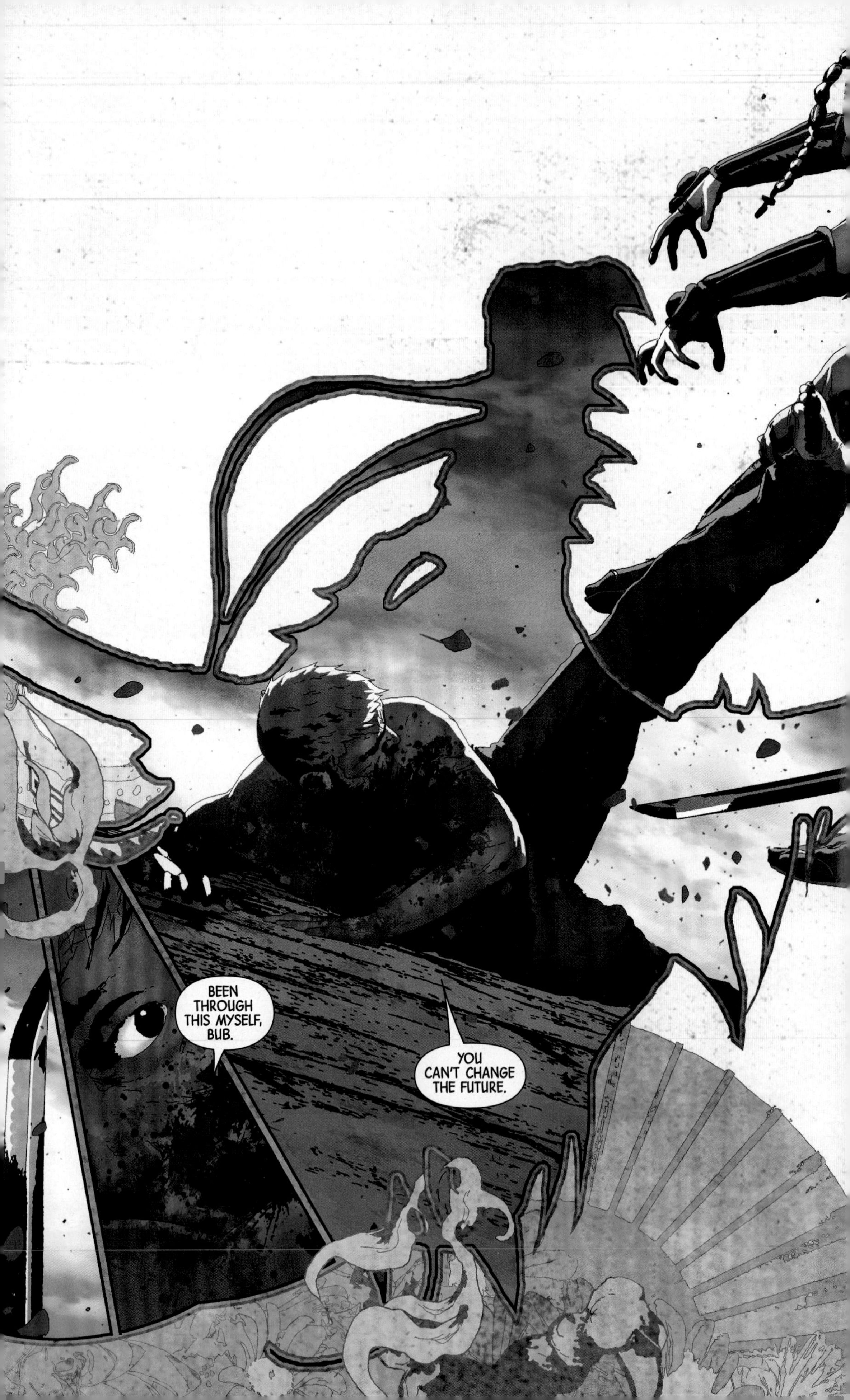
BEEN THROUGH THIS MYSELF, BUB.
YOU CAN'T CHANGE THE FUTURE.

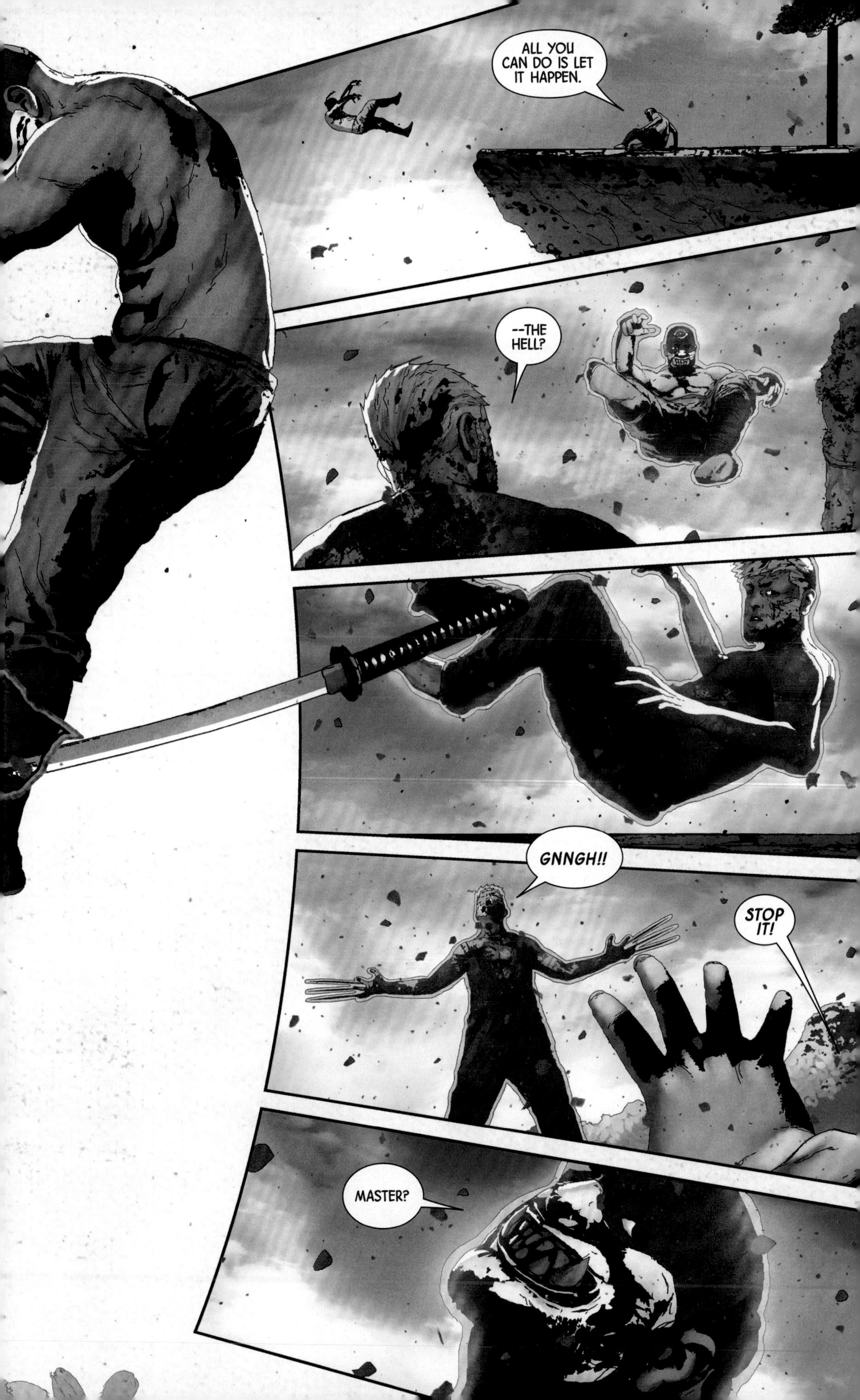
ALL YOU CAN DO IS LET IT HAPPEN.
--THE HELL?
GNNGH!!
STOP IT!
MASTER?

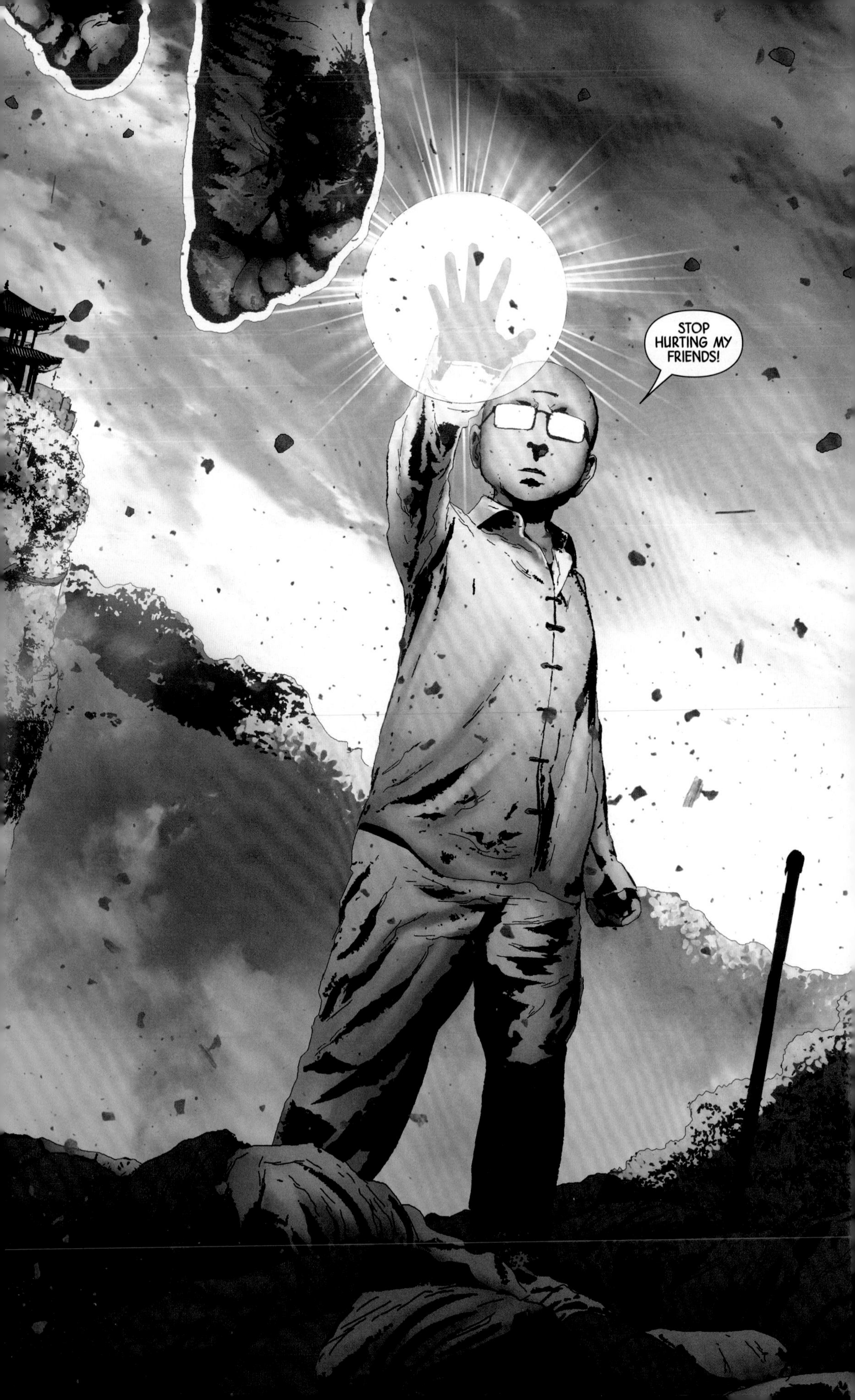
STOP HURTING MY FRIENDS!

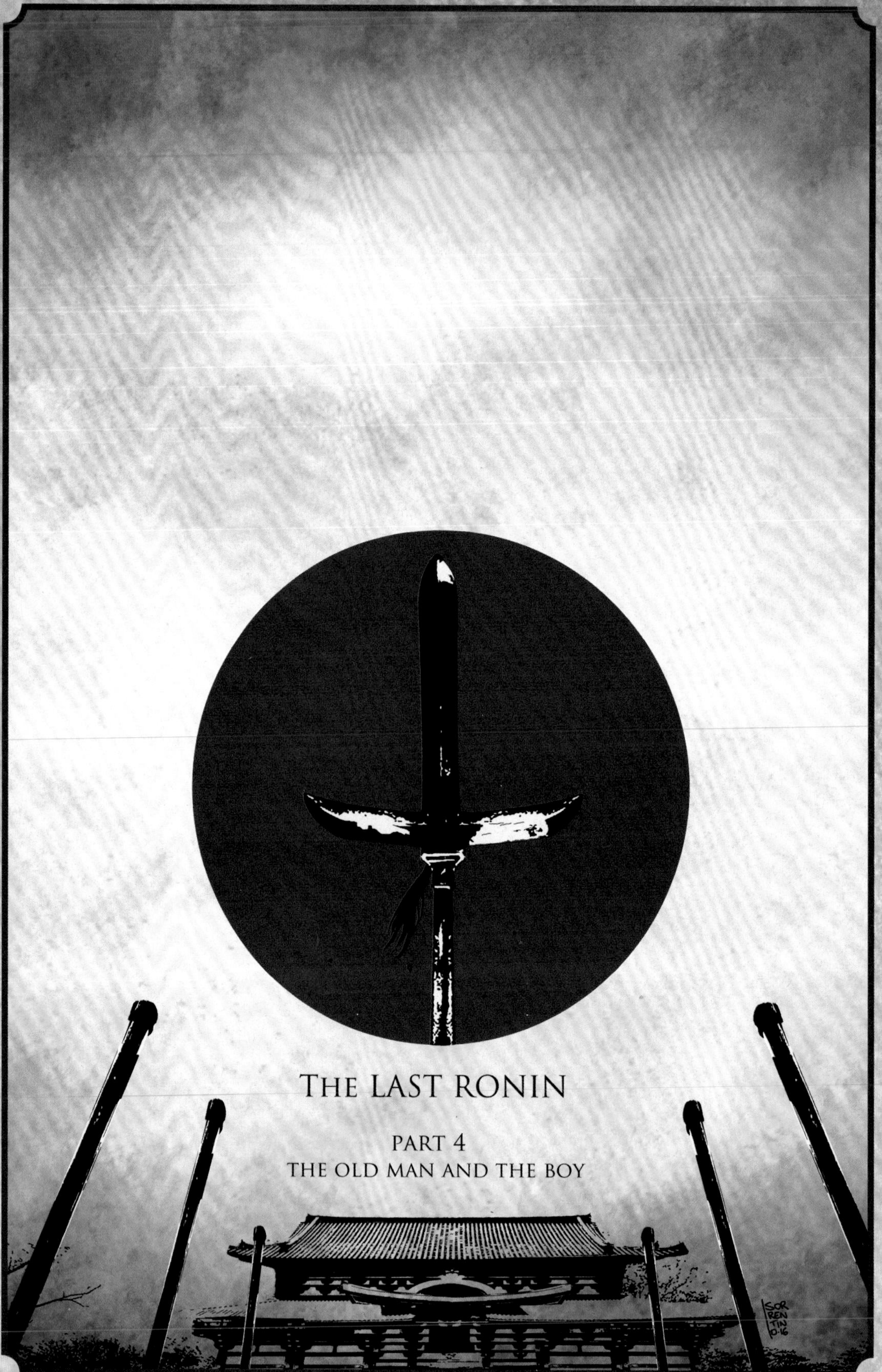
THE LAST RONIN
PART 4
THE OLD MAN AND THE BOY
SOR
REN
TIN
O·16

12

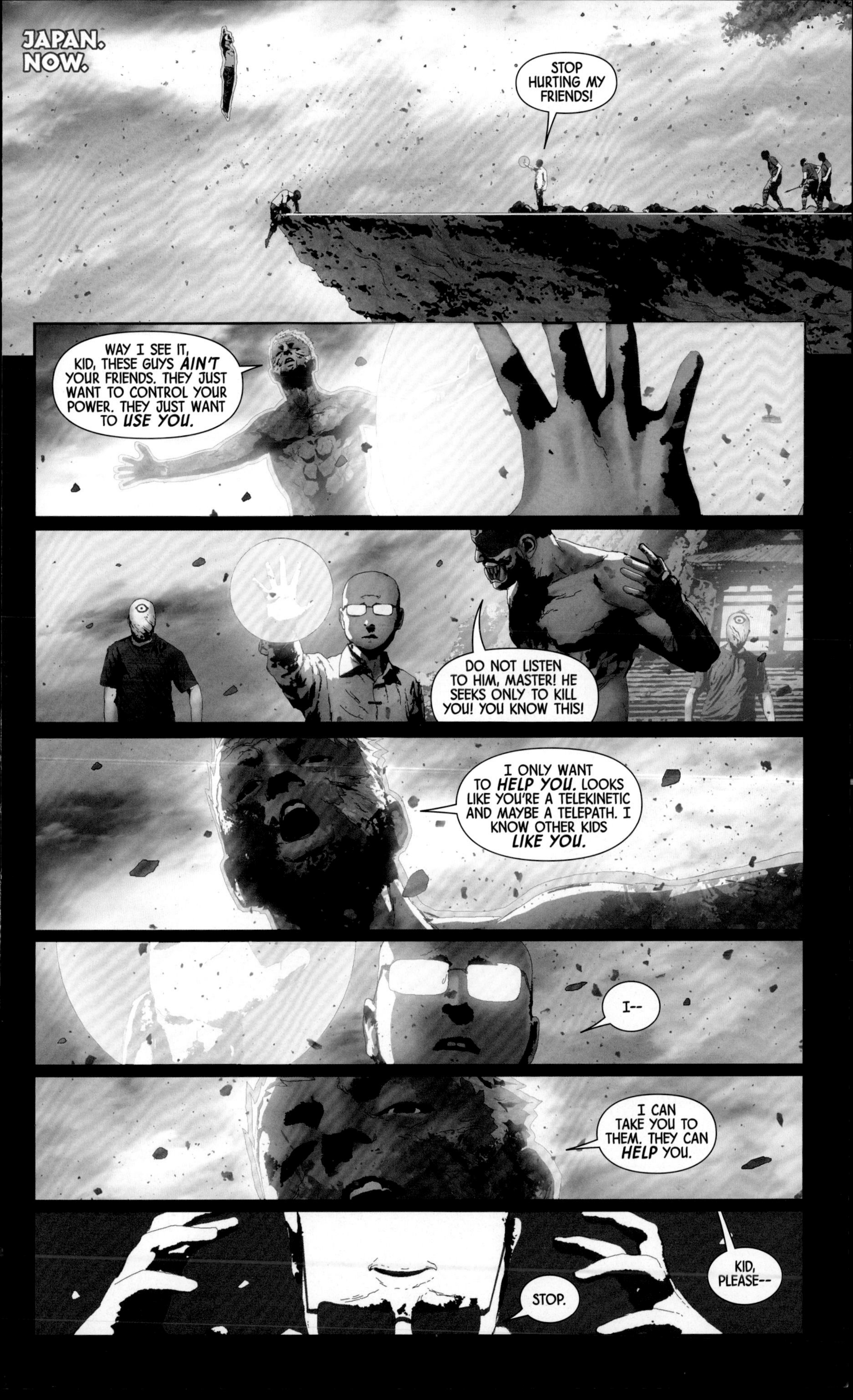
JAPAN. NOW.
STOP HURTING MY FRIENDS!
WAY I SEE IT, KID, THESE GUYS AIN'T YOUR FRIENDS. THEY JUST WANT TO CONTROL YOUR POWER. THEY JUST WANT TO USE YOU.
DO NOT LISTEN TO HIM, MASTER! HE SEEKS ONLY TO KILL YOU! YOU KNOW THIS!
I ONLY WANT TO HELP YOU. LOOKS LIKE YOU'RE A TELEKINETIC AND MAYBE A TELEPATH. I KNOW OTHER KIDS LIKE YOU.
I--
I CAN TAKE YOU TO THEM. THEY CAN HELP YOU.
STOP.
KID, PLEASE--

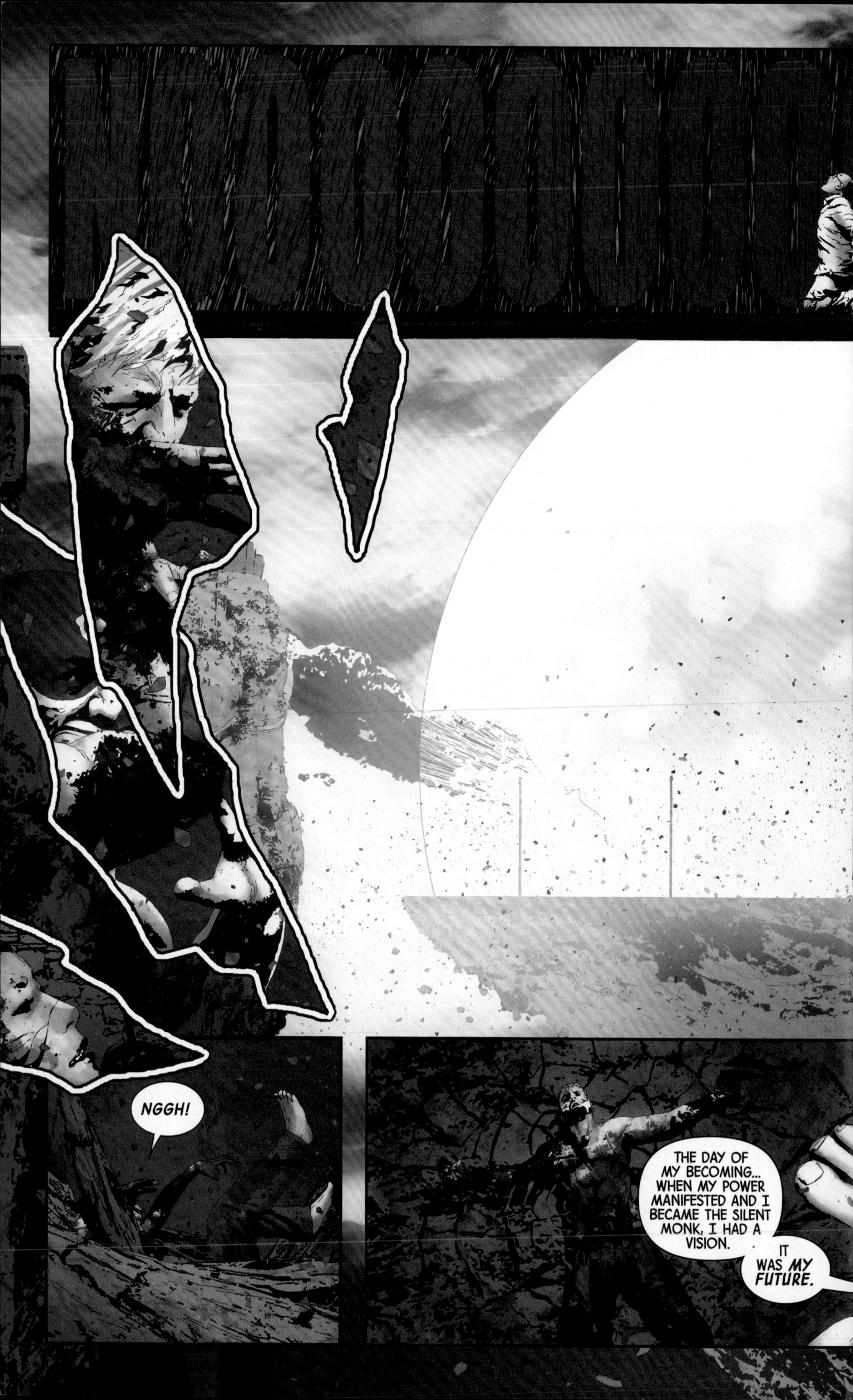
NGGH!
THE DAY OF MY BECOMING... WHEN MY POWER MANIFESTED AND I BECAME THE SILENT MONK, I HAD A VISION.
IT WAS *MY FUTURE.*

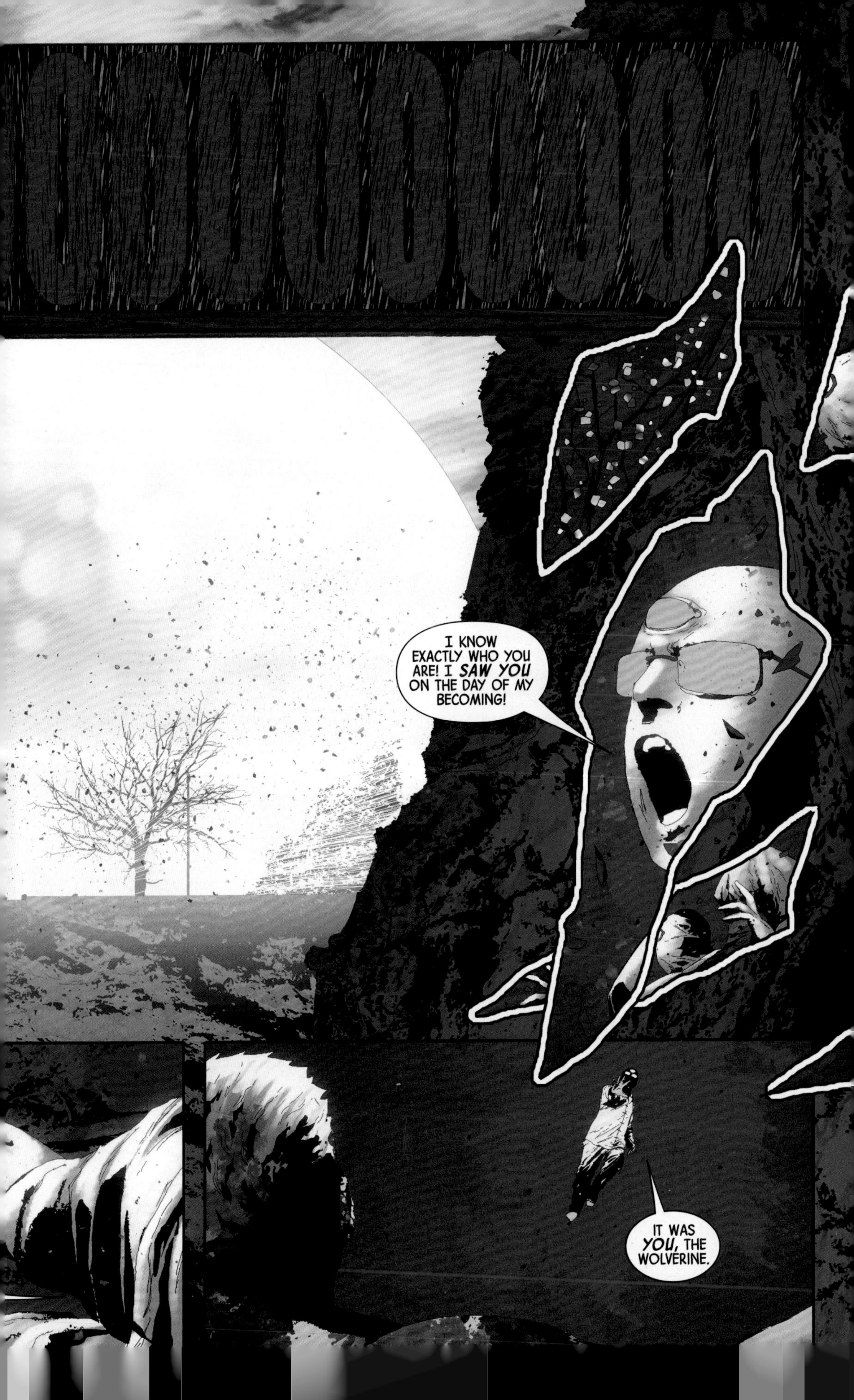
I KNOW EXACTLY WHO YOU ARE! I *SAW YOU* ON THE DAY OF MY BECOMING!
IT WAS *YOU,* THE WOLVERINE.

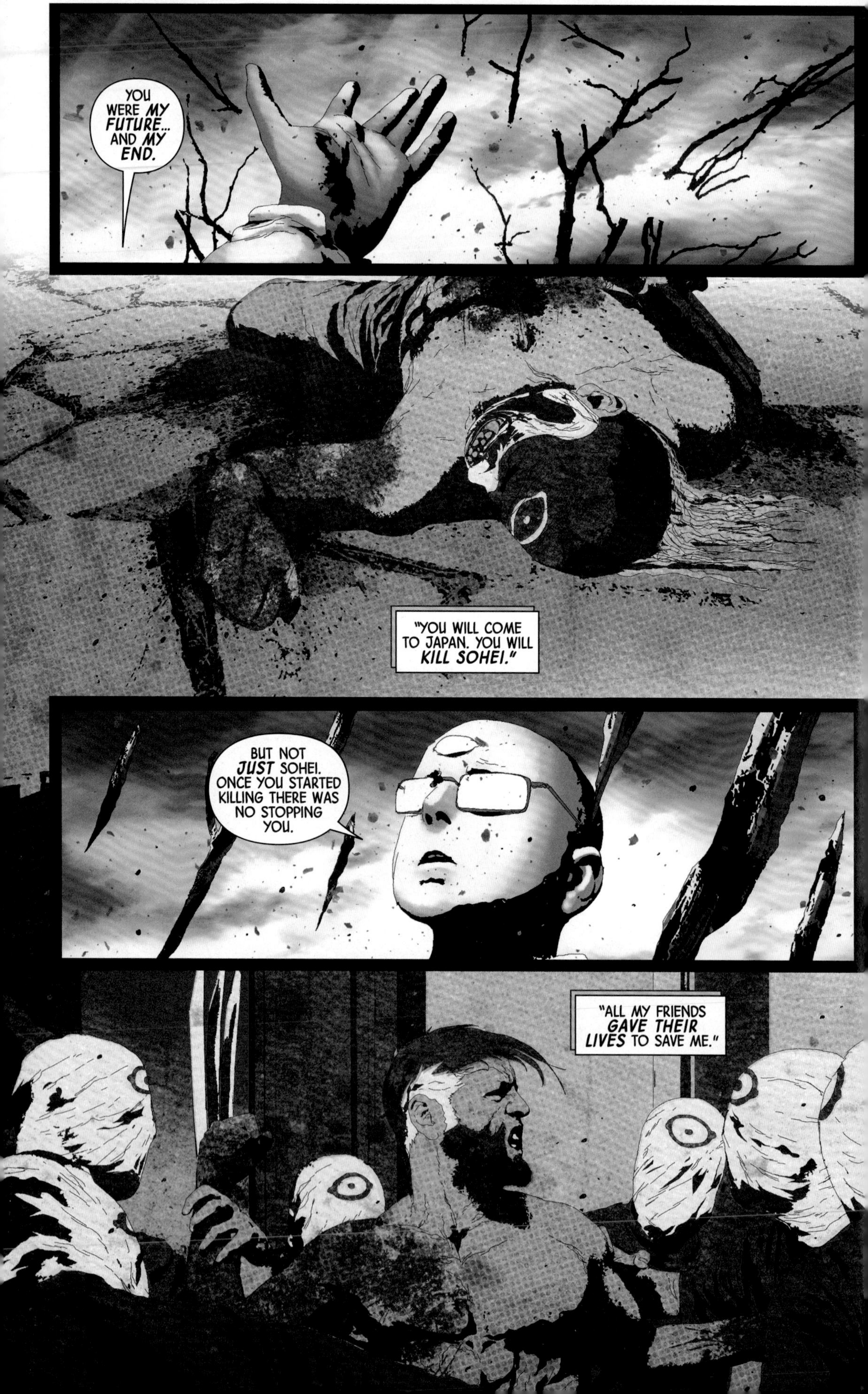
YOU WERE MY FUTURE... AND MY END.
"YOU WILL COME TO JAPAN. YOU WILL KILL SOHEI."
BUT NOT JUST SOHEI. ONCE YOU STARTED KILLING THERE WAS NO STOPPING YOU.
"ALL MY FRIENDS GAVE THEIR LIVES TO SAVE ME."

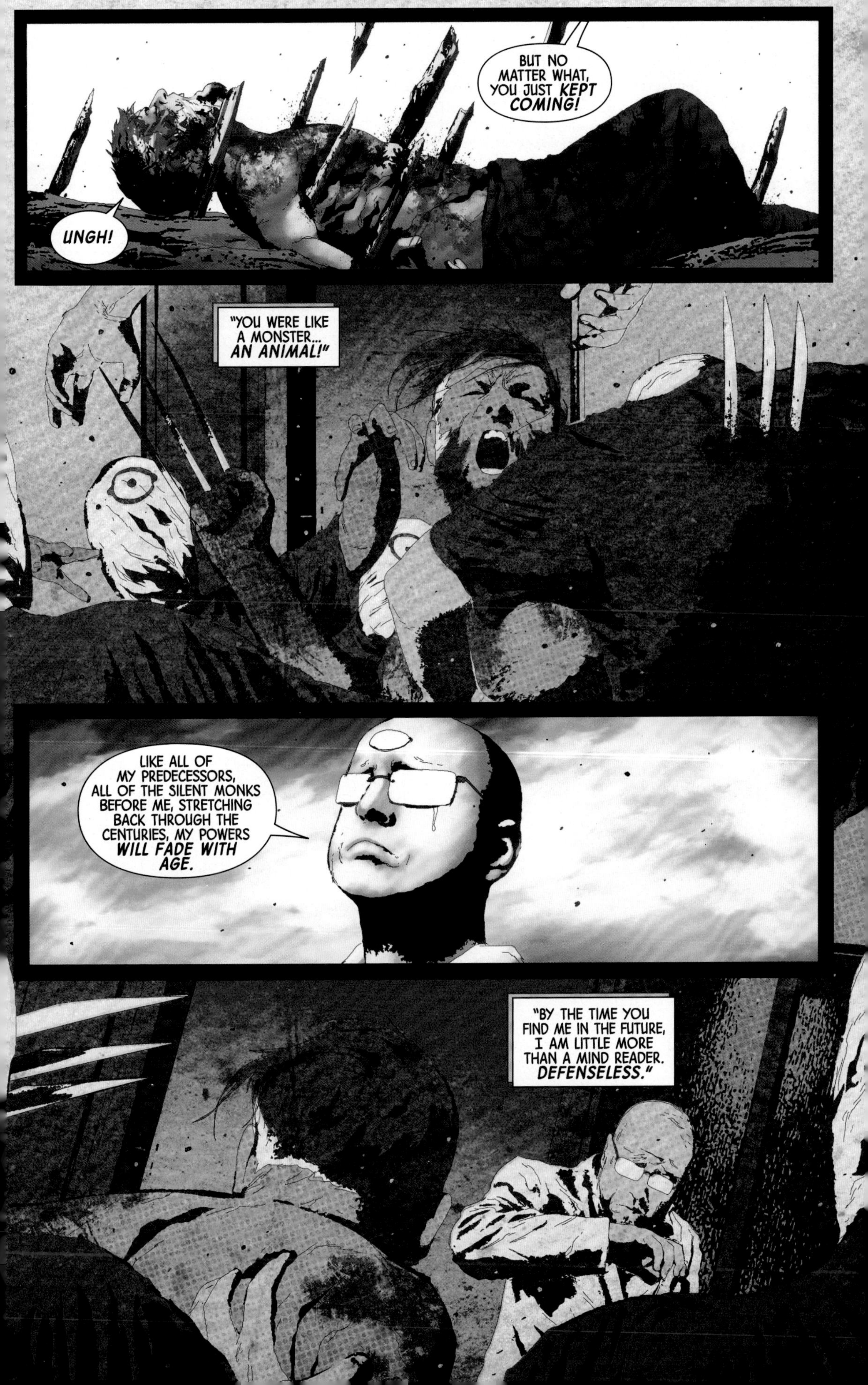
BUT NO MATTER WHAT, YOU JUST KEPT COMING!
UNGH!
"YOU WERE LIKE A MONSTER... AN ANIMAL!"
LIKE ALL OF MY PREDECESSORS, ALL OF THE SILENT MONKS BEFORE ME, STRETCHING BACK THROUGH THE CENTURIES, MY POWERS WILL FADE WITH AGE.
"BY THE TIME YOU FIND ME IN THE FUTURE, I AM LITTLE MORE THAN A MIND READER. DEFENSELESS."

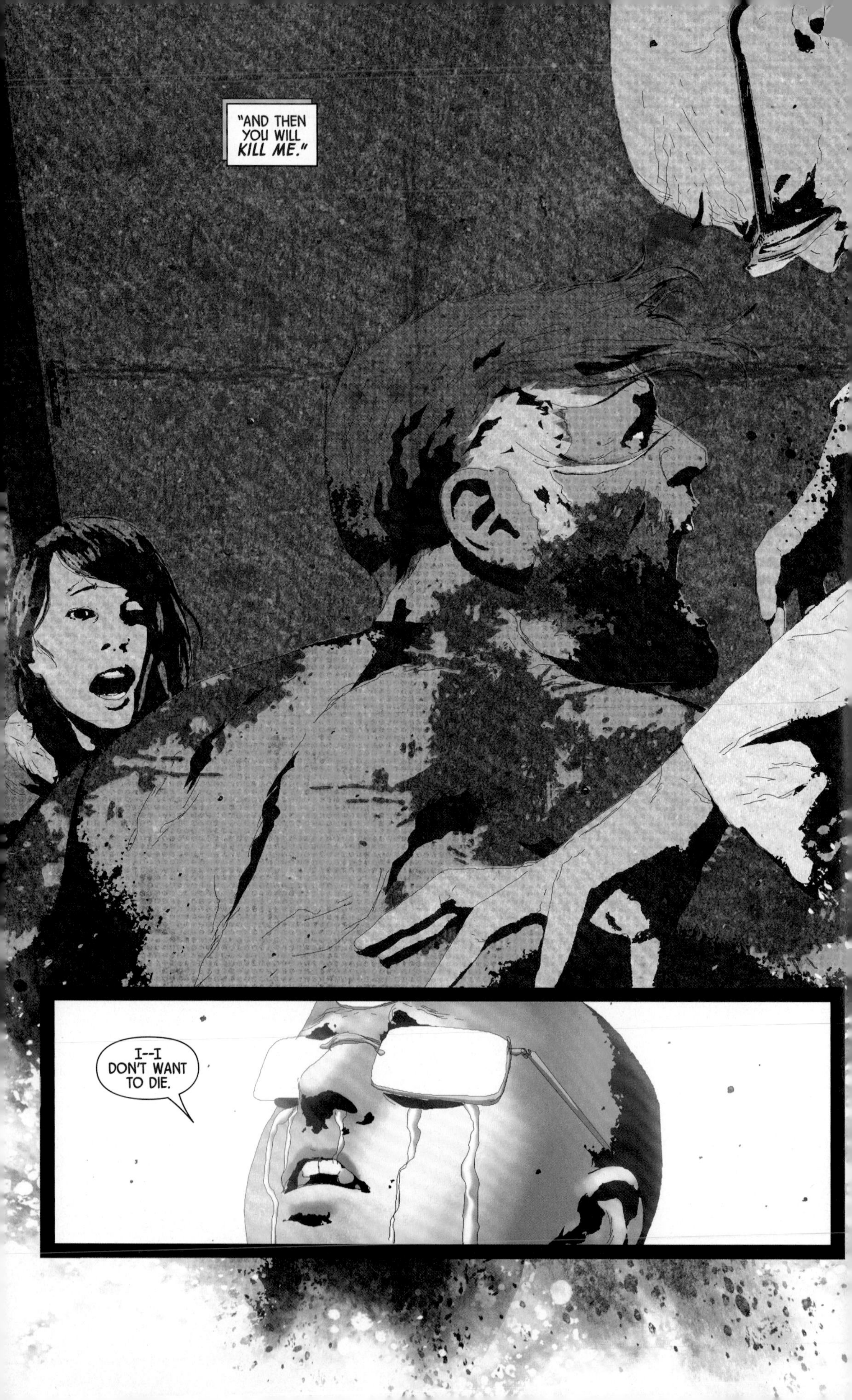
"AND THEN YOU WILL KILL ME."
I--I DON'T WANT TO DIE.

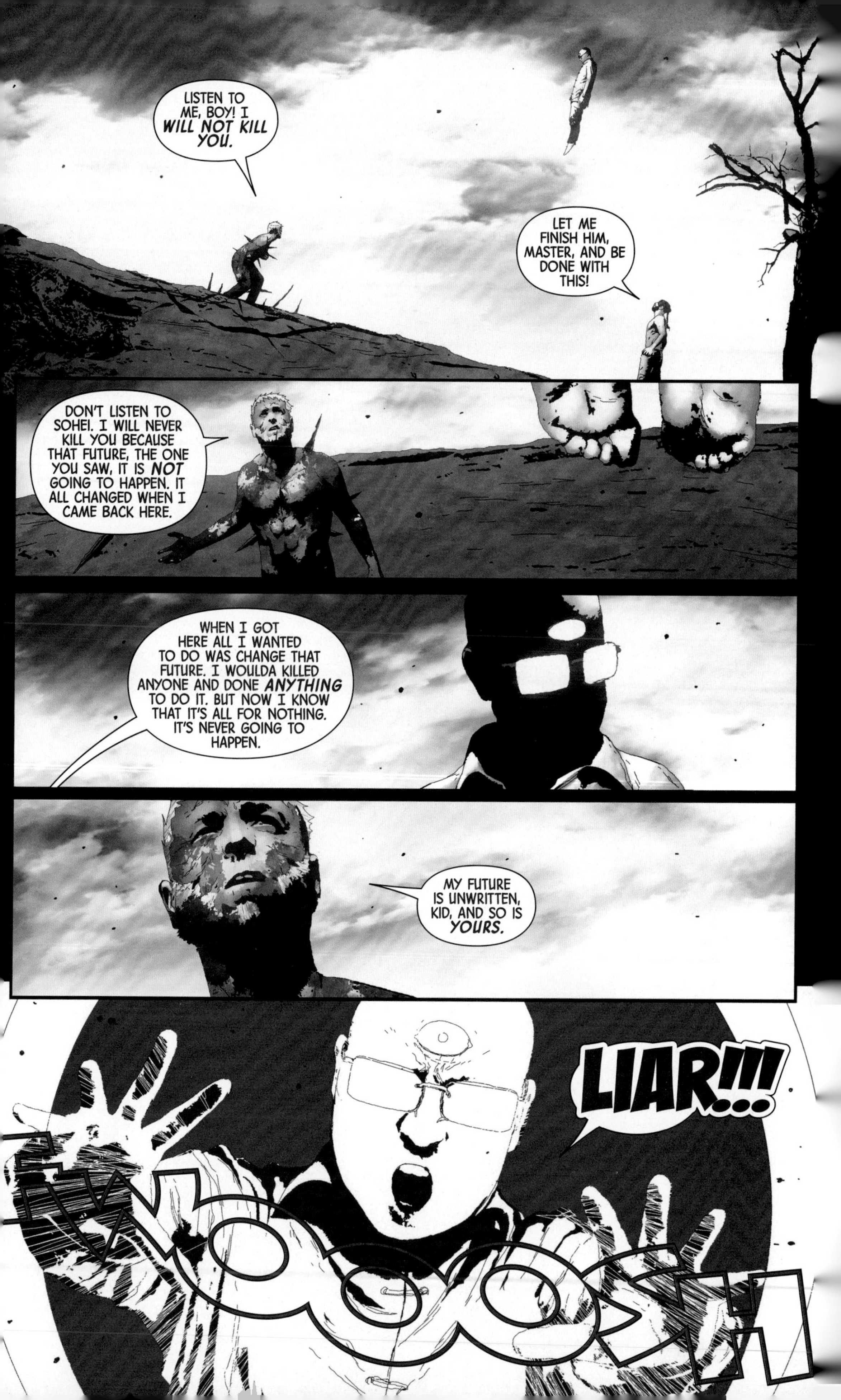

LISTEN TO ME, BOY! I WILL NOT KILL YOU.
LET ME FINISH HIM, MASTER, AND BE DONE WITH THIS!
DON'T LISTEN TO SOHEI. I WILL NEVER KILL YOU BECAUSE THAT FUTURE, THE ONE YOU SAW, IT IS NOT GOING TO HAPPEN. IT ALL CHANGED WHEN I CAME BACK HERE.
WHEN I GOT HERE ALL I WANTED TO DO WAS CHANGE THAT FUTURE. I WOULDA KILLED ANYONE AND DONE ANYTHING TO DO IT. BUT NOW I KNOW THAT IT'S ALL FOR NOTHING. IT'S NEVER GOING TO HAPPEN.
MY FUTURE IS UNWRITTEN, KID, AND SO IS YOURS.
LIAR!!!
FWOOOOSH

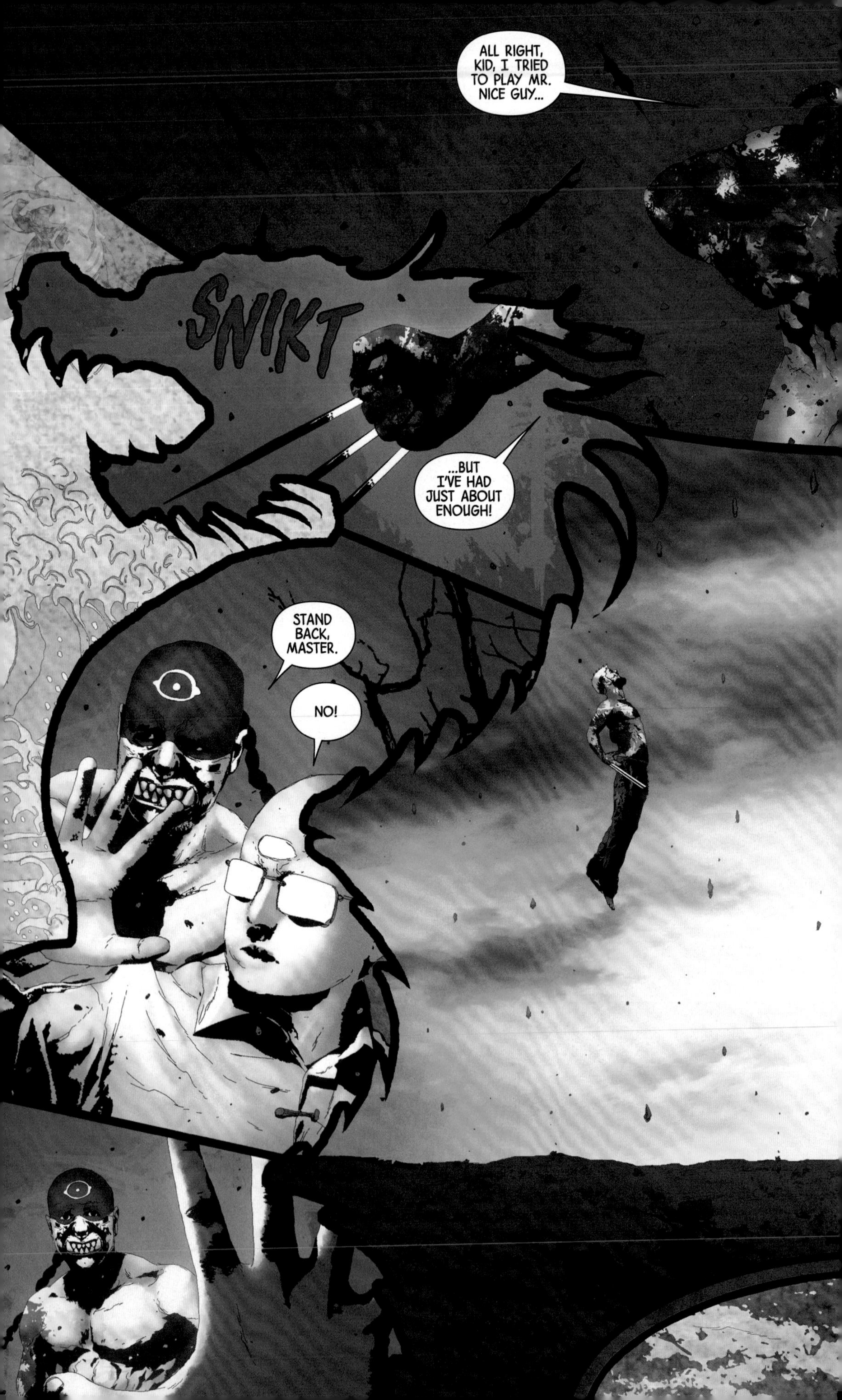
ALL RIGHT, KID, I TRIED TO PLAY MR. NICE GUY...
SNIKT
...BUT I'VE HAD JUST ABOUT ENOUGH!
STAND BACK, MASTER.
NO!

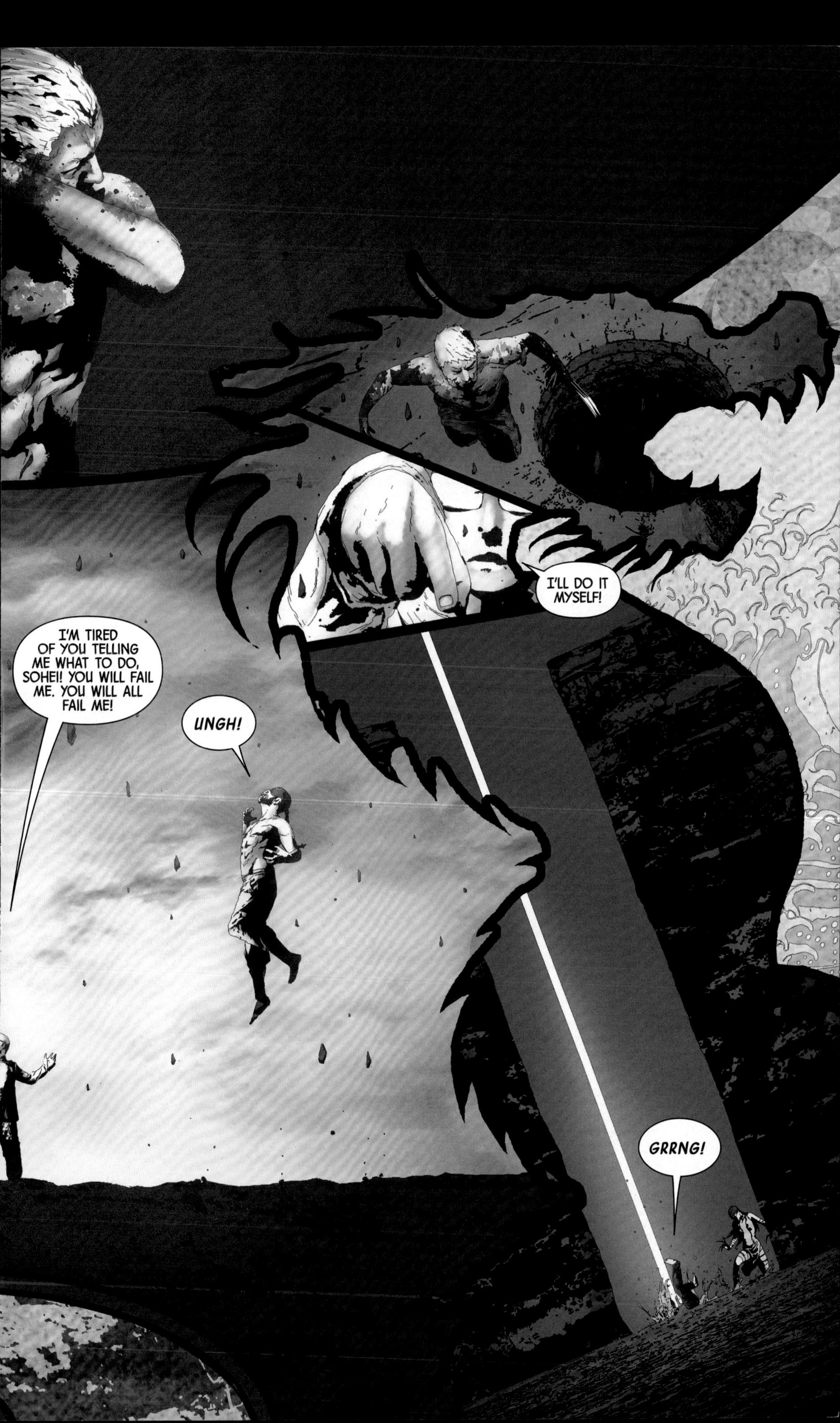
I'LL DO IT MYSELF!
I'M TIRED OF YOU TELLING ME WHAT TO DO, SOHEI! YOU WILL FAIL ME. YOU WILL ALL FAIL ME!
UNGH!
GRRNG!

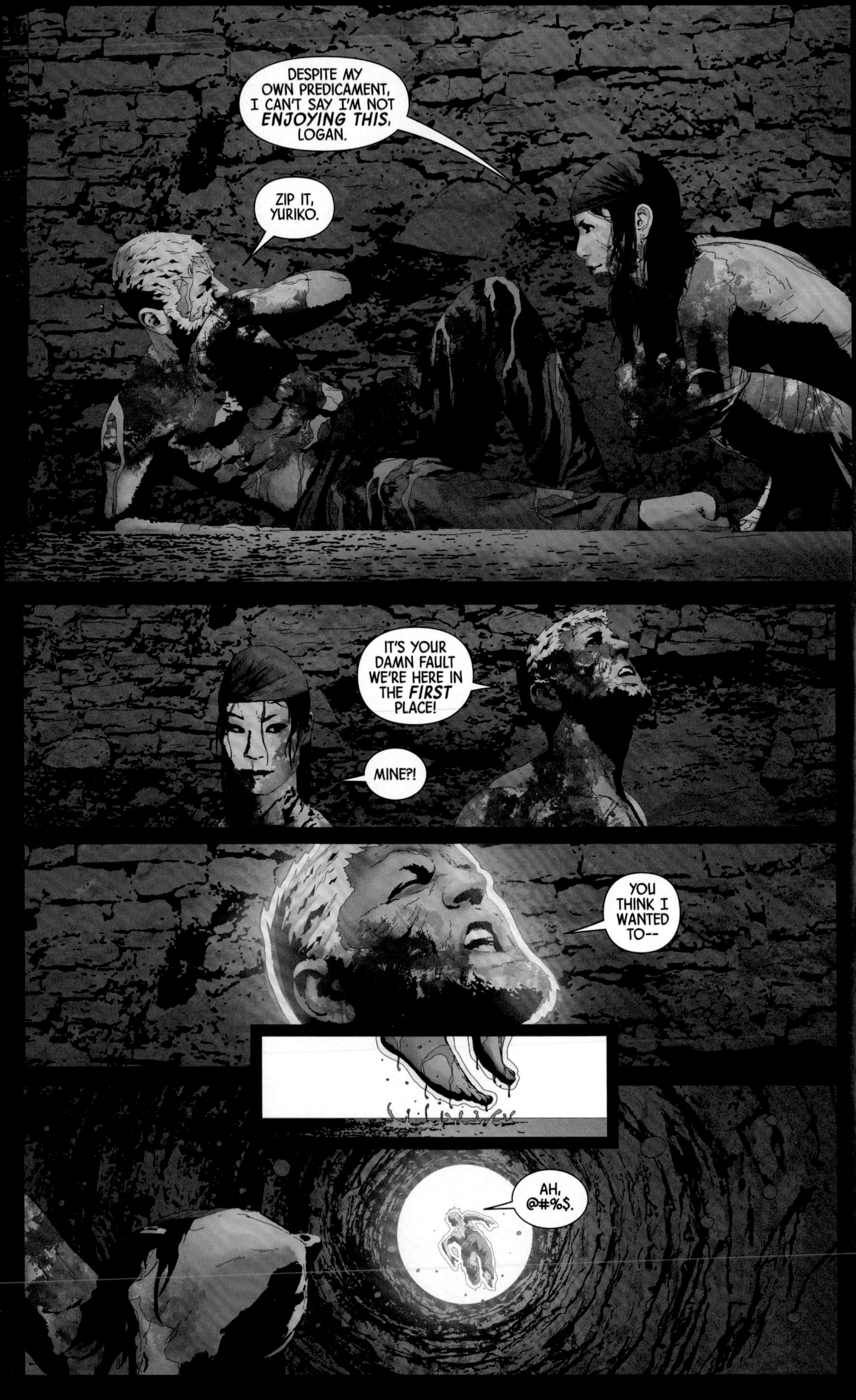
DESPITE MY OWN PREDICAMENT, I CAN'T SAY I'M NOT ENJOYING THIS, LOGAN.
ZIP IT, YURIKO.
IT'S YOUR DAMN FAULT WE'RE HERE IN THE FIRST PLACE!
MINE?!
YOU THINK I WANTED TO--
AH, @#%$.

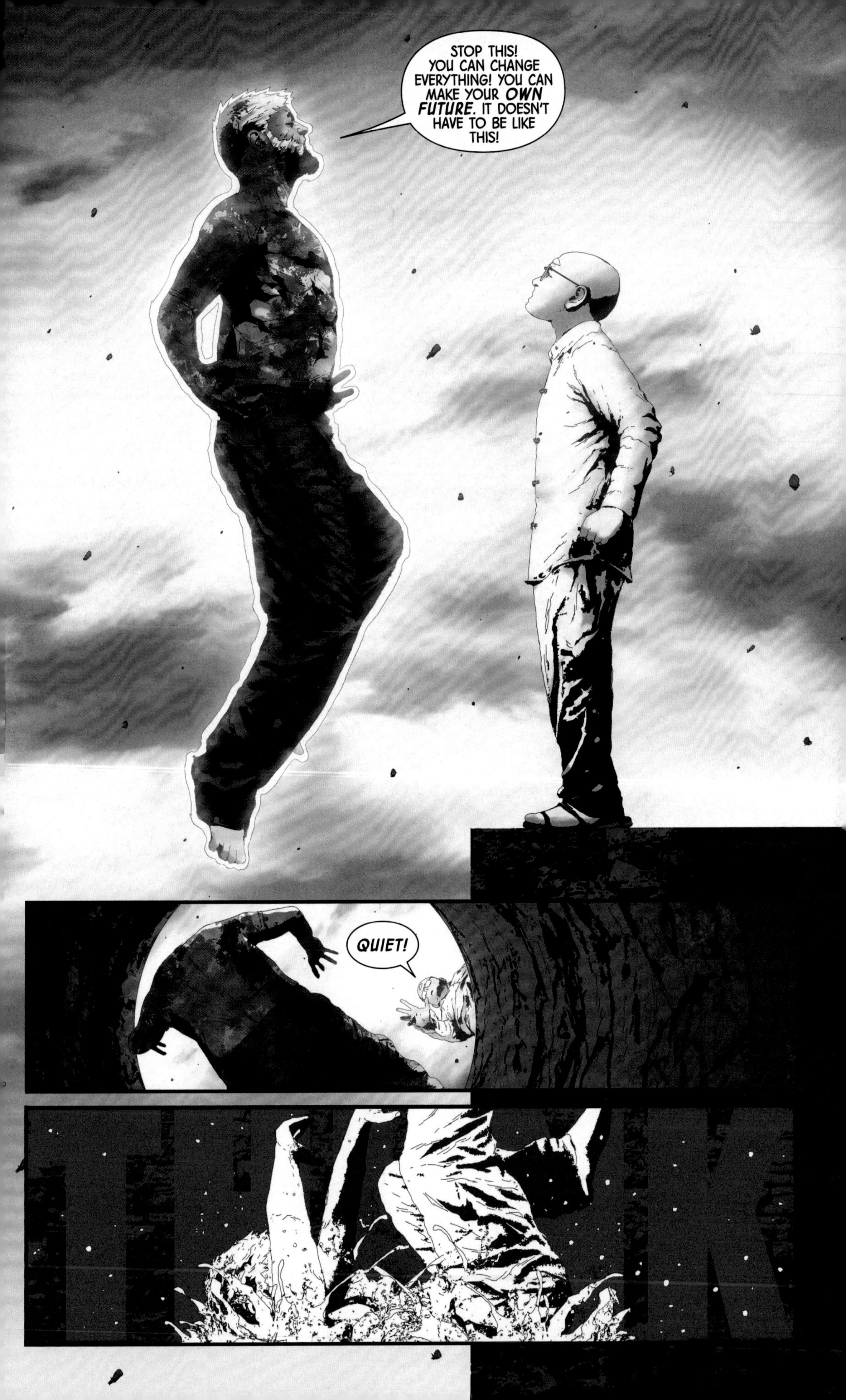
STOP THIS! YOU CAN CHANGE EVERYTHING! YOU CAN MAKE YOUR *OWN FUTURE*. IT DOESN'T HAVE TO BE LIKE THIS!
QUIET!

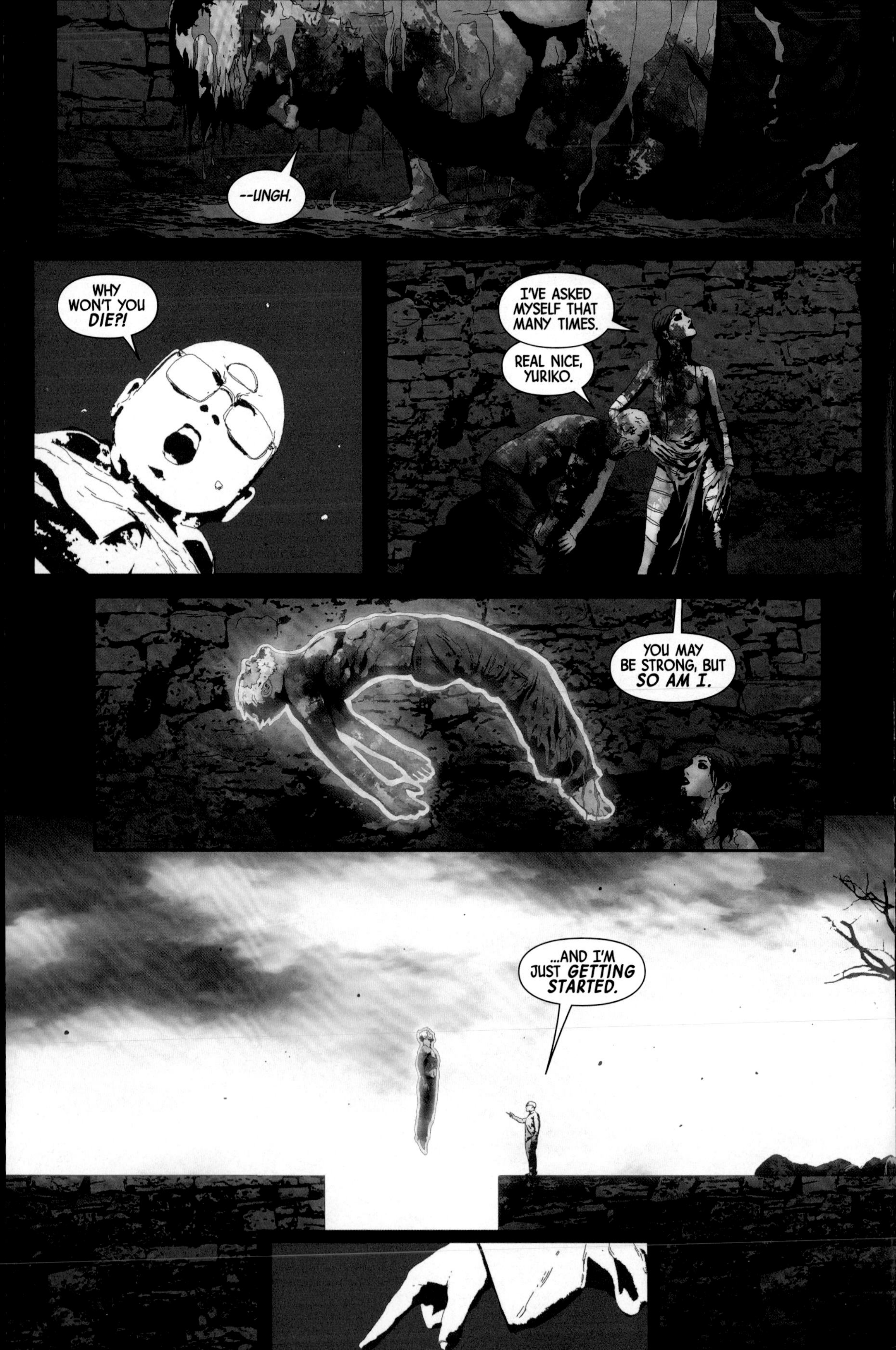
--UNGH.
WHY WON'T YOU DIE?!
I'VE ASKED MYSELF THAT MANY TIMES.
REAL NICE, YURIKO.
YOU MAY BE STRONG, BUT SO AM I.
...AND I'M JUST GETTING STARTED.

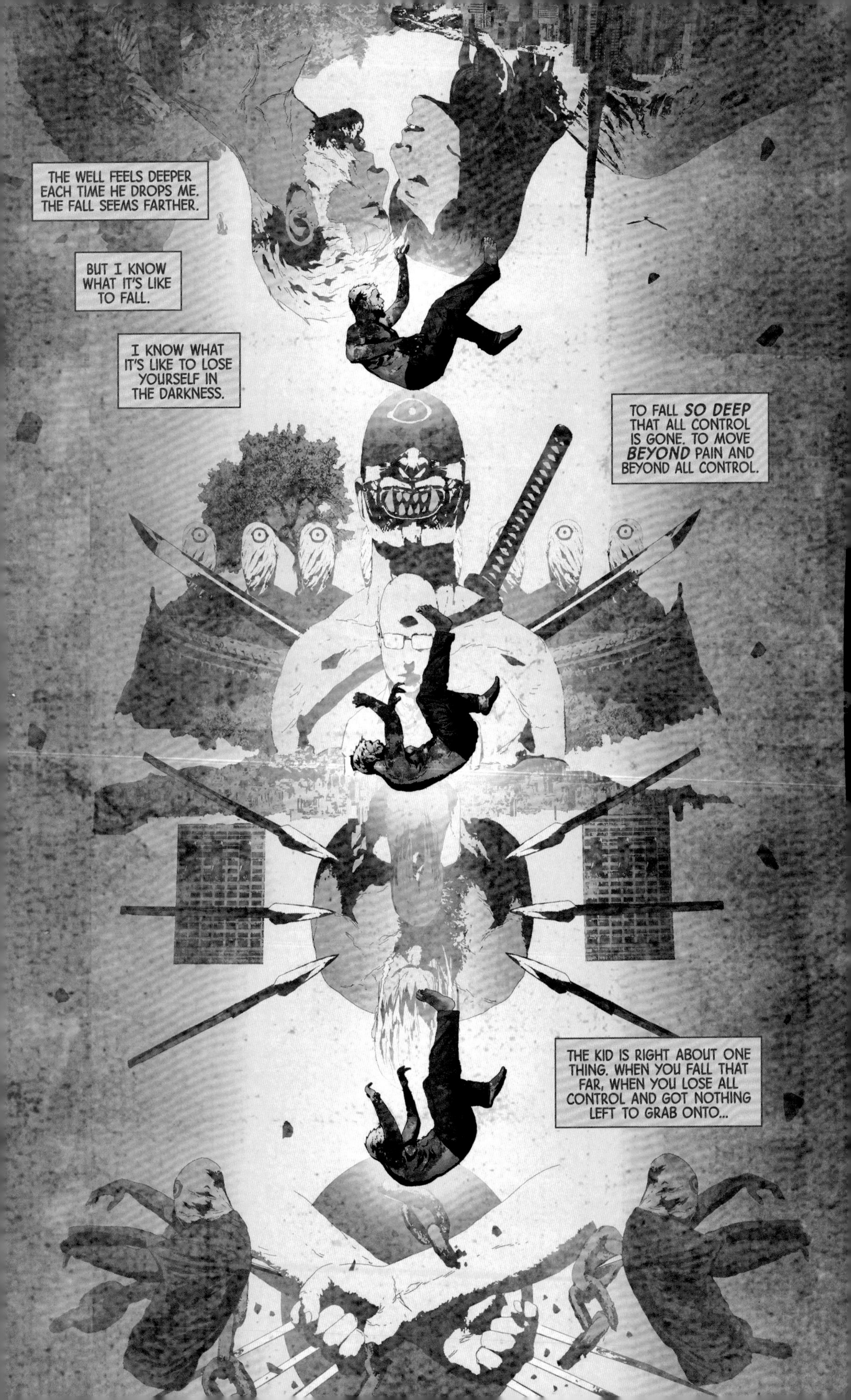
THE WELL FEELS DEEPER EACH TIME HE DROPS ME. THE FALL SEEMS FARTHER.
BUT I KNOW WHAT IT'S LIKE TO FALL.
I KNOW WHAT IT'S LIKE TO LOSE YOURSELF IN THE DARKNESS.
TO FALL SO DEEP THAT ALL CONTROL IS GONE. TO MOVE BEYOND PAIN AND BEYOND ALL CONTROL.
THE KID IS RIGHT ABOUT ONE THING. WHEN YOU FALL THAT FAR, WHEN YOU LOSE ALL CONTROL AND GOT NOTHING LEFT TO GRAB ONTO...

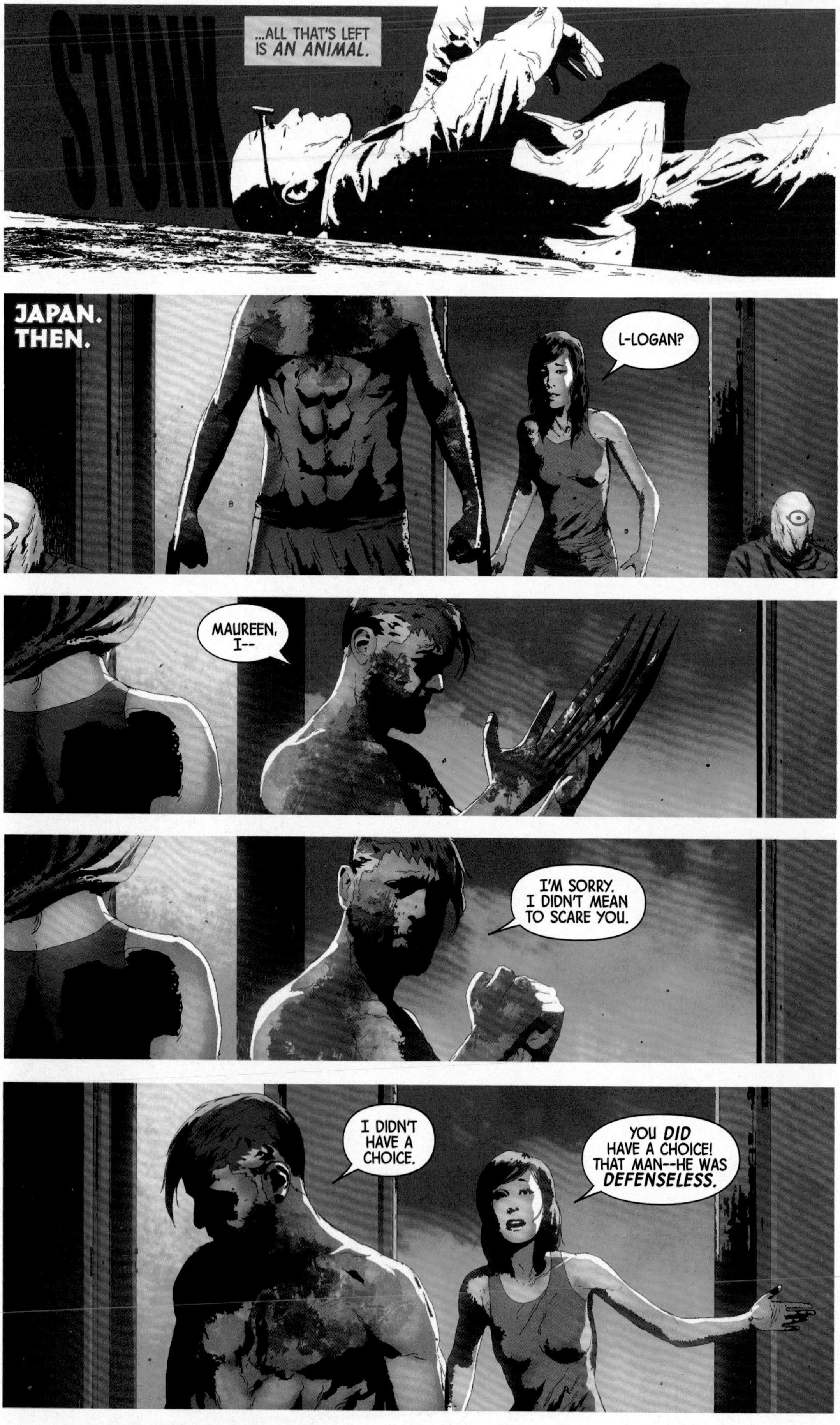
STUNK
...ALL THAT'S LEFT IS *AN ANIMAL.*
JAPAN. THEN.
L-LOGAN?
MAUREEN, I--
I'M SORRY. I DIDN'T MEAN TO SCARE YOU.
I DIDN'T HAVE A CHOICE.
YOU *DID* HAVE A CHOICE! THAT MAN--HE WAS *DEFENSELESS.*

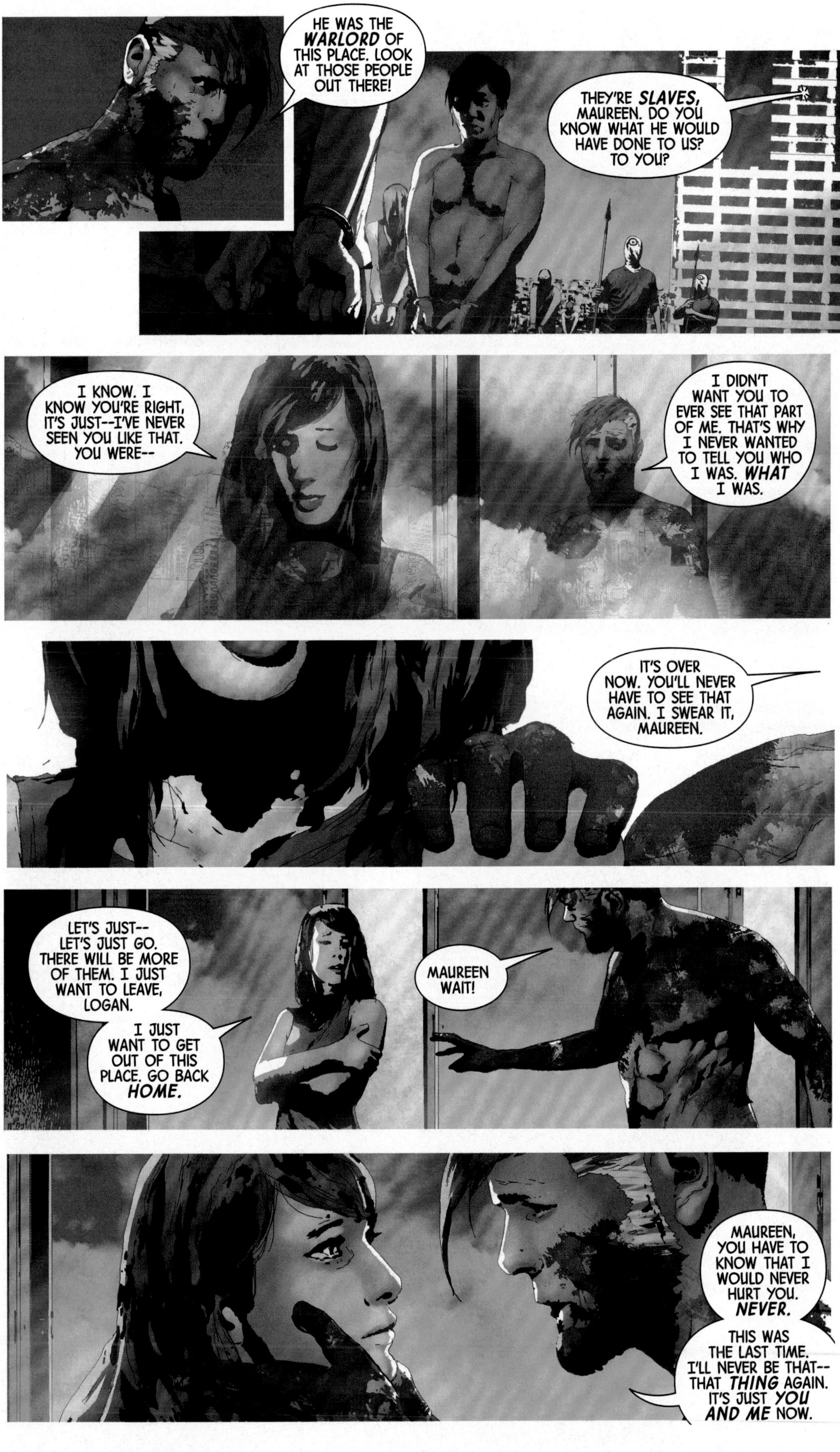
HE WAS THE WARLORD OF THIS PLACE. LOOK AT THOSE PEOPLE OUT THERE!
THEY'RE SLAVES, MAUREEN. DO YOU KNOW WHAT HE WOULD HAVE DONE TO US? TO YOU?
I KNOW. I KNOW YOU'RE RIGHT, IT'S JUST--I'VE NEVER SEEN YOU LIKE THAT. YOU WERE--
I DIDN'T WANT YOU TO EVER SEE THAT PART OF ME. THAT'S WHY I NEVER WANTED TO TELL YOU WHO I WAS. WHAT I WAS.
IT'S OVER NOW. YOU'LL NEVER HAVE TO SEE THAT AGAIN. I SWEAR IT, MAUREEN.
LET'S JUST-- LET'S JUST GO. THERE WILL BE MORE OF THEM. I JUST WANT TO LEAVE, LOGAN.
I JUST WANT TO GET OUT OF THIS PLACE. GO BACK HOME.
MAUREEN WAIT!
MAUREEN, YOU HAVE TO KNOW THAT I WOULD NEVER HURT YOU. NEVER.
THIS WAS THE LAST TIME. I'LL NEVER BE THAT-- THAT THING AGAIN. IT'S JUST YOU AND ME NOW.

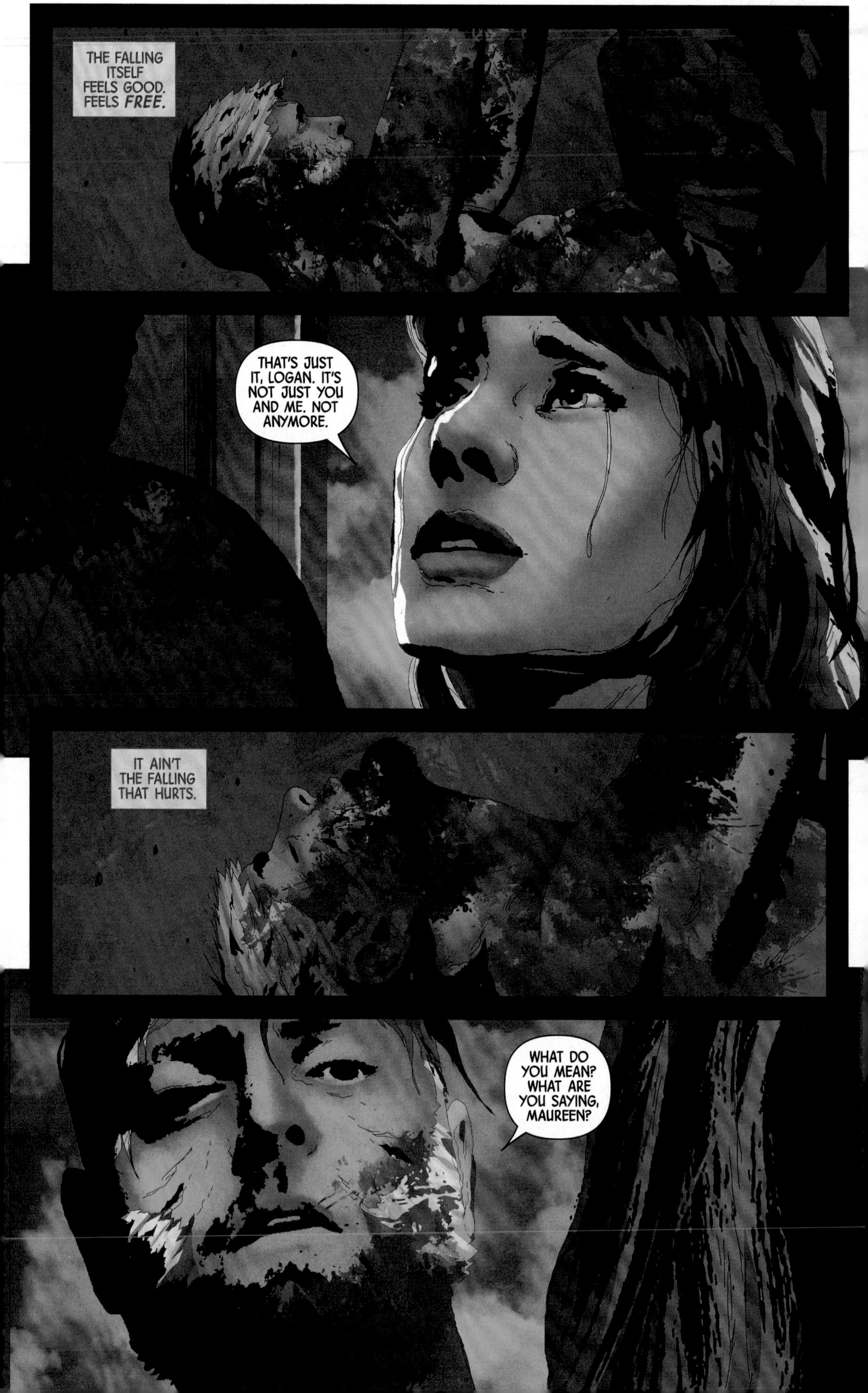
THE FALLING ITSELF FEELS GOOD. FEELS FREE.
THAT'S JUST IT, LOGAN. IT'S NOT JUST YOU AND ME. NOT ANYMORE.
IT AIN'T THE FALLING THAT HURTS.
WHAT DO YOU MEAN? WHAT ARE YOU SAYING, MAUREEN?

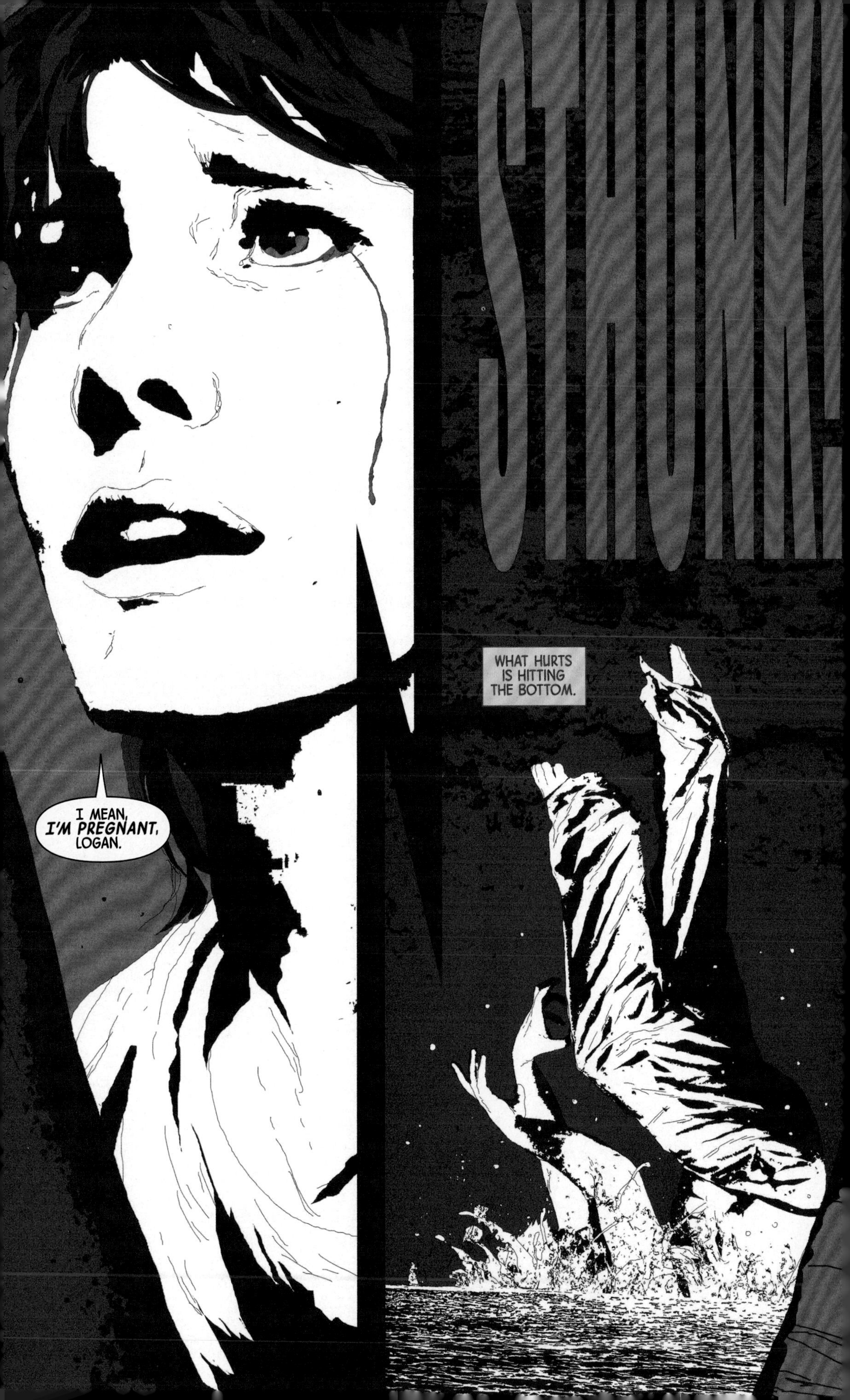
I MEAN, I'M PREGNANT, LOGAN.
STHUNK!
WHAT HURTS IS HITTING THE BOTTOM.

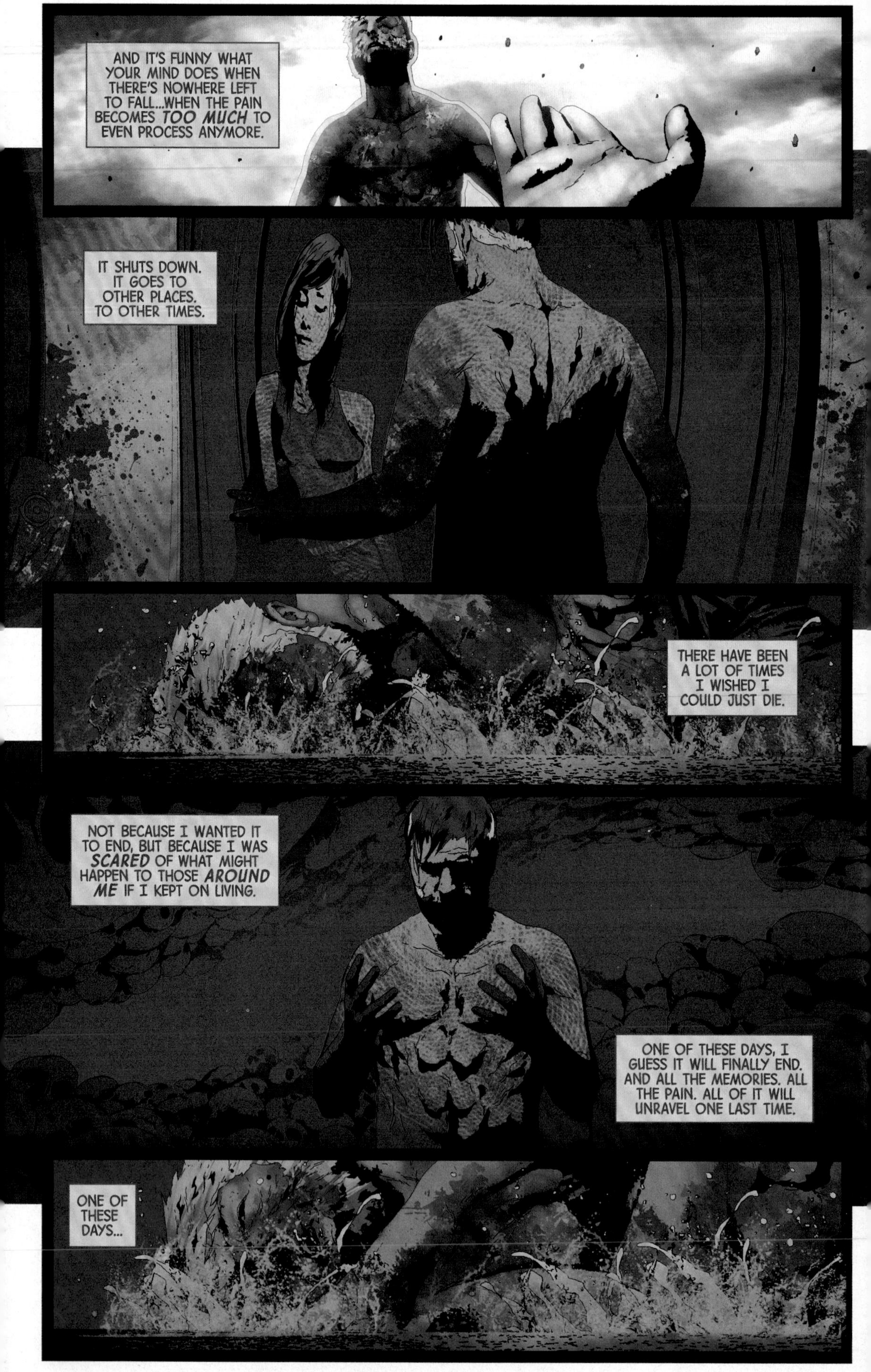
AND IT'S FUNNY WHAT YOUR MIND DOES WHEN THERE'S NOWHERE LEFT TO FALL...WHEN THE PAIN BECOMES TOO MUCH TO EVEN PROCESS ANYMORE.
IT SHUTS DOWN. IT GOES TO OTHER PLACES. TO OTHER TIMES.
THERE HAVE BEEN A LOT OF TIMES I WISHED I COULD JUST DIE.
NOT BECAUSE I WANTED IT TO END, BUT BECAUSE I WAS SCARED OF WHAT MIGHT HAPPEN TO THOSE AROUND ME IF I KEPT ON LIVING.
ONE OF THESE DAYS, I GUESS IT WILL FINALLY END. AND ALL THE MEMORIES. ALL THE PAIN. ALL OF IT WILL UNRAVEL ONE LAST TIME.
ONE OF THESE DAYS...

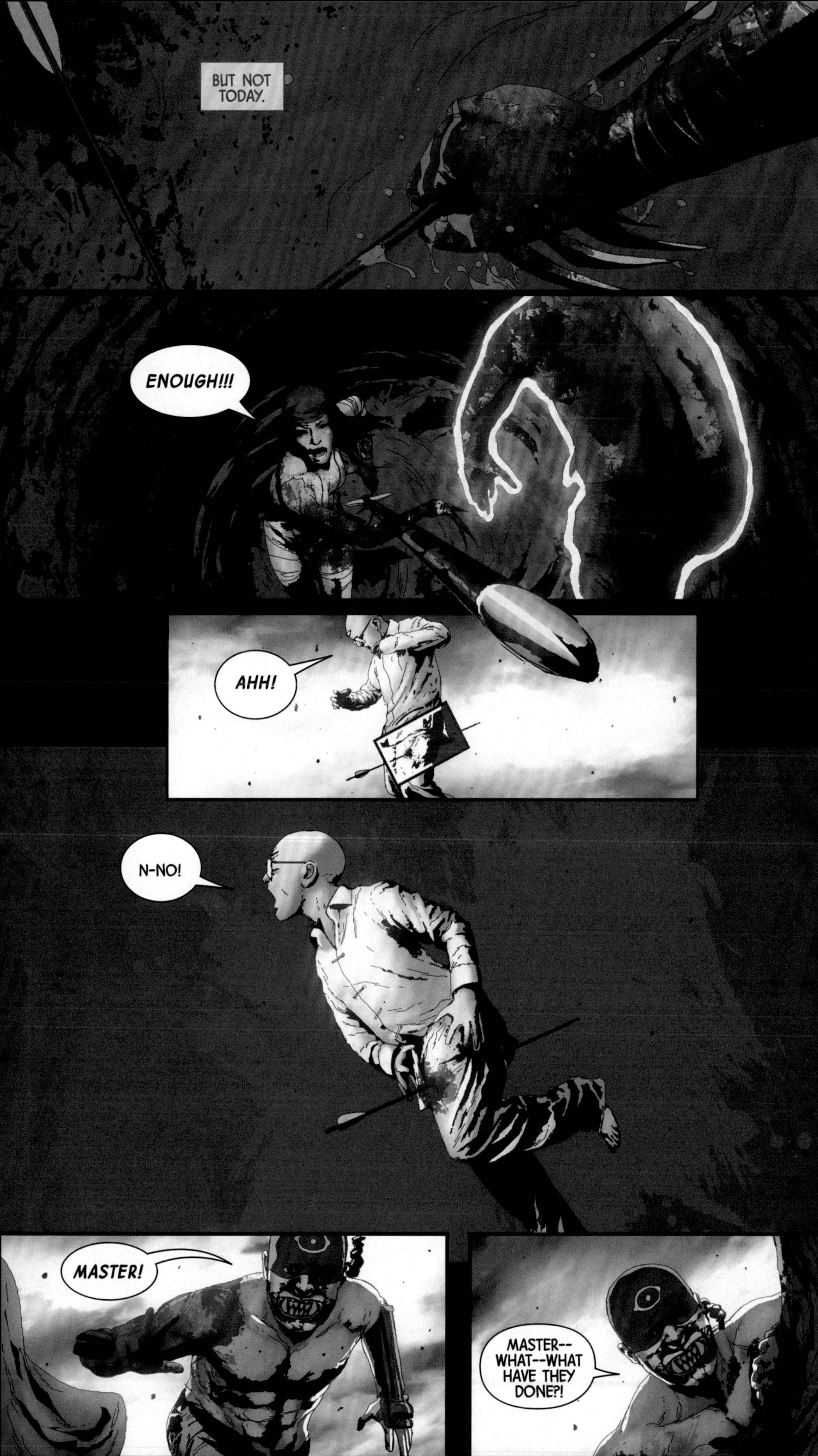
BUT NOT TODAY.
ENOUGH!!!
AHH!
N-NO!
MASTER!
MASTER-- WHAT--WHAT HAVE THEY DONE?!

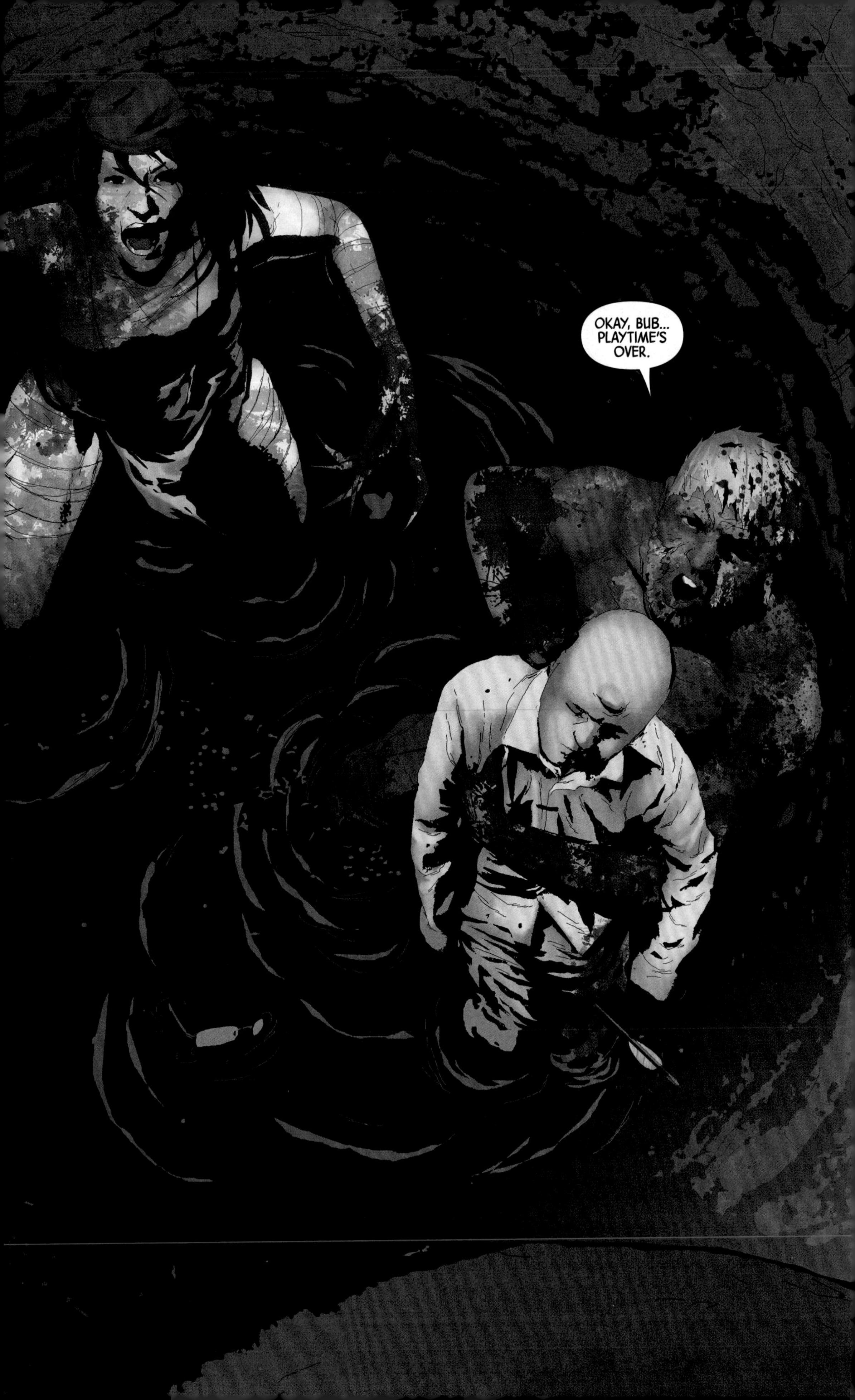
OKAY, BUB... PLAYTIME'S OVER.

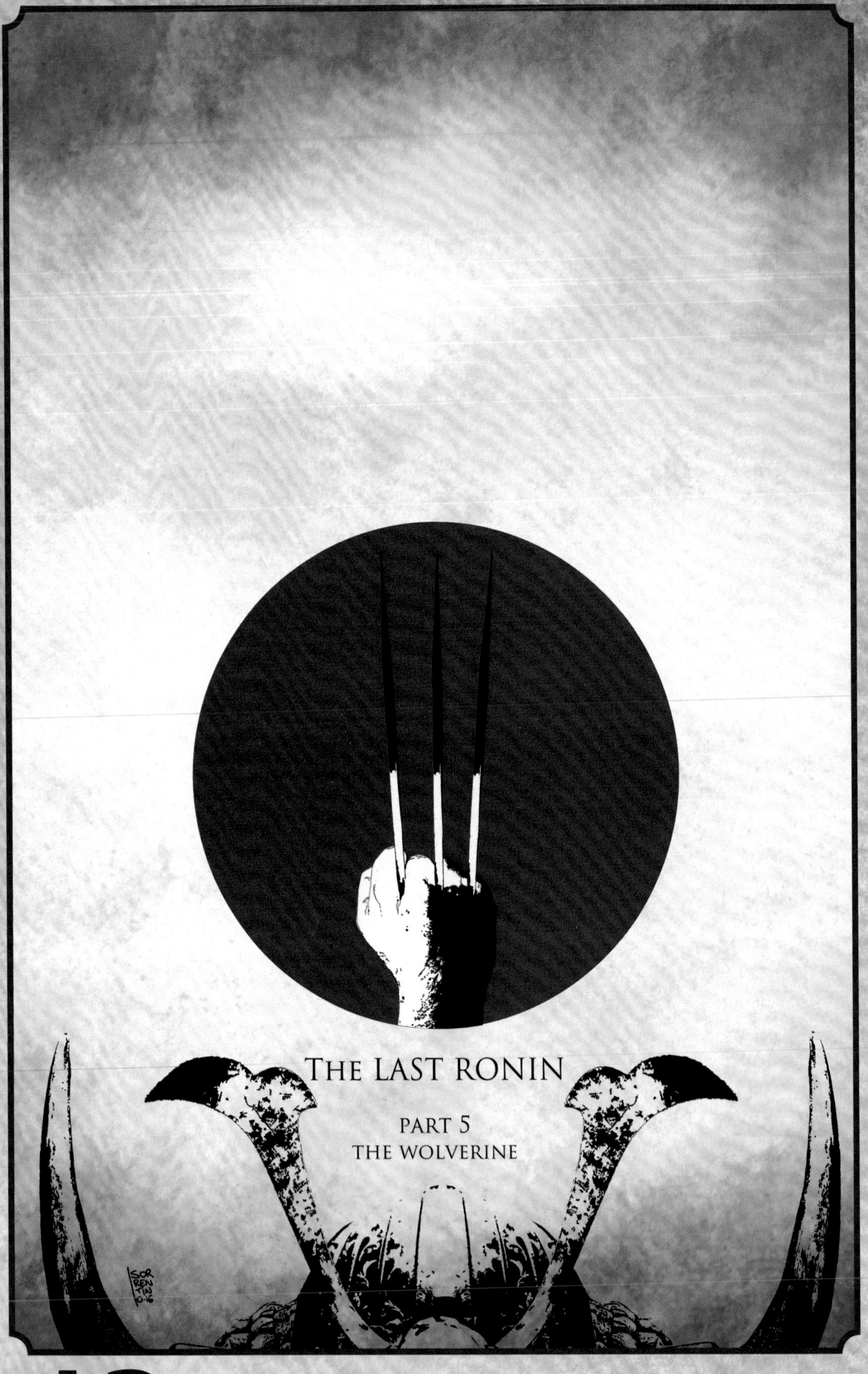
THE LAST RONIN
PART 5
THE WOLVERINE

13

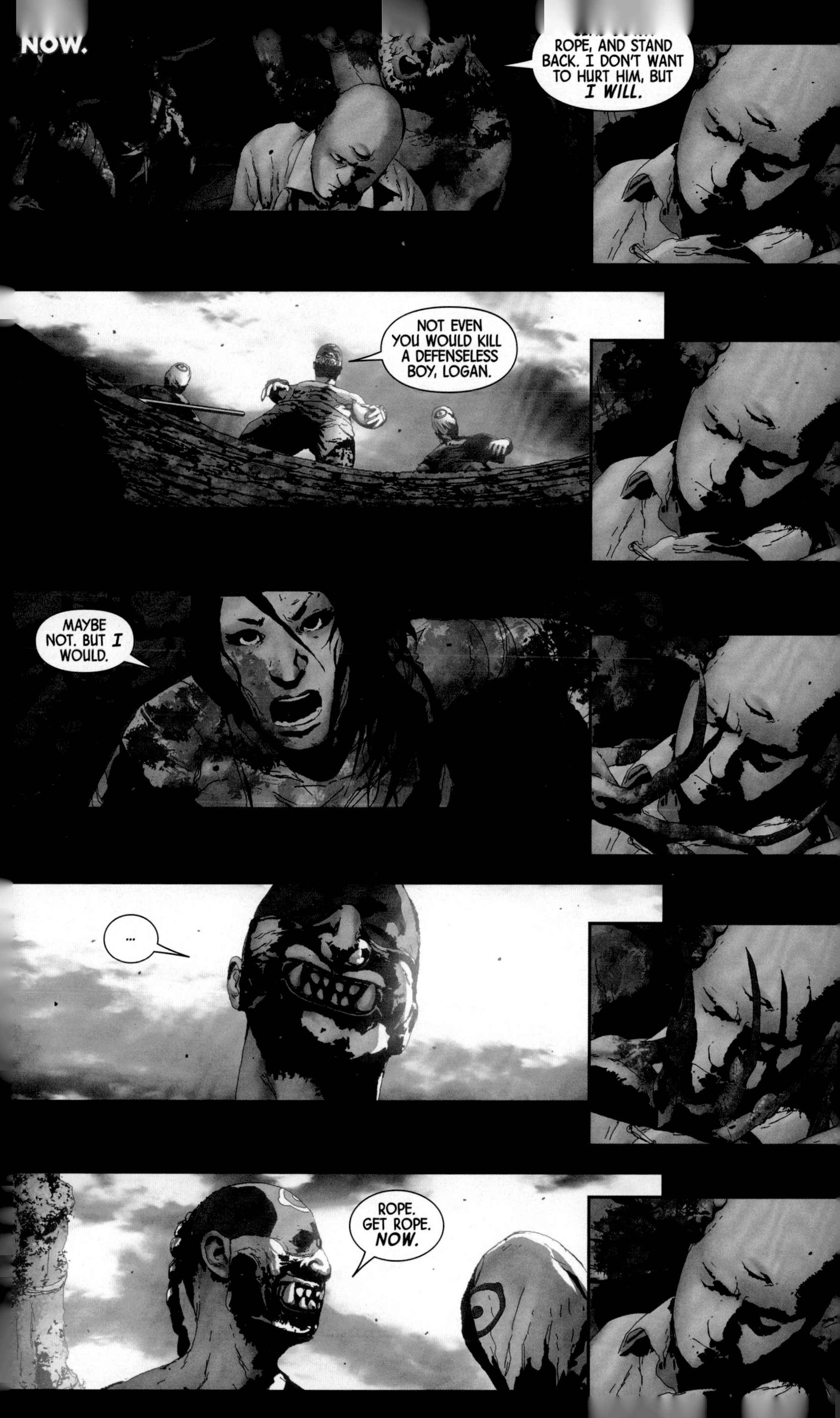
NOW.
ROPE, AND STAND BACK. I DON'T WANT TO HURT HIM, BUT I WILL.
NOT EVEN YOU WOULD KILL A DEFENSELESS BOY, LOGAN.
MAYBE NOT. BUT I WOULD.
...
ROPE. GET ROPE. NOW.

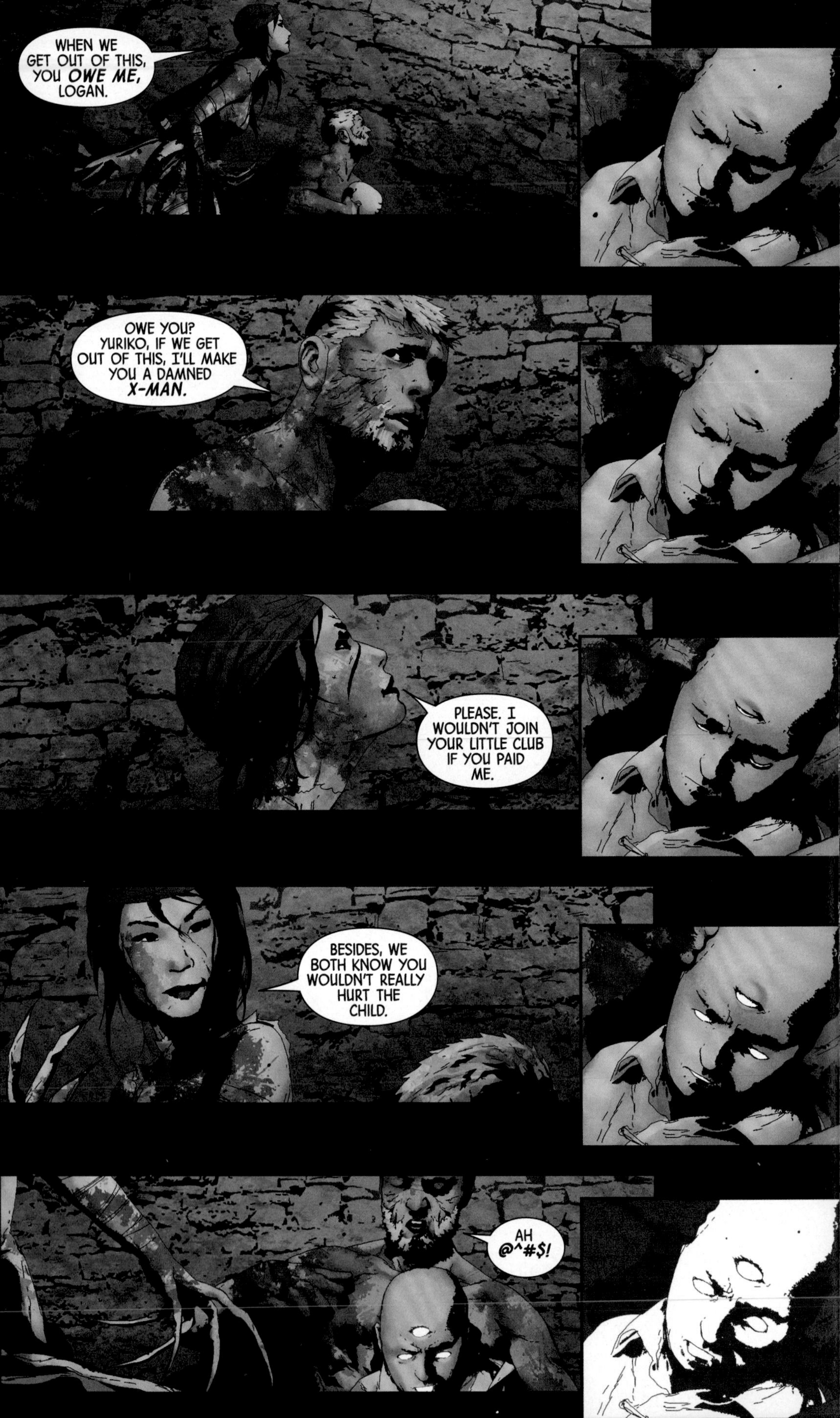
WHEN WE GET OUT OF THIS, YOU OWE ME, LOGAN.
OWE YOU? YURIKO, IF WE GET OUT OF THIS, I'LL MAKE YOU A DAMNED X-MAN.
PLEASE. I WOULDN'T JOIN YOUR LITTLE CLUB IF YOU PAID ME.
BESIDES, WE BOTH KNOW YOU WOULDN'T REALLY HURT THE CHILD.
AH @^#$!

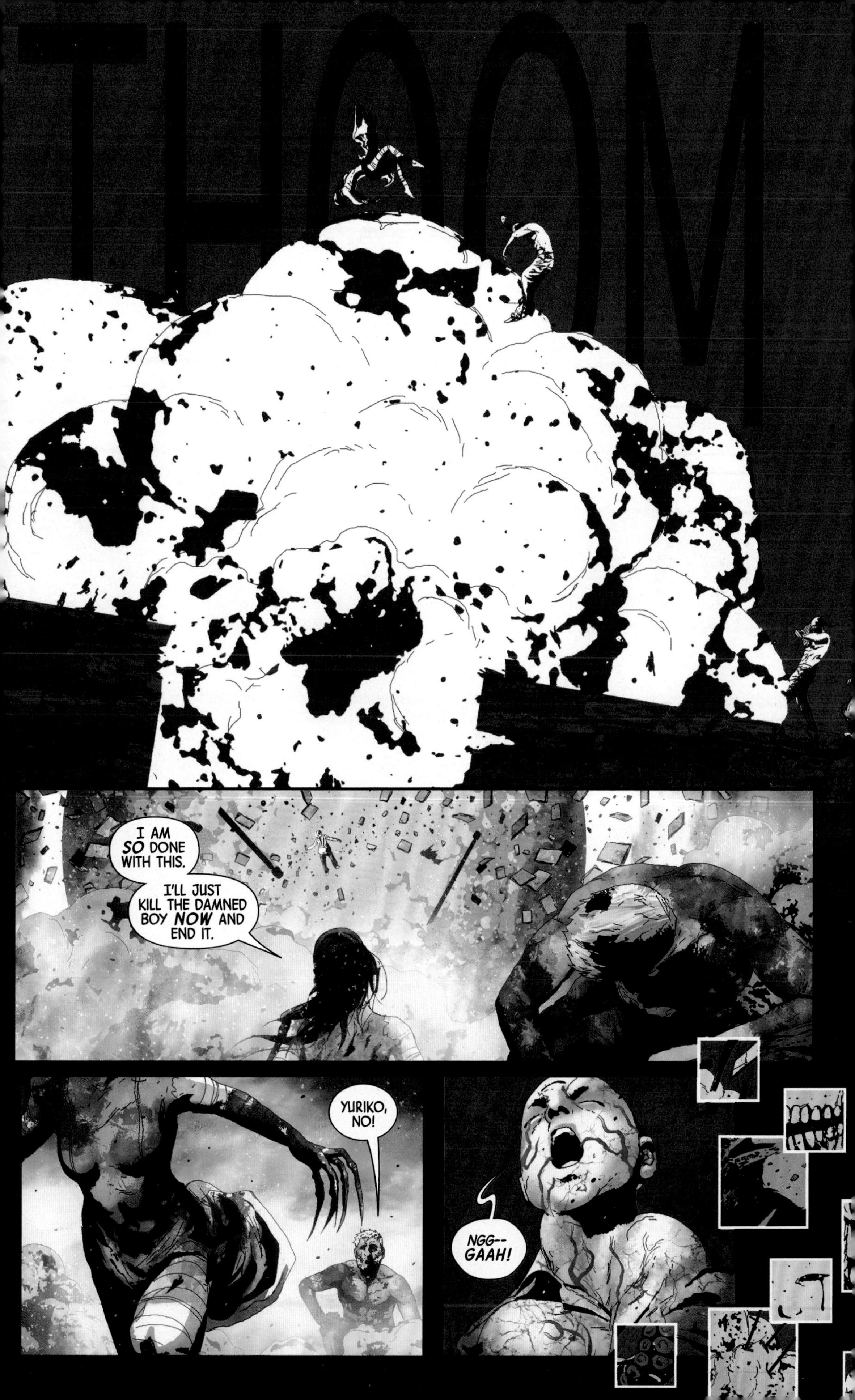
THOOM
I AM SO DONE WITH THIS.
I'LL JUST KILL THE DAMNED BOY NOW AND END IT.
YURIKO, NO!
NGG-- GAAH!

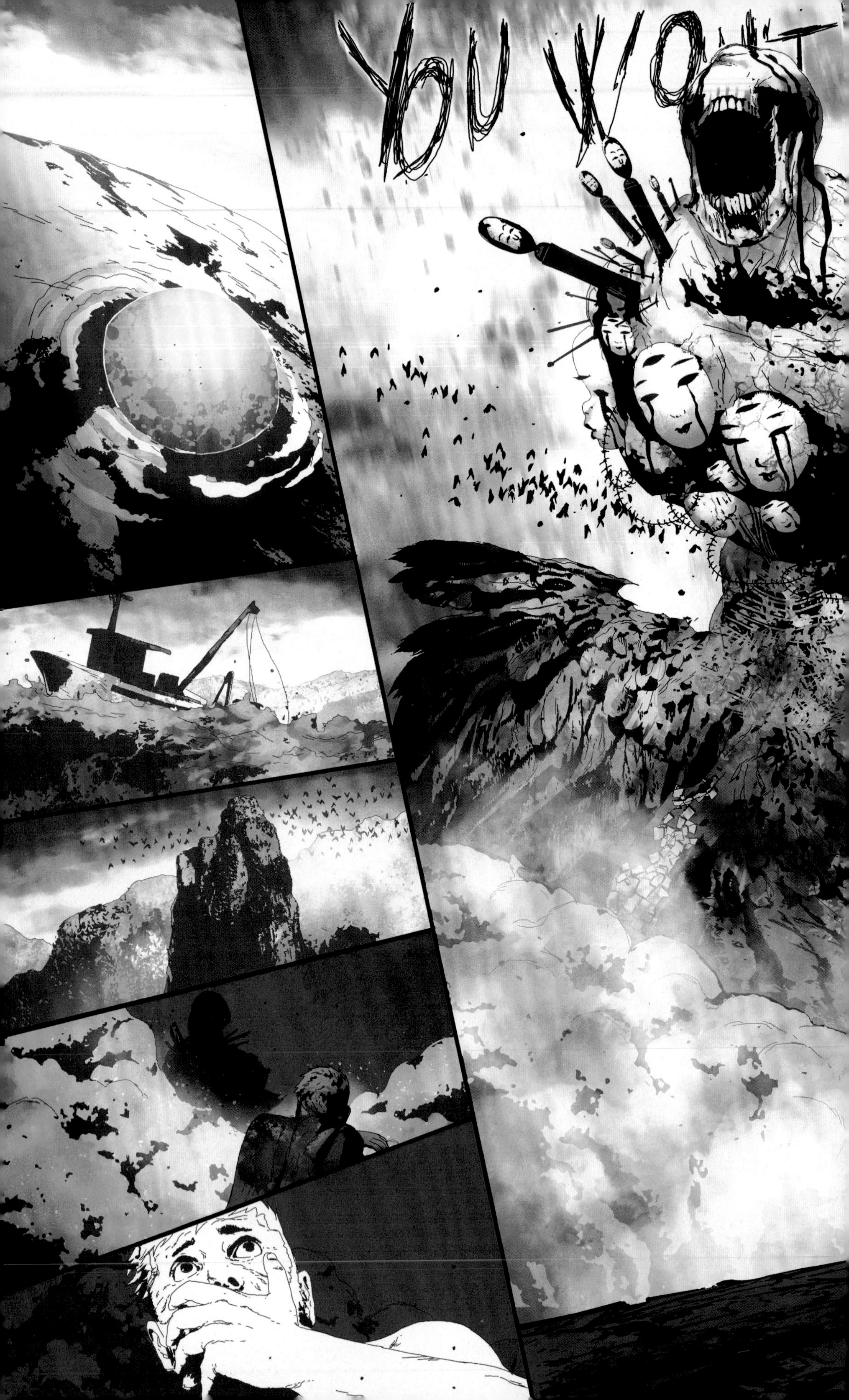
YOU WON'T

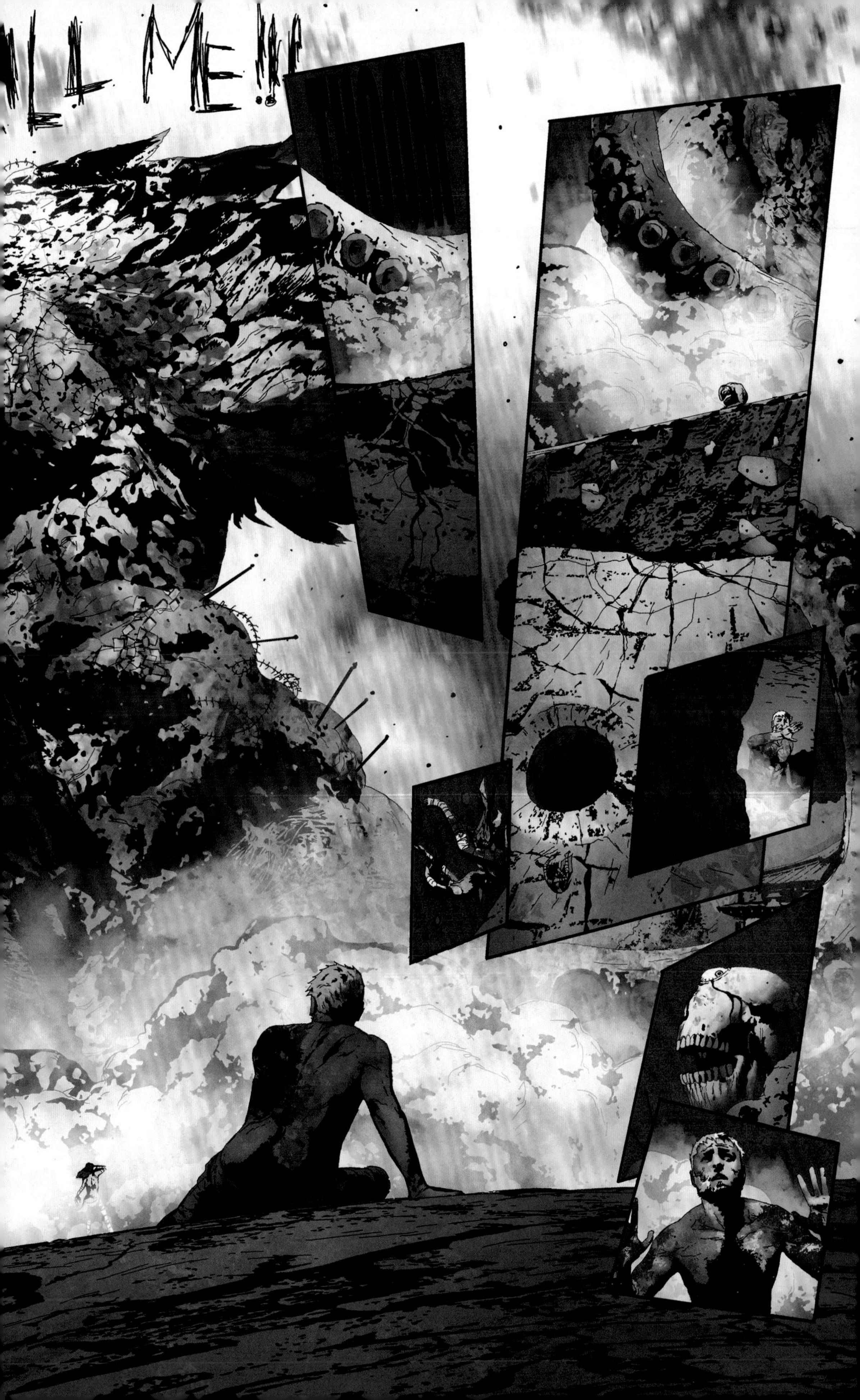
LL ME!!

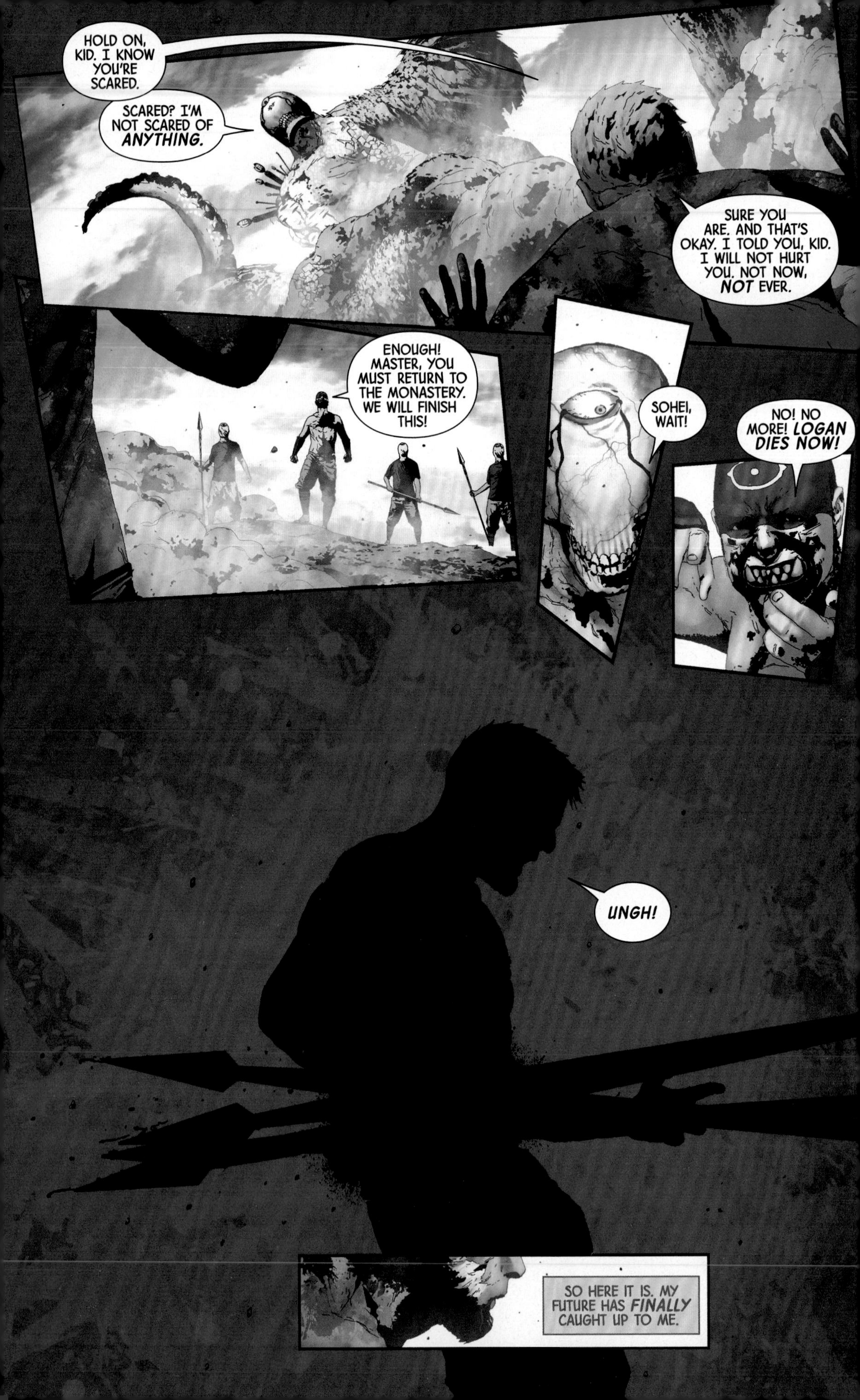
HOLD ON, KID. I KNOW YOU'RE SCARED.
SCARED? I'M NOT SCARED OF *ANYTHING.*
SURE YOU ARE. AND THAT'S OKAY. I TOLD YOU, KID. I WILL NOT HURT YOU. NOT NOW, *NOT* EVER.
ENOUGH! MASTER, YOU MUST RETURN TO THE MONASTERY. WE WILL FINISH THIS!
SOHEI, WAIT!
NO! NO MORE! *LOGAN DIES NOW!*
UNGH!
SO HERE IT IS. MY FUTURE HAS *FINALLY* CAUGHT UP TO ME.

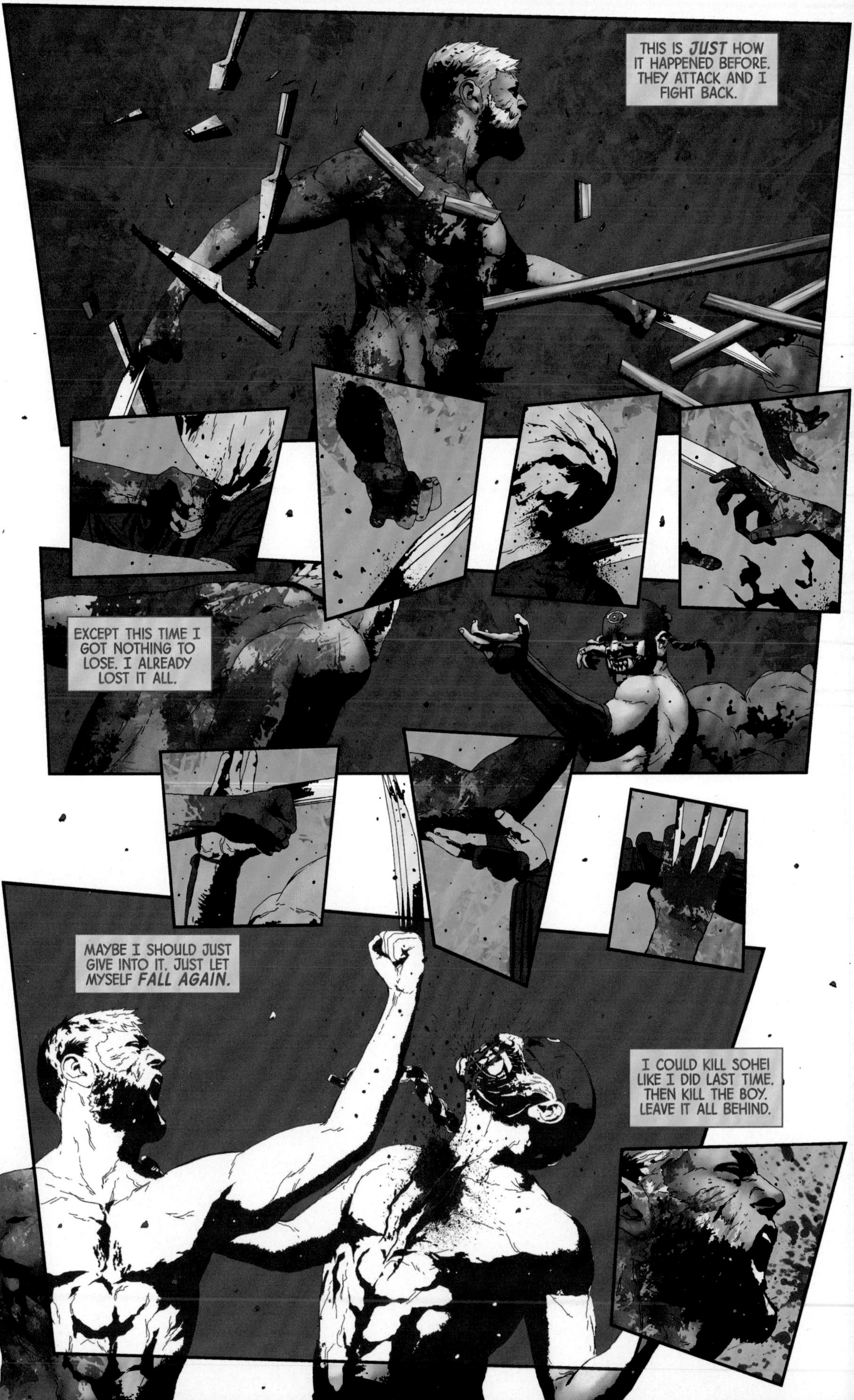
THIS IS JUST HOW IT HAPPENED BEFORE. THEY ATTACK AND I FIGHT BACK.
EXCEPT THIS TIME I GOT NOTHING TO LOSE. I ALREADY LOST IT ALL.
MAYBE I SHOULD JUST GIVE INTO IT. JUST LET MYSELF FALL AGAIN.
I COULD KILL SOHEI LIKE I DID LAST TIME. THEN KILL THE BOY. LEAVE IT ALL BEHIND.

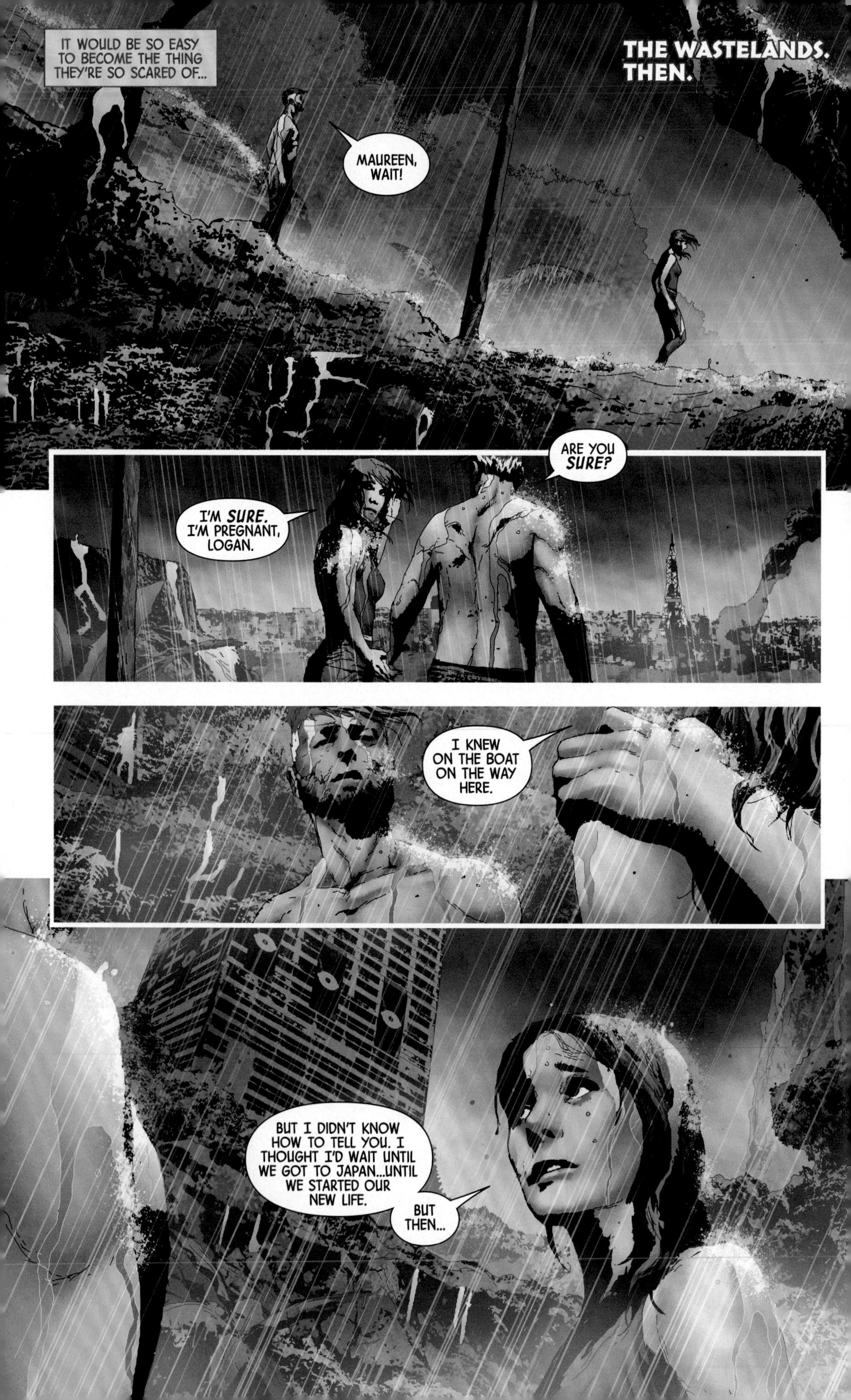
IT WOULD BE SO EASY TO BECOME THE THING THEY'RE SO SCARED OF...
THE WASTELANDS. THEN.
MAUREEN, WAIT!
ARE YOU SURE?
I'M SURE. I'M PREGNANT, LOGAN.
I KNEW ON THE BOAT ON THE WAY HERE.
BUT I DIDN'T KNOW HOW TO TELL YOU. I THOUGHT I'D WAIT UNTIL WE GOT TO JAPAN...UNTIL WE STARTED OUR NEW LIFE.
BUT THEN...

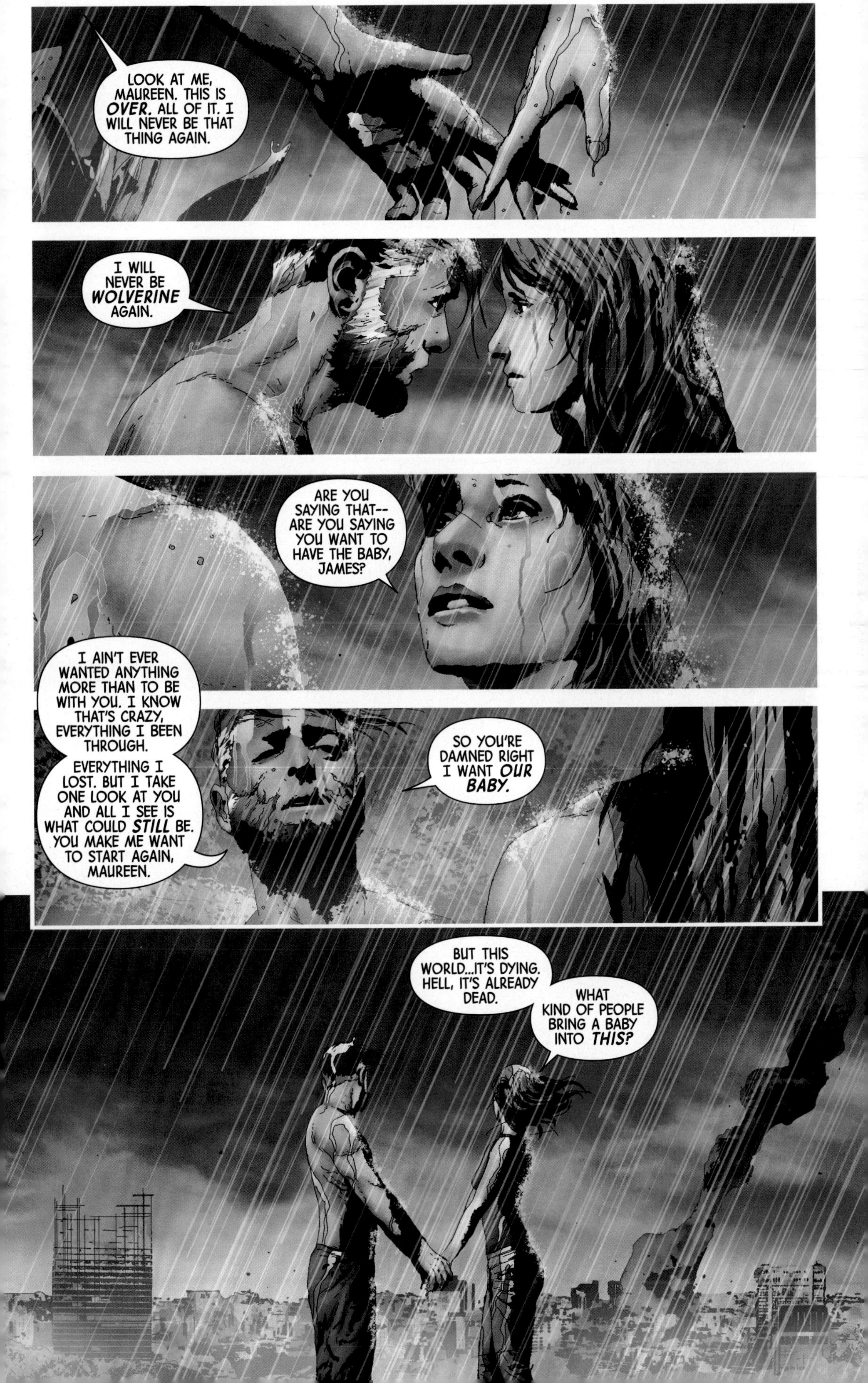
LOOK AT ME, MAUREEN. THIS IS OVER. ALL OF IT. I WILL NEVER BE THAT THING AGAIN.
I WILL NEVER BE WOLVERINE AGAIN.
ARE YOU SAYING THAT-- ARE YOU SAYING YOU WANT TO HAVE THE BABY, JAMES?
I AIN'T EVER WANTED ANYTHING MORE THAN TO BE WITH YOU. I KNOW THAT'S CRAZY, EVERYTHING I BEEN THROUGH.
EVERYTHING I LOST. BUT I TAKE ONE LOOK AT YOU AND ALL I SEE IS WHAT COULD STILL BE. YOU MAKE ME WANT TO START AGAIN, MAUREEN.
SO YOU'RE DAMNED RIGHT I WANT OUR BABY.
BUT THIS WORLD...IT'S DYING. HELL, IT'S ALREADY DEAD.
WHAT KIND OF PEOPLE BRING A BABY INTO THIS?

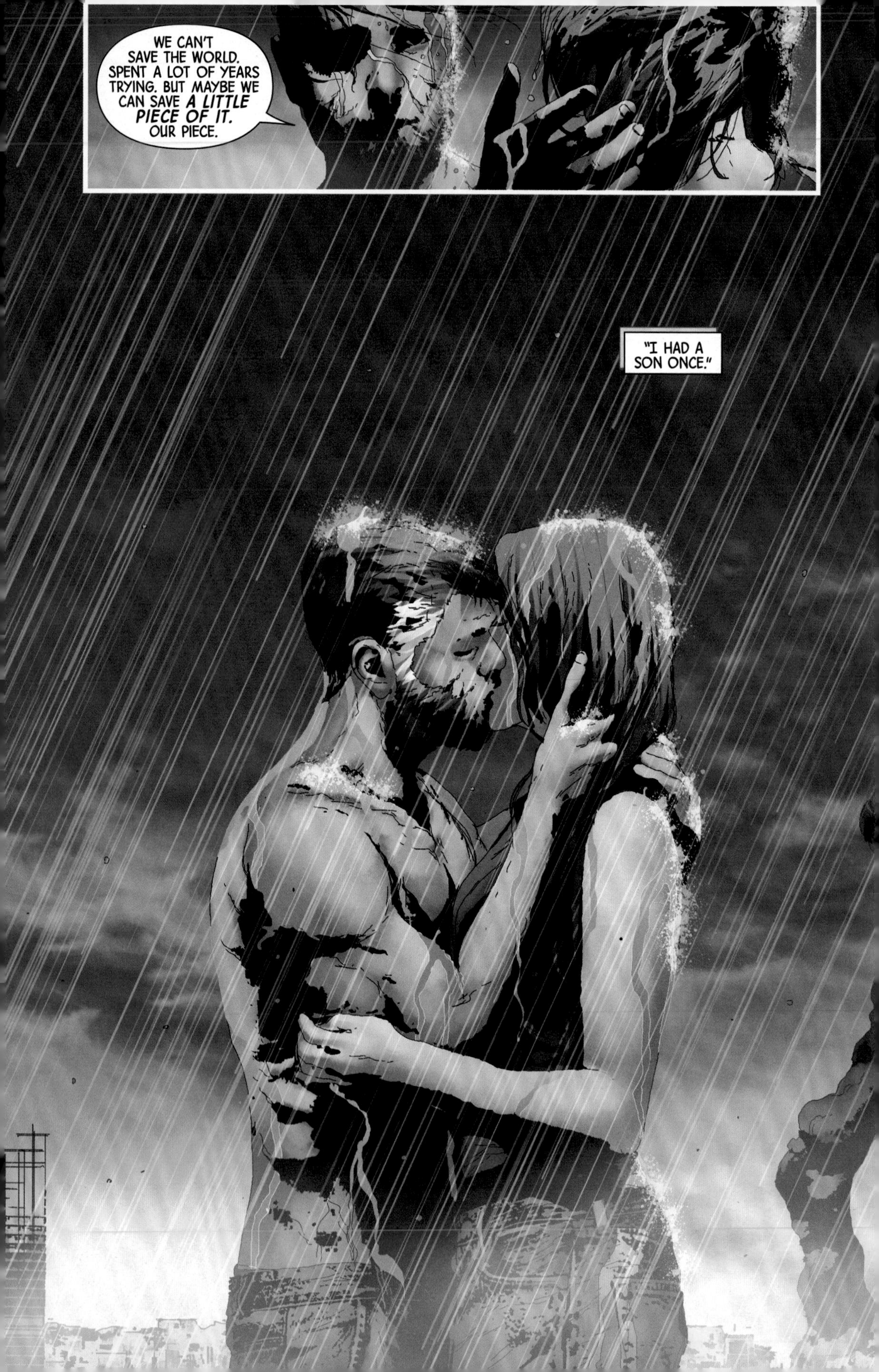
WE CAN'T SAVE THE WORLD. SPENT A LOT OF YEARS TRYING. BUT MAYBE WE CAN SAVE *A LITTLE PIECE OF IT.* OUR PIECE.
"I HAD A SON ONCE."

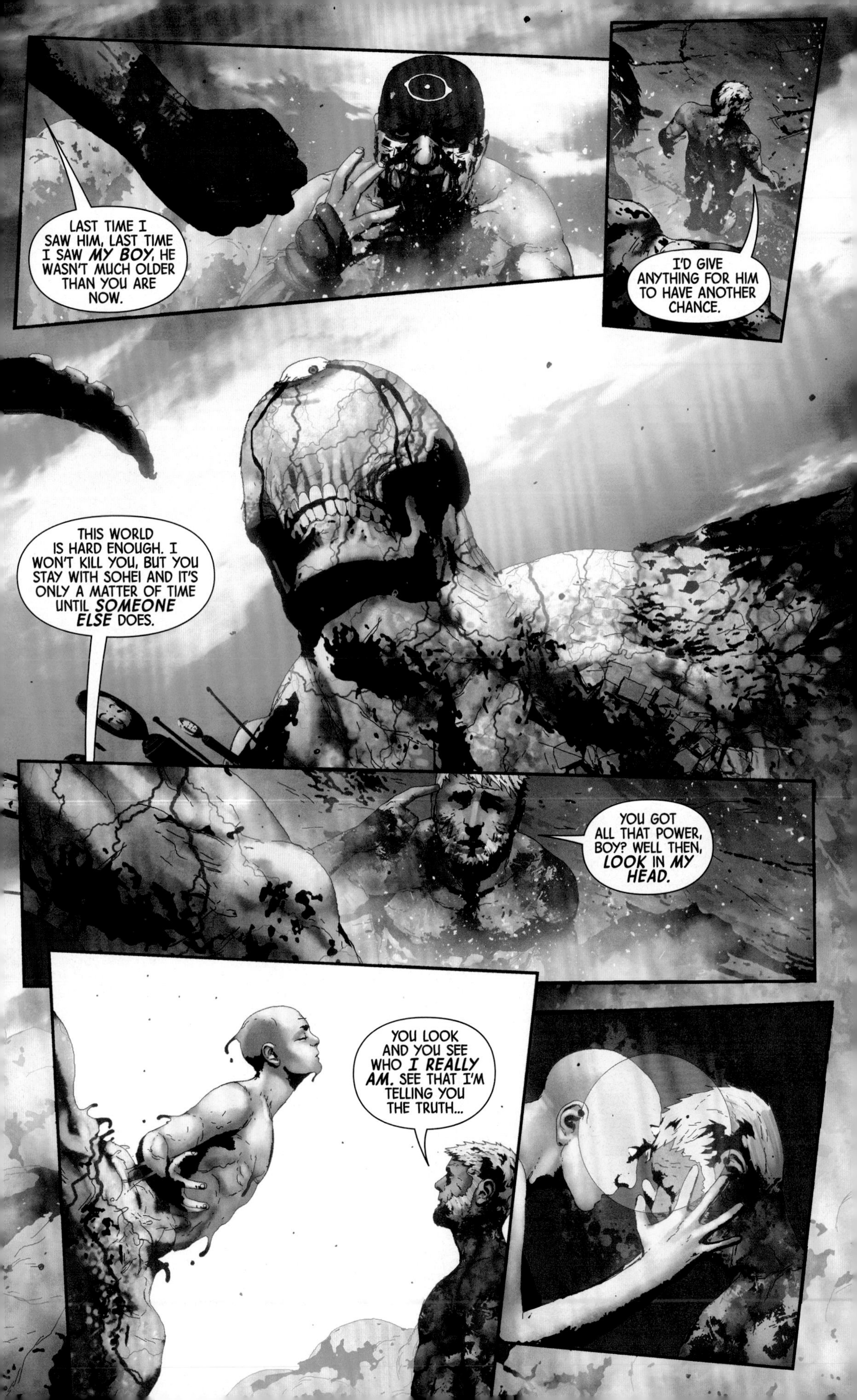
LAST TIME I SAW HIM, LAST TIME I SAW MY BOY, HE WASN'T MUCH OLDER THAN YOU ARE NOW.
I'D GIVE ANYTHING FOR HIM TO HAVE ANOTHER CHANCE.
THIS WORLD IS HARD ENOUGH. I WON'T KILL YOU, BUT YOU STAY WITH SOHEI AND IT'S ONLY A MATTER OF TIME UNTIL SOMEONE ELSE DOES.
YOU GOT ALL THAT POWER, BOY? WELL THEN, LOOK IN MY HEAD.
YOU LOOK AND YOU SEE WHO I REALLY AM. SEE THAT I'M TELLING YOU THE TRUTH...

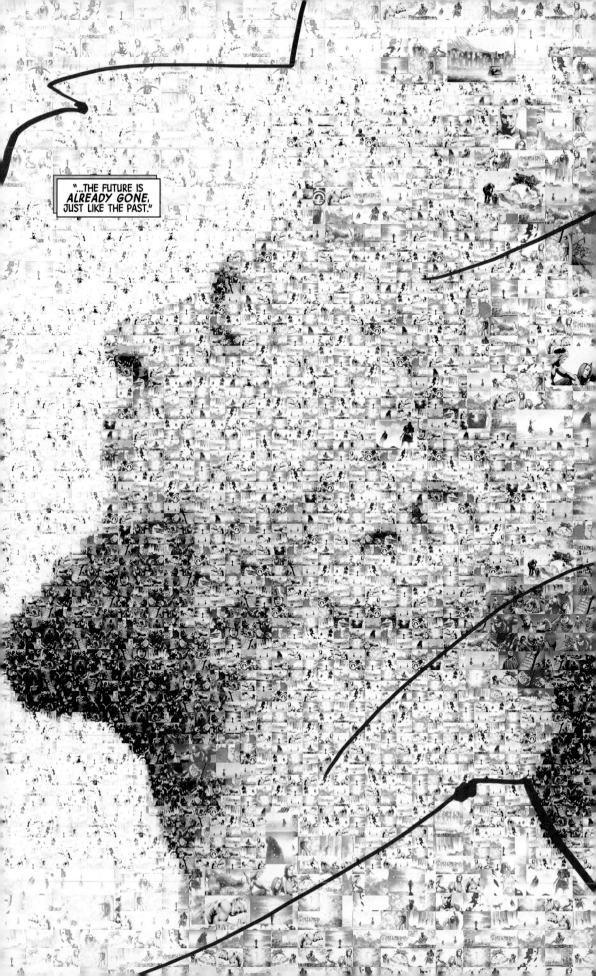

"...THE FUTURE IS *ALREADY GONE,* JUST LIKE THE PAST."

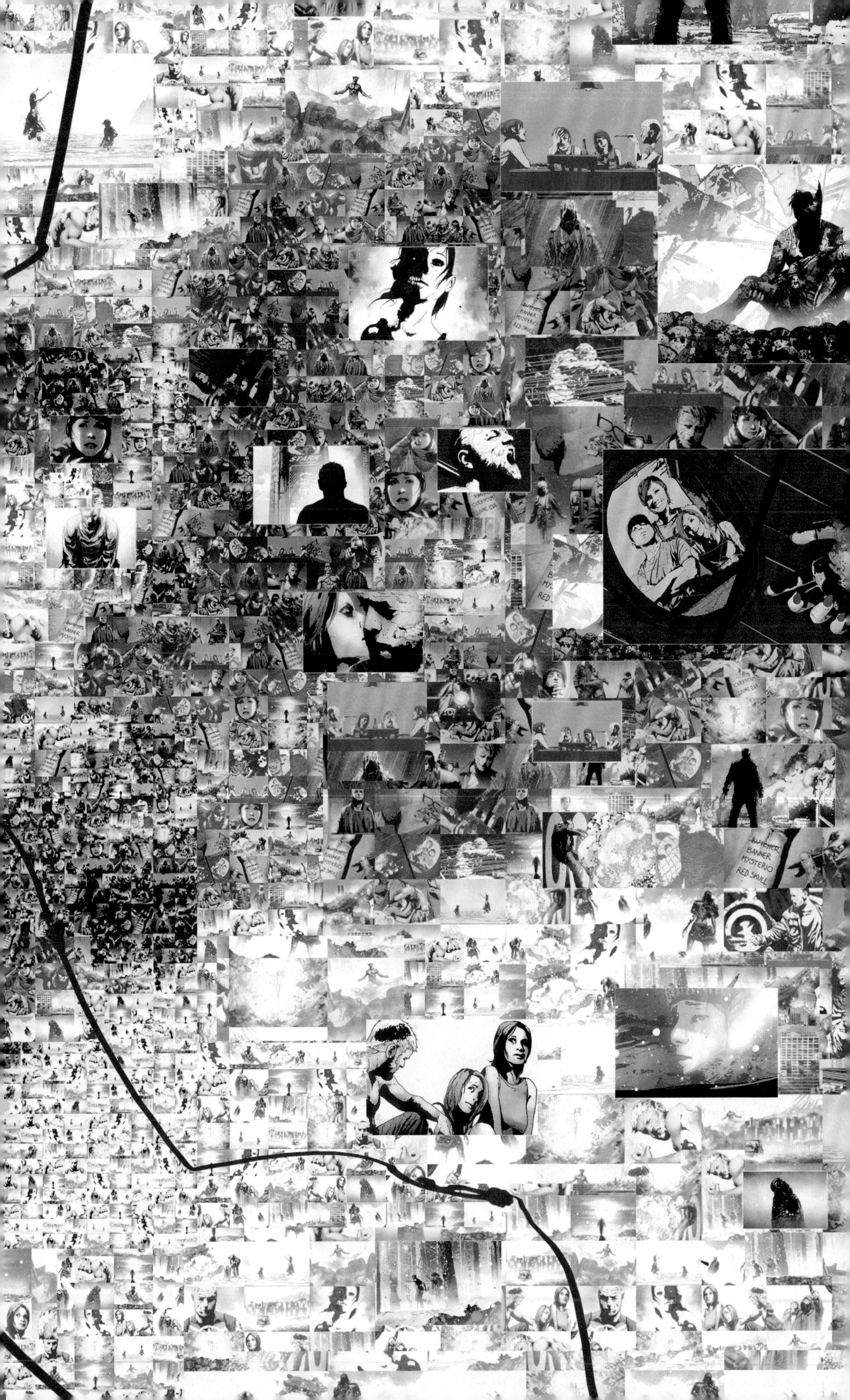
BUTCHER
BANNER
MYSTERIO
RED SKULL

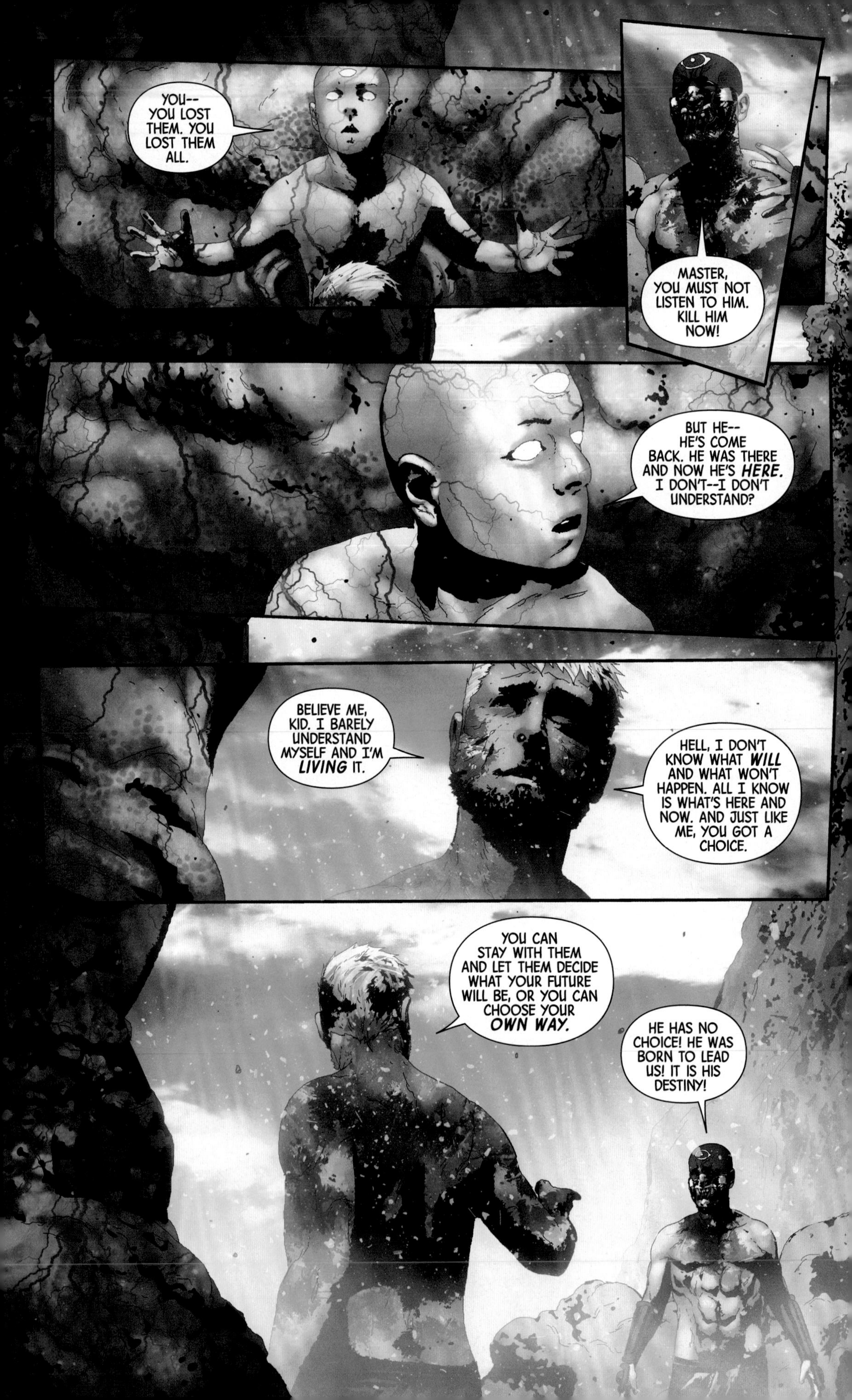
YOU-- YOU LOST THEM. YOU LOST THEM ALL.
MASTER, YOU MUST NOT LISTEN TO HIM. KILL HIM NOW!
BUT HE-- HE'S COME BACK. HE WAS THERE AND NOW HE'S HERE. I DON'T--I DON'T UNDERSTAND?
BELIEVE ME, KID. I BARELY UNDERSTAND MYSELF AND I'M LIVING IT.
HELL, I DON'T KNOW WHAT WILL AND WHAT WON'T HAPPEN. ALL I KNOW IS WHAT'S HERE AND NOW. AND JUST LIKE ME, YOU GOT A CHOICE.
YOU CAN STAY WITH THEM AND LET THEM DECIDE WHAT YOUR FUTURE WILL BE, OR YOU CAN CHOOSE YOUR OWN WAY.
HE HAS NO CHOICE! HE WAS BORN TO LEAD US! IT IS HIS DESTINY!

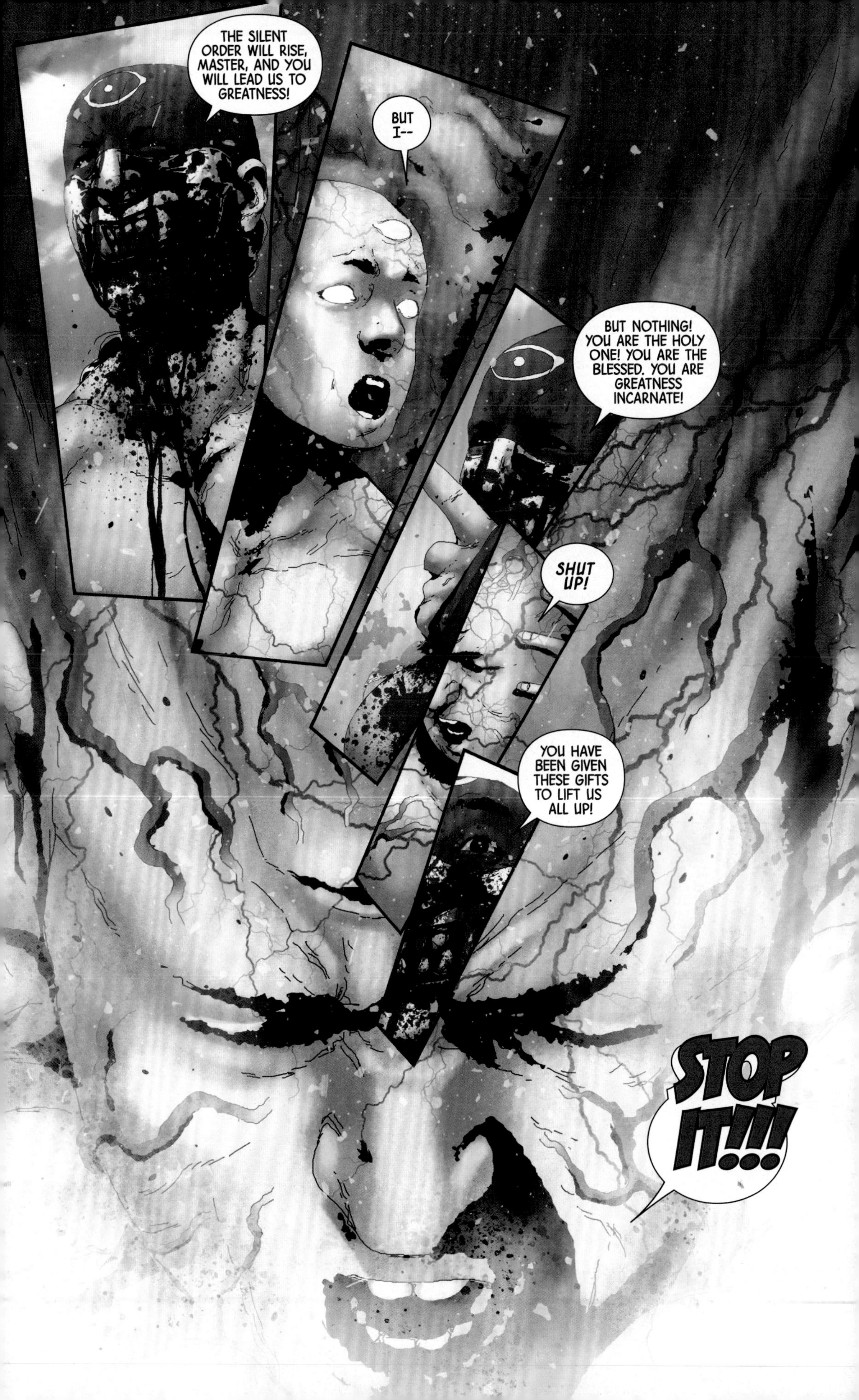
THE SILENT ORDER WILL RISE, MASTER, AND YOU WILL LEAD US TO GREATNESS!
BUT I--
BUT NOTHING! YOU ARE THE HOLY ONE! YOU ARE THE BLESSED. YOU ARE GREATNESS INCARNATE!
SHUT UP!
YOU HAVE BEEN GIVEN THESE GIFTS TO LIFT US ALL UP!
STOP IT!!!

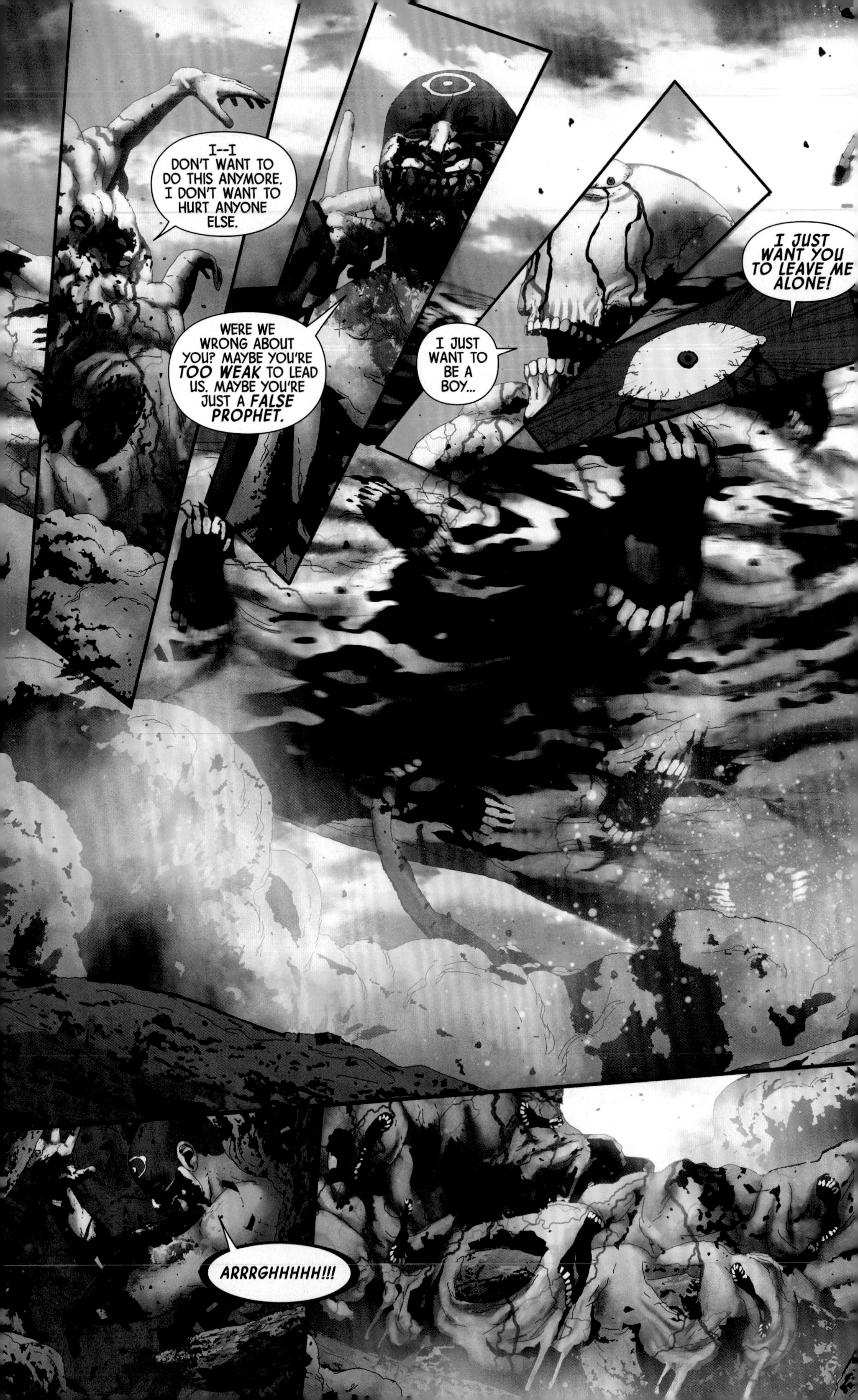
I--I DON'T WANT TO DO THIS ANYMORE. I DON'T WANT TO HURT ANYONE ELSE.
WERE WE WRONG ABOUT YOU? MAYBE YOU'RE TOO WEAK TO LEAD US. MAYBE YOU'RE JUST A FALSE PROPHET.
I JUST WANT TO BE A BOY...
I JUST WANT YOU TO LEAVE ME ALONE!
ARRRGHHHHH!!!

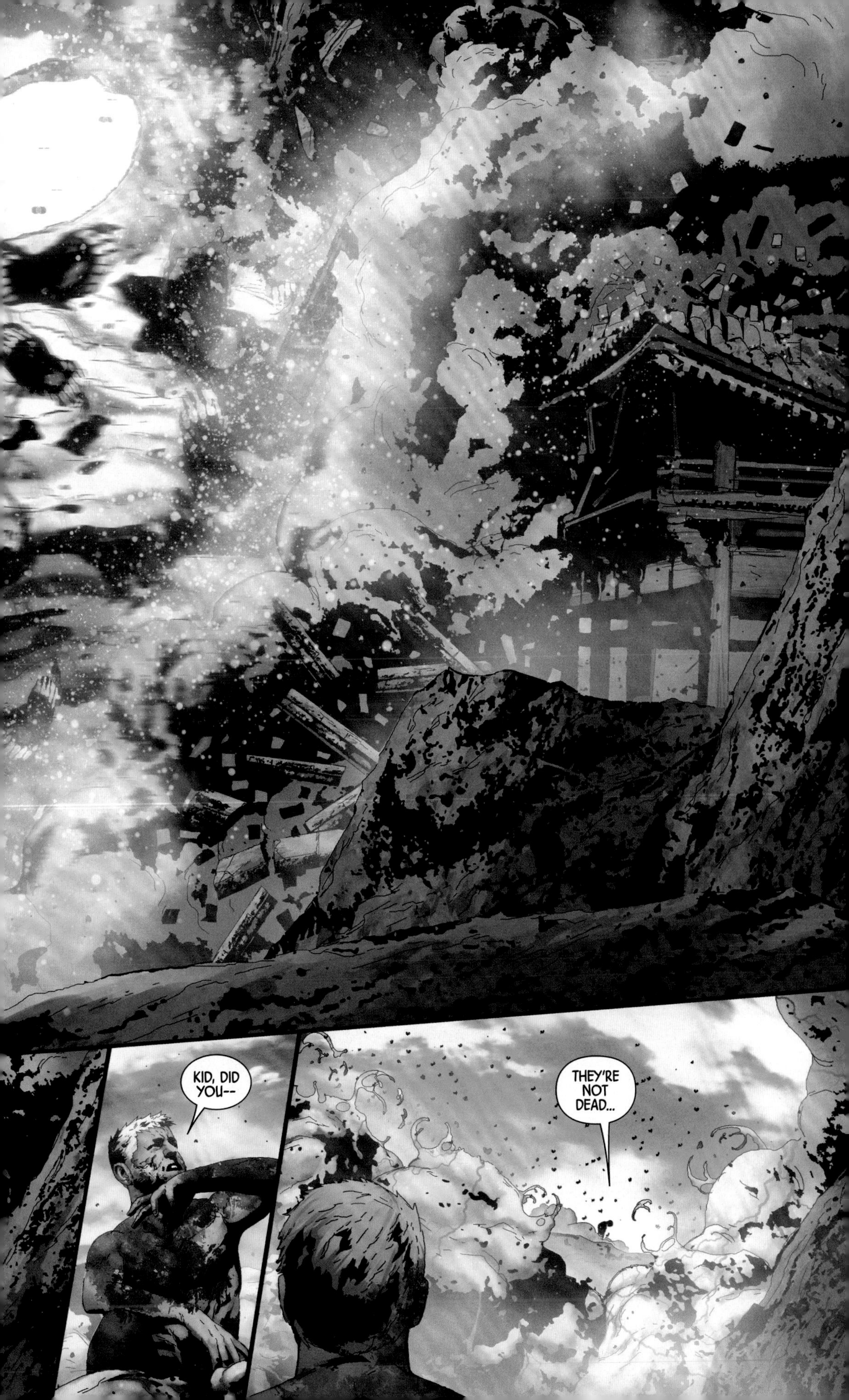
KID, DID YOU--
THEY'RE NOT DEAD...

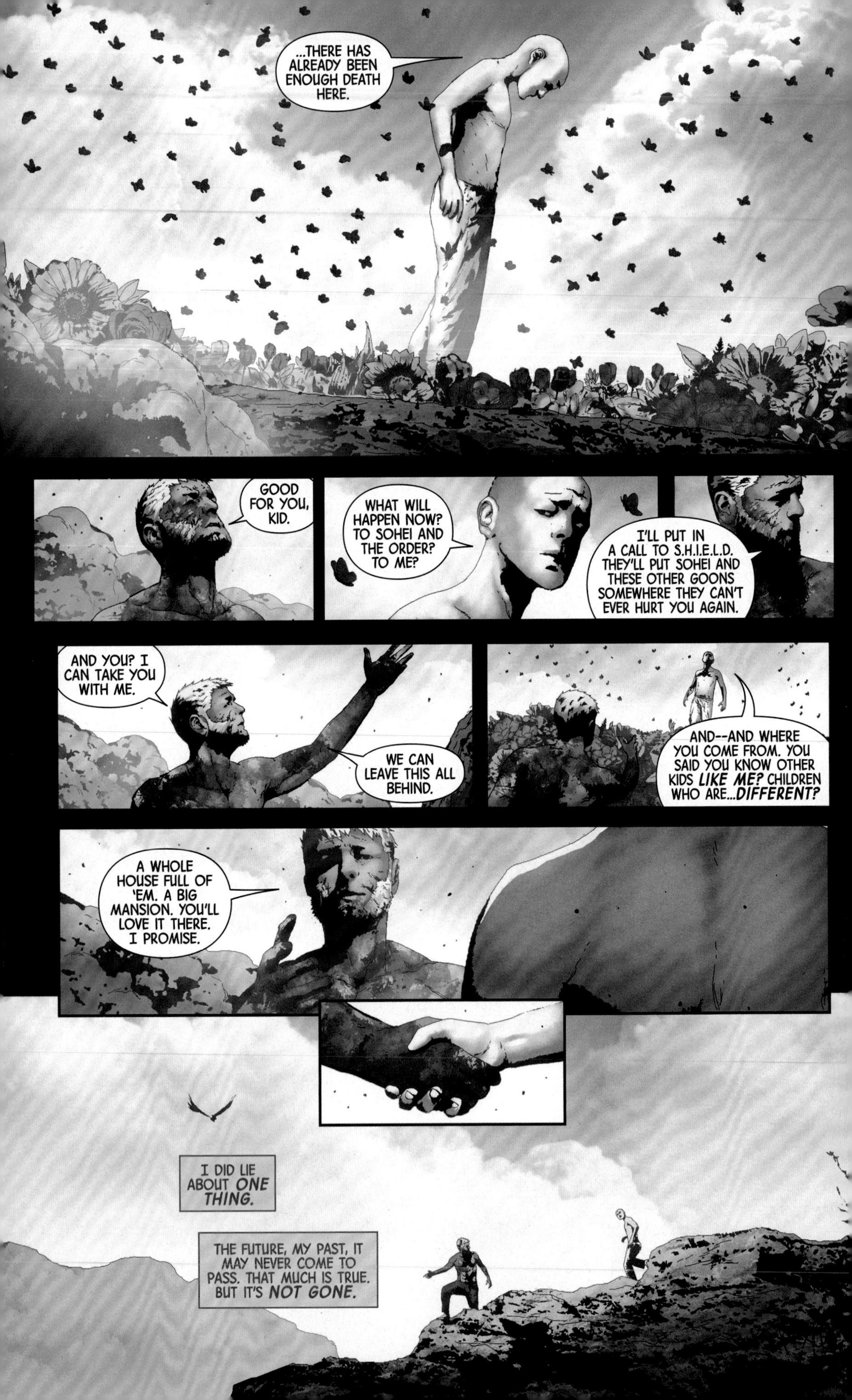
...THERE HAS ALREADY BEEN ENOUGH DEATH HERE.
GOOD FOR YOU, KID.
WHAT WILL HAPPEN NOW? TO SOHEI AND THE ORDER? TO ME?
I'LL PUT IN A CALL TO S.H.I.E.L.D. THEY'LL PUT SOHEI AND THESE OTHER GOONS SOMEWHERE THEY CAN'T EVER HURT YOU AGAIN.
AND YOU? I CAN TAKE YOU WITH ME.
WE CAN LEAVE THIS ALL BEHIND.
AND--AND WHERE YOU COME FROM. YOU SAID YOU KNOW OTHER KIDS LIKE ME? CHILDREN WHO ARE...DIFFERENT?
A WHOLE HOUSE FULL OF 'EM. A BIG MANSION. YOU'LL LOVE IT THERE. I PROMISE.
I DID LIE ABOUT ONE THING.
THE FUTURE, MY PAST, IT MAY NEVER COME TO PASS. THAT MUCH IS TRUE. BUT IT'S NOT GONE.

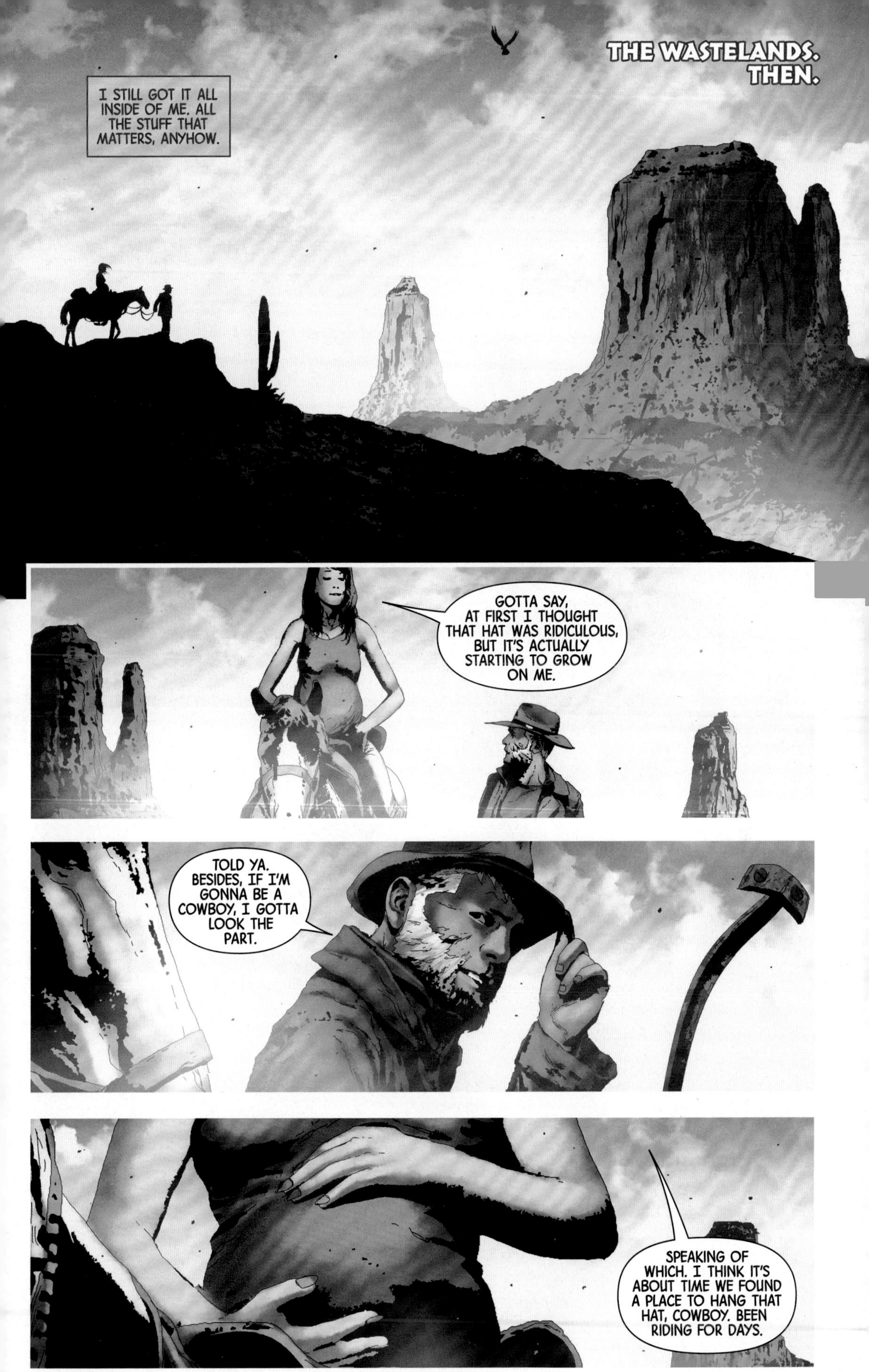
THE WASTELANDS. THEN.
I STILL GOT IT ALL INSIDE OF ME. ALL THE STUFF THAT MATTERS, ANYHOW.
GOTTA SAY, AT FIRST I THOUGHT THAT HAT WAS RIDICULOUS, BUT IT'S ACTUALLY STARTING TO GROW ON ME.
TOLD YA. BESIDES, IF I'M GONNA BE A COWBOY, I GOTTA LOOK THE PART.
SPEAKING OF WHICH. I THINK IT'S ABOUT TIME WE FOUND A PLACE TO HANG THAT HAT, COWBOY. BEEN RIDING FOR DAYS.

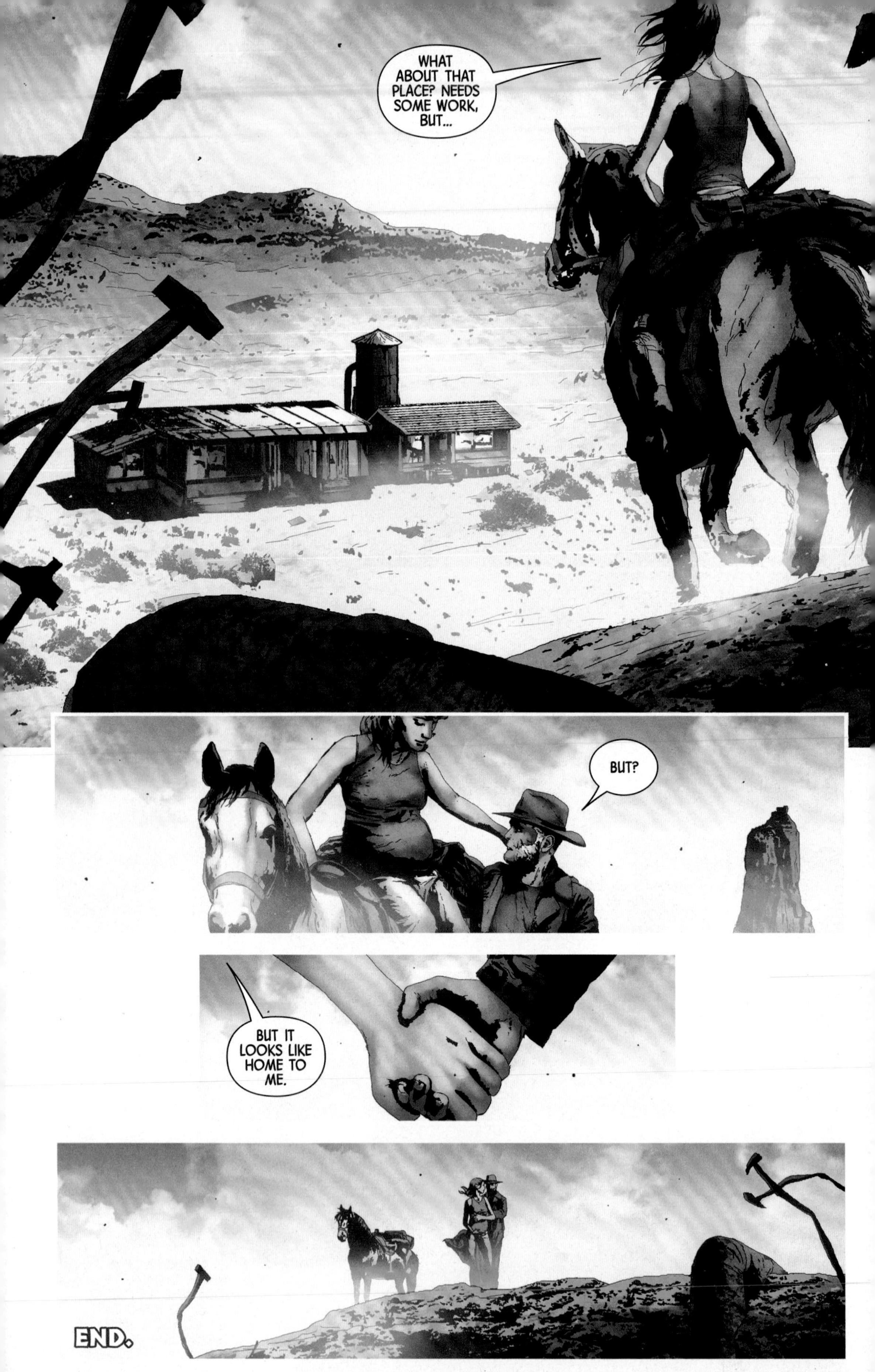
WHAT ABOUT THAT PLACE? NEEDS SOME WORK, BUT...
BUT?
BUT IT LOOKS LIKE HOME TO ME.
END.